A/C

Please return / renew by date shown.
You can renew at: **norlink.norfolk.gov.uk**
or by telephone: **0344 800 8006**
Please have your library card & PIN ready.

23. SEP 19.

4

THE NEXT STATION STOP

FIFTY YEARS BY TRAIN

PETER CATON

Matador
9 Priory Business Park
Kibworth Beauchamp
Leicestershire LE8 0RX, UK
Tel: (+44) 116 279 2299
Fax: (+44) 116 279 2277
Email: books@troubador.co.uk
Web: www.troubador.co.uk/matador

ISBN 978 1783060 504

British Library Cataloguing in Publication Data.
A catalogue record for this book is available from the British Library.

Main cover photo - The Tay Bridge

Typeset in 12pt Garamond by Troubador Publishing Ltd, Leicester, UK
Printed and bound in the UK by TJ International, Padstow, Cornwall

Matador is an imprint of Troubador Publishing Ltd

To my father, who introduced me to the pleasure of travelling by train, and to whom I am most grateful for his help with this book.

And to my nephew Ben, who just loves trains.

CONTENTS

Introduction   *ix*

Chapter 1   Cornwall in January   1
Chapter 2   Around Glasgow   13
Chapter 3   West Highlands in Search of Snow   20
Chapter 4   Over the Water to Kent   32
Chapter 5   To the Norfolk Coast   40
Chapter 6   The Cotswold Line   47
Chapter 7   High Speed to Edinburgh   52
Chapter 8   South Wales and Engineering Work   61
Chapter 9   Pendolino to the North West   71
Chapter 10   Heart of Wales Line   79
Chapter 11   Wrexham & Shropshire   89
Chapter 12   Mystery Trip   96
Chapter 13   An Eventful Trip to Cumbria   103
Chapter 14   Essex Coast Branches   116
Chapter 15   Three Yorkshire Resorts   128
Chapter 16   North Wales Circular   140
Chapter 17   Newton Abbot Newton Abbot   153
Chapter 18   Three Revived Railways   165
Chapter 19   Hampshire & Dorset   171
Chapter 20   To the Far North   178
Chapter 21   Three Treats to Finish   192
Chapter 22   Through Switzerland to Italy   203
Chapter 23   Back Through Germany   213
Chapter 24   Belgium Revisited   221
Chapter 25   Reflections   228

INTRODUCTION

Most introductions start by telling you what the book is about. I shall do the opposite and tell you what it isn't about. *The Next Station Stop* is not a book about either stations or trains – it's a book about travelling by train. It is both a travel and railway book. The subtitle gives you a clue. Regular travellers will recognise the main title; others will have to wait for the final chapter for the explanation (but I don't mind if you peep at the last couple of pages now).

A few years ago, under a pile of papers at the back of a drawer, I found a little red notebook that dated back to my childhood. The content wasn't something a teenage boy would have advertised to his friends. It would have been considered odd then and positively weird now. I never had a desire to collect locomotive numbers but used to record logs of our childhood journeys, transferring notes from scraps of paper to a red book that was considerably neater than any of my schoolbooks!

Discovering that little red notebook with its neatly recorded timings got me thinking – are today's train journeys better? To find out I decided to repeat them. I've travelled to the places we stayed at on childhood holidays and repeated days out, comparing journeys with those made over my fifty years of rail travel. I've written about the journeys, people met, places seen and what the trains were like. The result I hope gives a flavour of what it is like travelling by train and what has changed over the last fifty years.

My aim has been to write a book from the viewpoint of someone who enjoys travelling by train (usually!), but is neither an enthusiast nor spotter, which will appeal to both those with a specific interest in railways and the more general travel reader. I have included some interesting snippets of railway history and some comparisons from my father's old timetables, but this is by no means a heavy railway book. There are no engine numbers! I've tried to avoid using specialist railway language but a few common abbreviations were unavoidable and are explained at the end of this introduction.

My observations and experiences of journeys recent and past are recorded as they happened. Many travel writers make up or exaggerate incidents to add interest or humour, but tempting as it may be to embellish, with a scientific rather than journalistic training, I have kept to the truth. My observations, whether good or bad, are though often forthright.

At school I was the only person in our class whose family didn't have a car. We went everywhere by train. It was typical of our childhood that when we collected a pet rabbit Dad pushed it through the town with the cage in a wheelbarrow. Lack of a car wasn't allowed to preclude us from visiting anywhere, even if most of the day was spent on trains, buses and walking. Our holidays were always to places with railway stations.

Like most eighteen year olds, getting a car gave me the freedom to break away from parental constraints and travel how and where I wanted. As I've grown older though the pleasure of driving has waned and sitting back watching the countryside pass by as someone else 'takes the strain' seems far more attractive. Before they became cynical teenagers I often took our two boys on trains, although as a professional coach driver my wife Deb can be even harder to persuade that there's an alternative to the car. Travelling frequently across the UK for work (I run a glue factory in Purfleet, Essex) and for football (following West Ham), I use the train whenever I can. Unlike driving, with the opportunity to work, eat, read, or just relax, time travelling on a train isn't wasted.

Each chapter describes a journey, comparing what has changed from childhood travels. I've aimed to make them as varied as possible, with some concentrating more on the modern journey, others more nostalgic and all interspersed with observations on people and places. The final three chapters describe trips by train to Milan and to Belgium, repeating journeys made in earlier years and comparing European train travel with the UK.

Every so often I have referred to or quoted from my three previous books, which all involved train travel. For *Essex Coast Walk* I used public transport to get to and from each walk, taking me on rural branch lines to the coast. *No Boat Required* took me to tidal islands in all four corners of England,

Wales and Scotland, with some wonderful train journeys, some of which I described in the book. *Stand Up Sit Down* is a very different book, considering the arguments for and against allowing standing at football matches and including visits to the twenty-three English league clubs retaining terraces – by train of course.

Information was obtained from numerous sources, too many to mention, although I've put a few acknowledgements in the text. I've researched as much as reasonably possible and made every effort to ensure that facts are accurate, but will be happy to be corrected if otherwise. Sometimes, like the number of arches on Worcester's viaduct, I've been out and checked for myself. I will however mention Transport Consultant Barry Doe, who has provided me with details of restaurant cars from his annual surveys and assisted with ticketing queries, and the internet forum *www.railforums.co.uk,* whose members have responded to various requests for information. The excellent website *www.seat61.com,* an invaluable resource for train travel across the world, helped me plan my European journeys.

A selection of colour photographs span the fifty years of my train travel. The oldest are from my father's colour slides and date back to the days of steam. Intermediate years are from my own colour prints and the remainder were mostly taken on my travels for the book. Several show shots at the same location taken many years apart. None have been digitally altered.

My parents' choice of holiday destinations and days out weren't always (ever?) the most common, but they took us to most parts of Britain, giving us experience of our country that friends who always went to the Mediterranean missed. I have written a little about the places I've been back to, looking at how they've changed and sometimes wondering why we stayed there. If the accommodation I chose was interesting (good or bad!) I've mentioned it. On each trip I've indulged another of the pastimes I enjoy, and included a walk, sometimes short, sometimes longer.

The Next Station Stop takes the reader on a tour of Britain's railways, experiencing beautiful and sometimes remote parts of our wonderful country, but also visiting some of our lesser known lines. Join me on a 10,000 mile journey and see what's changed in 'Fifty Years by Train'.

Map of my Journeys

A few terms and abbreviations:

HST: High Speed Train – 125mph diesel trains which were introduced in the 1970s and still run on many routes.

DMU: Diesel Multiple Unit – Train consisting of one or more coaches powered by on-board diesel motors rather than pulled by a locomotive.

Sprinter: A family of DMUs introduced by British Rail in the 1980s and 90s and sometimes a generic name for a modern DMU.

Pacer: Basic DMUs introduced by British Rail in the mid 1980s.

Voyager: High speed multiple unit diesel trains which were introduced on cross country routes in 2001.

Pendolino: High speed tilting electric trains which were introduced by Virgin in 2002.

'142', '153; '158' etc: Numbers allocated to various classes of DMU trains.

CHAPTER ONE

CORNWALL IN JANUARY

London – Penzance – St Ives – Falmouth – Newquay – Looe

It seems fitting for a travel book to begin at a famous London railway terminus. *Essex Coast Walk* had started at Liverpool Street and *No Boat Required* at Paddington, where tonight once again I was to join the overnight train to Cornwall. I was starting my travels on one of Britain's great trains – the Night Riviera.

Emerging from the warmth of the Underground to the late evening cool of the station concourse, I turned to my left. There, already waiting at Platform One, was Paddington's most romantic train; an old fashioned diesel locomotive gently ticking over, ready to haul seven coaches with sleeping passengers 300 miles to the far west of England. As I did with my father on our childhood journeys, I walked to the front to see the engine – *Restormel Castle*, a Class 57, which dates from almost as long as my train travels, albeit a new engine inside the original 1965 body shell. In today's railway of fixed units, this was a throwback to the journeys of my youth.

At the appointed hour of ten thirty, the doors were opened and passengers welcomed on board. The friendly attendant showed me to my berth and took my order for breakfast – bacon roll, muesli or croissant. A recent addition to the sleeper is television screens and comfortably ensconced in my little air conditioned cabin, I enjoyed an episode of *The Simpsons* before settling down for the night. Snuggled under a warm blanket, I thought what I always do on a sleeper – that this is just a wonderful way to travel. I felt the jolt as we moved off at 23.45, but asleep by midnight, was to wake up in Cornwall. Why would anyone want to fly?

This wonderful service nearly closed in 2005, when the government asked bidders for the new franchise to consider other options. With the train needing a £5 million subsidy, it was said not to be cost effective, but users argued that this figure didn't take account of the benefit the overnight link made to the region's economy. A Save Our Sleeper campaign was launched, with the backing of many West Country MPs, and when FirstGroup were awarded the new franchise they announced it would continue. Publicity over the threatened withdrawal helped increase usage and in 2010 First Great Western announced that additional coaches were being added to cater for greater demand, which they thought was due to people wanting to save money on London hotel costs. The train is now profitable and although quiet today, the attendant told me that most of the year it's fully booked.

My dozen or so previous journeys on the Night Rivera were all in fairly recent years, often as a convenient way to visit my grandma in Torquay, when I'd double back from Plymouth. A single coach used to be detached here and passengers could continue to sleep as it stayed in the platform until 8am, but this ceased as part of the cost saving when the sleeper was saved. The handful of passengers didn't justify the costs of an attendant and shunter, so it wasn't an unreasonable sacrifice to help keep the train running.

Despite its good rail links, we never had a childhood holiday in Cornwall, just once a few days in St Ives with friends. Since then we've been many times, including five family holidays staying by Fistral Beach in Newquay. I took the boys on the sleeper, with Deb driving down the night before. The early arrival gave us an extra day in Cornwall and the journey an exciting start to the holiday, contrasting with difficulty in keeping children entertained on a long car trip. While the Plymouth portion was running we changed there, once nearly being carried to the sidings when the shunter set off with us still on board – a moment of excitement for the children but panic for Dad! On the last two occasions we changed at Bodmin Parkway, enjoying breakfast in the Signalbox Café, before heading on to Newquay.

After sleeping well I was woken at 7am by a knock on the door, the attendant bringing my breakfast of croissant and strawberry jam. There was no repeat of the little embarrassment of my last trip when the steward hadn't heard my call to wait, and opened the door to a sight of semi-nakedness and my hurried attempts to pull up underpants, an operation which invariably takes at least twice as long when performed with urgency. As we'd pulled into Penzance the steward told me she'd been doing this job for ten years and never got tired of the views. I assumed she meant the sea and not gentlemen's bottoms!

We drew into St Erth at the same time as the single coach train from St Ives, from which five passengers emerged into the dark morning. A misty dawn was breaking as we passed St Michael's Mount, lights in the castle glowing dimly across the water. Just a handful of passengers remained to alight at Penzance, where a five coach Voyager was waiting to depart for Glasgow.

Penzance was still waking – workers waiting for buses, a lorry delivering boxes to Shoe Zone and children stopping to buy chocolate on their way to school. With no showers on the sleeper and a while to pass before I started heading back east, I sought out the local leisure centre for a quick swim. Emerging refreshed, both the town and I had woken up, although the rain had become decidedly heavier. Putting off thoughts of walking along the shore to Marazion and St Michael's Mount, I wandered round the town but found little of interest. Six ladies drinking coffee round a table in a cosy café whose windows were already starting to steam, looked to be having a more enjoyable time.

Back at the station I bought a 'Ride Cornwall' ticket, which for just £10 allowed a day's travel on all Cornwall's trains and most of its buses. The 9.40 Cross Country train to Manchester was about to depart and I jumped on board, choosing a seat that was booked between Birmingham and Stoke-on-Trent. I wondered how many others would occupy the seat on its 383 mile journey. Helen the guard announced all 25 stops, but that there'd be no catering until Plymouth. An 'at seat service' (a trolley) would then be available, but she failed to mention that there'd be no hot food – for a journey of 8 hours. Virgin used to run the cross country services, and whilst their catering wasn't brilliant, since Arriva took over it's become abysmal.

St Erth village is some distance away, so I spent the wait for the St Ives train on the station. With a booking office and buffet in the original granite buildings, wooden canopies, and gardens tended by local volunteers, it has changed little, remaining a proper living railway station, not simply a platform where trains stop. A notice explained that connections for St Ives can't be held due to the limited turn round and thirty minute service, which seemed fair enough, although less acceptable was the American spelling 'traveling'.

The 4¼ mile branch to St Ives is one of our most scenic railways, and even in constant rain the run alongside the Hayle Estuary and on the cliffs of St Ives Bay was a spectacular ride. Winter may be the best time to enjoy it, as on our last journey the train had been packed with passengers using the park and ride facility at Lelant Saltings. Even today the single coach was more than half full, the usual handful of passengers augmented by a class of young schoolchildren, their excited chatter filling the train. The guard stopped to talk to them, just a couple of minutes of his time that will have added to their enjoyment of the day. As we pootled down the estuary a dozen shelducks waddled half heartedly away, almost disdainful that a train of this size didn't merit them taking to the air. Estuary turned to sea as we passed Carbis Bay, where the guard said he'd seen seals earlier in the week. Today just the obligatory one man and his dog walked on the expanse of sand.

St Ives station, whilst beautifully situated just above Porthminster Beach, is a disappointment. The Victorian buildings where once the Cornish Riviera Express terminated on summer Saturdays, were demolished in 1971, to be replaced by a short concrete platform and bus shelter. Sad it may be, but were it not for such economies the line may not have survived.

In the holiday season, St Ives, whilst a beautiful town, can be spoilt by the number of tourists. Although in summer cars are restricted, visitors being encouraged to use the park and ride, it's not truly car-free, and the people throng the narrow streets. January was perhaps a better time to appreciate the quaint streets, steep alleys, and picturesque harbour. The rain having stopped, I walked to my favourite spot, the tiny St Nicholas' Chapel on the cliff beyond the town, with magnificent views to beaches below.

Seven of us boarded the train for the return to St Erth, one more getting on at Carbis Bay and buying a ticket to Falmouth. Once again the shelducks waddled away as we passed, but three herons remained statuesque on the water's edge.

The 11.48 from St Erth stops at most stations to Newton Abbot and was busy with local traffic. A two car Class 150, it was an inferior train to that on the St Ives branch, but can't run as a single coach, so the branches get the better trains. Whilst not as scenic as the branches, the Cornish Main Line is an interesting ride, and I enjoyed a pasty looking out at ruined tin mines as we passed Camborne and Redruth.

A one minute connection in Truro proved inadequate, the Falmouth train pulling out just as I crossed the bridge. The man on the ticket barrier told me, '*it's a strange beast the Falmouth line*'. As the two trains operating have to pass midway, it has to be cancelled if more than seven minutes late and won't wait more than two. I pointed out that this would have been enough for me and the man from Carbis Bay, but the one minute connection isn't advertised, so it doesn't wait.

The wait gave me just time to walk into Truro, the busy centre befitting its county town status, and for a quick glimpse at the beautiful cathedral. On our last visit here *City of Truro* had been displayed statically but in steam in the town centre, and my son allowed to shovel coal into the fire box.

The clientele on the 12.50 to Falmouth Docks were distinctly different to those on all the other Cornish trains. Only here did I see the baseball caps and body piercings that one usually associates with less rural counties. Marketed as The Maritime Line, it's probably the least scenic of the branches, although passes through pleasant countryside with occasional views to the River Fal.

It's the only Cornish branch to run with two trains, the twenty nine services a day a considerable improvement on the eleven from the 1986 timetable. Doubling the service has resulted in a similar increase in passengers, and not relying on holiday traffic, the Falmouth branch thrives all year round. The trains pass at Penryn, where a loop was reinstalled in 2009, and in a unique arrangement to save the cost of a bridge, the two platforms are end to end on one side of the track. The station serves a campus of University College Falmouth and was busy with students. Penmere, the next station, is painted in traditional Great Western chocolate and cream, and immaculately maintained by the Friends of Penmere.

Extraordinarily for a town of its size, Falmouth actually has three stations; Falmouth Town and Docks, as well as Penmere. Most passengers left at Town, only one other staying with me for the extra half mile to the end of the line. This short section was temporarily closed for five years in 1970, and on my only previous visit trains terminated at Town station, which was then known as The Dell. Due to the gradient drivers weren't permitted to leave their cabs to change ends, so the trains ran on to Docks to reverse anyway.

With the deepest harbour in Western Europe, Falmouth is an active maritime town boasting a proud history. Commerce and the university add to local use, making the branch the busiest in Cornwall. With the missed 'connection' having reduced my stay to half an hour, I had just time for the short walk down to the docks where the Royal Fleet Auxiliary ship *Argus* loomed above the wharf.

Whilst just a single platform, Falmouth Docks station retains some character and a full length canopy, although it's hardly as grand as the original three track granite terminus. An attractive mosaic illustrates the links between the railway and the town's maritime heritage, and can be forgiven for depicting an HST which don't run on the branch. This wasn't as out of place as the rear unit of two linked '153s' that arrived with a couple of passengers, its London Midland City branding seemingly lost in rural Cornwall.

Back at Truro, I watched the Cornish Riviera Express arrive from Paddington, before boarding the 14.41 to Par. A London bound HST, the quiet coach made a welcome haven from the under-floor engine noise of the smaller trains. The greater acceleration of Voyagers allows them to make the journey from Penzance to Plymouth six minutes quicker, but I'd gladly take a bit longer and enjoy the superior comfort of a thirty-five year old train. There were no baseball caps here, and the well spoken couple opposite chatted about chamber music at Wigmore Hall and opera at Glyndebourne. An observation, albeit without statistical basis; there seem to be more well heeled people on the trains from Cornwall to London than anywhere else.

With an hour in Par I walked the mile or so to the beach, picking up a Danish pastry on the way. At the western end of the beach is a china clay plant that until recently used to pump slurry into coasters, with dried powder being taken by rail. The view to the left is rather more attractive, with cliffs heading out to Gribbin Head beyond which is the Fowey Estuary. On our last Newquay holiday I'd taken the train to Par and walked round the coast to Fowey, where the rest of the family joined me for fish and chips. Today I just sat on the beach to eat the very sticky cake – well, ample stickiness to my fingers but not quite enough to hold the cherry that dropped forlornly onto the sand.

Another single coach formed the 16.10 to Newquay, eight of the ten passengers having joined from the connecting London train. The guard checked tickets to see whether anyone needed the request stops, but although we were all going to Newquay it stopped at them anyway. Then we got the full safety announcement about unattended baggage and reporting suspicious items – hardly necessary for ten of us on one coach in Cornwall, where every other guard had shown common sense discretion to dispense with the scripted announcement. Like airline safety demonstrations, overuse eventually leads to no one listening.

The next time I saw the little train was later that evening on the television news. It had collided with a car on a level crossing. No one was hurt and the car driver was being interviewed – *'I've been rushed off my feet all day and was not aware that there was a warning at the crossing. I don't often come down that road. I was travelling fairly slowly and out of the blue saw the train. I slammed on the brakes, but it was coming too fast and hit me. It was quite overwhelming how close I was. I am very thankful to be alive.'* As far as I know being 'rushed off your feet' is not a defence for ignoring warning signs, three big red flashing lights and endangering lives. Should she not have been arrested, not talking to a reporter? And why did she slam on the brakes? Surely either you stop before the crossing or accelerate to get away – you don't halt on the track then blame the train for coming too fast. Should this lady really be driving?

As I ate an excellent carvery dinner in the Griffin Inn, two retired gentleman on the next table were talking about their day visiting Exeter. Travelling for just £5 they'd enjoyed the train ride and a couple of hours in the city. I chatted to a lady who I took to be the proprietor. She'd lived in Newquay all her life and told me how fish used to be brought up from the harbour on a tramway. Once an extension of the railway, with a rope operated incline to the harbourside, this has now been opened up as a walkway. As a child she recalled the circus arriving by train each summer, with elephants, lions and tigers processing from the station, and excited children following behind. It was a big day in the town but she always worried the tiger would get out.

The Holmwood Guest House provided all I needed for the night and at a very reasonable price, my only criticism that they ask for breakfast to be ordered the night before and I never know what I want until morning. A large bowl of hot porridge was an excellent choice. Dave, the owner, told me they get quite a few guests arriving by train, although a lot now fly, and some have had to alter arrangements with there being no Sunday train service in winter.

First job of the morning was to find out if the trains were running after last night's mishap. Local television said no, there was no one to ask at the station, but the helpful lady at National Rail Enquires said yes they were. To check for myself I waited for the 10.13 to arrive, then set off for a morning walk down the old tramway and along one of our favourite stretches of Britain's coast. Half a dozen hardy souls were surfing on Towan Beach, but after a windy walk round the headland I found Fistral Beach deserted, bar another 'one man and his dog' (or were the ones from Carbis Bay following me round Cornwall?). Huge Atlantic rollers pounded the beach, the white surf bright in sunshine, but too rough for even the bravest surfer.

Once a family holiday destination, Newquay has become Britain's premier surfing centre and a popular stag and hen party venue. The typical visitor now spends their time on the waves and in the nightclubs, rather than with buckets and spades on its sandy beaches. Of course some families and older people still come, the latter especially out of the main season, but in the 25 years we've been visiting there has been a marked change in the resort's emphasis. Latterly there's been some effort to attract families back and we still find that with the contrast between a busy town and the quieter coasts either side, plus of course having its own railway, Newquay provides all that's needed for a holiday.

Although a little more extensive than St Ives, with just a single platform Newquay station is a shadow of its former self. At least it still has a booking office (albeit summer only) and café, but most of the buildings and the carriage sidings are now a car park. It is however the only Cornish branch to still have long distance trains, summer services running from the North and London. With limited capacity, on summer Saturdays local services make way for a succession of HSTs bringing thousands of mainly young people to the resort.

The thirteen passengers who boarded the 13.03 to Par contrasted with the queuing system employed on summer Saturdays. Several left us at stations on the way, carrying shopping from a morning in Newquay. A lady behind me read *Three Little Pigs* to her young granddaughter, which with much patience and imagination she made last all the way to Par. My journey was spent enjoying another pasty and the changing scenery – green fields to heathland to china clay works, then a fast flowing stream through a wooded valley as we descended to Par. Single track as far as Goonbarrow Junction, where clay wagons and a strange looking shunting engine stood in a siding, the Newquay branch suits a little train, and the packed HSTs which gingerly traverse it in summer seem as lost as the London Midland '153' looked in Falmouth.

The two coaches of the 13.57 from Par were almost full. It arrived five minutes late, and lost another two by Liskeard. I'd assumed the Looe connection would wait and wasn't best pleased to see it pull out just as I reached the platform. The man in the booking office said I should have asked the guard to call ahead to get it held, but how was I to know? With more than an hour until the next train to Looe I walked into the town, but found it rather ordinary.

Back at the station, as I took a photo of the Looe platform, the signalman called out from his box opposite. Would I like to take some photos inside? We chatted for a few minutes, with just a moment of concern when he thought he saw a senior manager getting off the London train and feared being caught with an unauthorised visitor. As I glanced round for places to hide he realised it was a false alarm and while I snapped away he pulled at levers sending passing HSTs on their way. This traditional signal box had changed little throughout the days of my railway travelling, but he said it would be gone in ten years, with everything controlled centrally from Didcot. In 1960 a train from Paddington to Penzance would be controlled by 185 signal boxes. Now there are just fourteen. On our childhood journeys almost every signal we passed was the old fashioned semaphore type, but with the change to colour lights the semaphore signal on Liskeard's platform is now the first encountered by a train from London.

Liskeard to Looe is perhaps our most eccentric branch line. Right from the start things are a little odd. Instead of the traditional bay for a branch, the Looe platform is at right angles to the main line, but facing due north, the opposite direction to its destination. Originally a goods line running from Bodmin Moor to the coast, and built partly over an old canal, in 1879 passenger services to Looe commenced from Moorswater just west of Liskeard. However, with no connection to the main line and a long walk to Liskeard centre, it was hardly convenient. In 1901, Joseph Thomas, a local engineer, came up with an ingenious solution. A horseshoe curve was built, initially heading north, crossing under the main line, descending steeply and eventually turning 360° to reach the original Looe line.

Coombe Junction, where the lines met and trains still have to reverse before continuing to Looe, has become famous as one of the least used of all our railway stations. Only two trains a day bother to run back the extra few yards to stop there, and the guard told me this is just to save having to go through the closure process. He'd only ever seen half a dozen people use it, all enthusiasts who wanted a ticket showing the name.

I can however claim to have been a genuine user. On a 1970s family day out from Devon, we first walked from Liskeard to Dobwalls miniature railway, then back to the nearest station – Coombe Junction. From here we'd travelled to St Keyne, then walked to Causeland, visiting a wishing well on the way. I don't recall the well being very exciting! The renamed station, St Keyne Wishing Well Halt, suits the line admirably, even if it does sound more like somewhere Thomas the Tank Engine might call at.

My more recent journeys to Looe had been in summer when the train was full with tourists, sometimes with standing room only, but on a dull January afternoon just four passengers boarded another single coach '153' for the 30 minute ride down the wooded East Looe valley. The guard apologised that I'd missed the connection, saying they used to be able to use discretion but are now told when to go or wait. In a time-honoured ritual, he got out at the junction to change the points, while the driver walked through the train from cab to cab. Two buzzes from the guard told her not to stop at the intermediate stations, all of which are request only and sparsely used. So there's a change from my childhood travels – we never saw a lady train driver. Approaching Looe the river becomes tidal, widening as it meets the West Looe, and in a spectacular entry to the town the train skirts its bank. Late afternoon sunshine gave a beautiful light on the still water, contrasted against the dark wooded hillside behind.

Looe remains a working fishing port and from the breakwater I watched a little blue boat, *The Galatea*, returning to harbour followed by a flock of squawking gulls. On the beach two boys practiced rugby with their dad. Four girls dipped their feet in the sea, screaming as small waves covered their ankles. A log in the RNLI window showed that the last lifeboat call out had been on January 1st, to the report of a body in the river. The action recorded, '*Removed one fancy dress costume*'. Contrasting with the summer hoards, only locals walked through the narrow streets.

I'd planned just an hour in Looe and then to travel on to Plymouth, but the missed connection in Liskeard meant a change of arrangements if I was to get back to Penzance for the sleeper. I could have boarded at Plymouth, but didn't fancy a cold evening waiting for the almost midnight departure. Instead I enjoyed a leisurely dinner at the Golden Guinea, an atmospheric old pub dating from 1632, with the rare treat of trifle for dessert.

The 18.33 back to Liskeard was surprisingly busy with fifteen passengers, mostly youngsters off for a Friday evening out. Presumably they get a bus or taxi home. Like both the St Ives and Falmouth branches, there are now more trains to Looe than at any time in the line's history. Only Newquay has fewer trains than shown in the 1962 Western Region timetable, although even the current six is an increase from just four a few years ago. Other than the trains themselves, perhaps the biggest change in Cornwall's railways has been this, an increase in both services and passengers. Anyone seeing the packed summer trains or their importance to locals throughout the year, would understand Transport Minister Barbara Castle's comments when refusing Beeching's plan to close the St Ives and Looe branches, that to do so would be '*the economics of Bedlam*'. I'd been impressed with the Cornish railways and pleased to find them welcoming, efficiently run and well used, even in January.

Back at Liskeard I changed to *The Cornishman*, one of First Great Western's named trains. Commendably they've kept some individuality, which is often lost on our modern railway. Arriving at a very wet Penzance, *Tintagel Castle* was waiting to haul the sleeper back to London. On a Friday night the seven coaches (four sleepers, two seated and a buffet car) were to be busy; the first time they had been since Christmas, Tamsin my friendly attendant told me. Strangely though I'd been able to book the cheapest fare, a mere £49 (less than a night in a hotel with the bonus of being transported 305 miles), whereas on the quieter outward train had to pay £79. A father was boarding with his young daughter, setting off for a weekend in London. How excited she looked. I wandered down to the buffet, securing their last remaining chocolate muffin and chatting to the lady serving, then met the sleeping car attendant who'd looked after me on the journey down. Everyone was so friendly and genuinely pleased to help their passengers. At the start of this chapter I wrote about sleepers – 'what a wonderful way to travel'. Now I must add – the Night Riviera – what a wonderful train.

CHAPTER TWO

AROUND GLASGOW

London – Glasgow – East Kilbride – Troon – Balloch

Our first family holiday that I remember well was in 1970 to Troon, on the Ayrshire coast. Two weeks spent either on the sandy beach or on various trips by train and boat, were perfect for a nine year old. We'd travelled from Euston to Glasgow, changing from electric to diesel engines at Crewe, a journey that took about six hours. The fastest Pendolino does it in just four hours eight minutes.

I visit the Glasgow area several times a year for work, although have to confess that for the first few trips I flew – then I discovered the sleeper and now wouldn't go any other way. After an evening at home it's a relaxed journey to Euston, I'm asleep in my cabin by midnight and wake at 7am just as we approach Glasgow. With time for breakfast then a short train ride, I can arrive at a customer for a 9am meeting. Flying just doesn't compare, the hour in the air being a fraction of the total journey time. To drive to the airport, park, pass security, pick up a hire car and struggle through the Glasgow traffic, would mean getting up at 4am. Plenty of business people do it, but I wonder how many would prefer the sleeper if only they gave it a try.

Another bonus of the sleeper is that rather than having to rush back to the airport, once my meetings are finished I'm free to explore Scotland. While others struggle with check-in queues, x-rays and metal detectors, I've spent evenings by sea, lochs and mountains, either returning to Glasgow or getting a sleeper back from further afield. For this trip I was visiting a customer in East Kilbride, then spending a few days travelling around Glasgow and the West Highlands.

As a regular passenger I buy a block of ten single tickets, which are valid for any Scottish sleeper, with a good discount. As a bonus they're First Class, which allowed me to wait in the warmth of the Virgin lounge at Euston, with free drinks and snacks. More importantly, First Class guarantees a private berth, whilst cheaper tickets can mean sharing with a stranger. First Class also tends to be quieter, especially in summer when American tourists in shared berths have that annoying tendency to talk just too loudly.

It was a long walk down Platform 15. The 'Lowland Sleeper' has sixteen coaches, half for Edinburgh and half for Glasgow, the train splitting at Carstairs. The 'Highland Sleeper', which leaves Euston around three hours earlier, is actually three trains in one, portions for Aberdeen, Inverness and Fort William dividing in the night at Edinburgh. Having run in this form since the late 1980s, when separate overnight trains stopped running from both Euston and Kings Cross, the service was recently threatened after Transport Scotland issued a consultation suggesting changes or withdrawal of the sleepers. A promise from Westminster of £50 million funding for new or refurbished trains was matched by the Scottish Government, and they will soon have their own franchise, securing the future of this historic link between Scotland and London. With an annual usage of 274,000, a five year increase of 31%, there's clearly a demand for the sleepers.

There was snow on the platform at Euston, but none in Glasgow where I followed my usual routine: shower, left luggage, visit to Boots to buy the item I invariably forget (this time a comb), toasted croissant with strawberry jam in Franco's Italian café on the station concourse, a quick walk to see the Clyde, then board the 8.42 to East Kilbride. Often as I've travelled through Glasgow's suburbs and into the countryside, I've thought that the stops on this 11½ mile line have an almost poetic ring – Crossmyloof, Pollokshaws West, Thornliebank, Giffnock, Clarkston, Busby, Thorntonhall, Hairmyres, East Kilbride. Perhaps a modern day Flanders and Swan could put them to music?

Diesel operated, but with long term plans for electrification, the trains always seem to be well used, with school children, commuters and shoppers making use of what I've found to be a very reliable half hourly service. After Clarkston the line becomes semi-rural, and today, with sunshine breaking through morning mist to cast its rays across frost covered countryside, was probably the most beautiful of my many journeys to East Kilbride.

After a couple of hours discussing glue, with business completed I could concentrate on travelling. The two coach train back was almost full by Glasgow, the guard having spent the journey rushing up and down to sell tickets, breaking off in mid-transaction to release the doors at each stop.

Back in Glasgow, I made the short walk to Queen Street station, where on the lower platforms I found another difference between modern rail travel and that of my youth. In those days it was considered that people were capable of using stairs without instruction. Now, in the days of 'health & safety gone mad', a constant loop helpfully announces, *Customers are reminded to always use the hand rail and take care on the stairs'*. With such assistance I successfully negotiated the staircase, but managed to cross the platform and board the 13.23 to Balloch by the simple action of placing one foot in front of the other without any instruction whatsoever.

After running through a tunnel to Partick, the three coach electric train ran along the banks of the Clyde, passing the impressive exhibition centre and with a view to Ibrox Park over the river. This journey to the southern end of Loch Lomond I'd done a couple of times after meetings, but first made on our Troon holiday when we caught the *Maid of the Loch* paddle steamer to Tarbet Pier, then an Oban train back from Arrochar and Tarbet station.

The *Maid of the Loch*, the last paddle steamer built in Britain, was constructed on the Clyde, then dismantled and brought by rail to Balloch, where she was reassembled and launched in 1953. With space for 1,000 passengers, she was by far the largest ship ever to sail on the loch. Previously vessels had been brought from the Clyde up the River Leven, on one occasion schoolchildren being given the day off school so they could board a steamer and weigh her down enough to pass under a bridge!

Our trip on a real steam ship was one of the highlights of our childhood holidays, and more than 40 years later I clearly recall going down to a lower deck with my sister and watching steam hissing in the engine room with shiny pistons pumping. Sadly, cost pressures meant she was taken out of service in 1981 and this historic ship has been moored at Balloch ever since. The long process of restoration has been continuing for some years and the ship is now regularly open as a restaurant and wedding venue. It was hoped that she will finally be steamed again in 2013.

Balloch Pier station, which served mainly to connect with sailings on the loch, closed in 1986, so I walked the half mile from the new terminus to the pier where *Maid of the Loch* is berthed. Her red funnel standing out against the blue sky, and with snow clad mountains in the background, she made a splendid sight. There are plans to move the recently closed 10¼ inch gauge Isle of Mull Railway to Balloch, serving both the pier and nearby shopping centre. Hopefully before too long it will be possible to take a miniature steam train to the end of the loch, then once more to cruise on a paddle steamer around the islands of Loch Lomond.

With the sun shining and sky blue, before travelling back to Glasgow I went for a stroll along the wooded eastern banks of the loch. Much of the waterside isn't accessible, but with the water perfectly still and snow capped mountains in the distance, the path below Balloch Castle made a beautiful walk.

I saw the guard only once on the 15.53 back to Glasgow, a contrast to the East Kilbride line. With six coaches and most of the stops having no ticket issuing facilities, some passengers undoubtedly travelled for free. ScotRail probably lose less than the cost of old fashioned booking offices and ticket inspectors, but a proportion of regular local passengers will know they've got a good chance of a free journey.

Delayed by a cash machine that decided to go through the full process of requiring PIN number and various options for withdrawal of cash before telling me it had run out, I almost missed the six coach train to Troon. It was full with returning commuters and I got virtually the last seat. The brand new, bright and airy Class 380 electric trains on the Ayrshire Coast line are a huge improvement from the DMUs that ran until electrification in 1986, and a significant step up from the old electric units they recently replaced.

We crossed the Clyde, then headed east through Paisley and into the countryside where evening mist hung over lochs and fields. As I wrote in

No Boat Required on my way to Dumfries, '*Even away from the more famous mountains, almost every train journey in Scotland has scenery that deserves looking out the window, but I was the only one to be doing so today.*' While I enjoyed the views, the Ayrshire commuters read, slept or rang home to discuss dinner arrangements. The lady opposite was having cottage pie. At Kilwinning the line splits, our train continuing south towards Ayr. The other branch to Ardrossan and Largs we'd used on our 1970 holiday, catching boats to the islands of Arran and Cumbrae.

The South Beach Hotel provided a huge bedroom and good dinner at a reasonable price. They cater mainly for golfers, but January and February are very quiet. Most guests only stop a day or two and I was told it would be unusual for anyone to stay a week in Troon, let alone the two we had in 1970. Three hotels have closed in the last few years and most of the bed & breakfasts are gone. Troon, like much of Scotland, is now a short break destination.

My wandering on a cold evening and brisk morning walk on the beach, suggested that it's a pleasant little town that happens to be by the sea, but no longer a holiday resort. One of the aims of my travels was to find out if the seemingly obscure places we'd stayed at on childhood holidays were an unusual choice then, or whether forty years later the towns had changed. With its sandy beach and good position for trips out, it seems that Troon was an excellent choice in 1970, but is no longer a family holiday destination. The half hourly train service to Glasgow taking only 40 minutes, 10 minutes quicker and more frequent than before electrification, must be a factor in Troon's change from resort to commuter town.

The station is still staffed, and seeing my hat, the booking clerk said they didn't get many West Ham fans round here. We contrasted our team's fortunes, mine top of their league but only because the other 23 clubs were even worse, and his, Kilmarnock, playing well but not winning. The attractive station retains its original Victorian architecture and was refurbished for the Open Golf Championship in 2004, when an estimated 100,000 people used it in one week.

As I waited for the Glasgow train a two coach '156' from Stranraer to Kilmarnock pulled into the other platform. I'd been to Stranraer on a cold January day for my tidal island travels, writing in *No Boat Required*:

'Changing at Kilwinning, I joined the Stranraer train and what I lovely ride it was. First running close to the sea with views across the Firth of Clyde to Arran and its snow covered mountains, then as we approached Girvan, the famous rock of Ailsa Craig, often picked out by TV cameras from golf at Troon or Turnberry. Leaving the sea we headed inland, climbing to the remote station of Barhill, then across wild and snowy moorland with views to the hills of the Southern Uplands. Like the Dumfries line, the route passes through scenery that in England would have National Park status, but this single track line was wilder and more remote – it could easily have been in the far north of Scotland, not this little known corner of the south west.'

Had there been time I would have liked to have repeated the journey, but wanted to return to Glasgow for a ride on one of our more unusual railways, before heading further north.

Affectionately known as 'The Clockwork Orange', the Glasgow Subway was only the third underground railway in the world (after London and Budapest), and the only one to be hauled by a giant cable driven by a surface steam engine. Converted to third rail electric in 1935, the line's four foot gauge and narrow eleven foot tunnel bore, are unique to Glasgow. It was taken over by Glasgow Corporation in 1936, and renamed Glasgow Underground, but many users refused to use the new name and in 2003 'Subway' was officially reinstated. Before a complete renovation in 1977 all the stations had island platforms, so only the side of the trains that passengers saw received a full coat of paint.

I joined at St. Enoch, which once served St. Enoch main line station, from where trains ran on the Midland route to Leeds and London. After closing in 1966, the services using its twelve platforms were diverted to Glasgow Central. Despite protests, the station and hotel were demolished in 1977, the rubble being used to help fill in Queen's Dock, on which the Scottish Exhibition and Conference Centre were built.

Subway trains run in both directions, taking 24 minutes to complete a circuit of the 15 stations. I find the designation of inner and outer circle, rather than clockwise and anticlockwise, a confusing way to show the direction, but worked out which platform to use to go the long way round to Buchanan Street, adjacent to Queens Street station. It's hard to write about the Subway without using the word diminutive. The little orange three coach trains look more the type one might find on a pier or theme park, than carrying 13 million passengers a year under a major city.

My outer circle train was quiet, only a couple of passengers joining at Ibrox which is somewhat busier when Rangers are at home. I'm not sure how the Subway copes with crowds of 50,000 at Ibrox Park, but in 2007 it was threatened that it would be closed on match days. The problem wasn't overcrowding, but Rangers supporters performing the 'bouncy bouncy', a boisterous celebration when fans jump and down, which it was feared could derail a train.

At Govan a group of disabled children and their helpers left the train, being met on the platform by a member of Subway staff. The driver gave them a friendly peep on the horn as we pulled away. The busiest stations were Hillhead (which I still automatically associate with the suffix 'by-election' after Roy Jenkins historic victory in 1981) and Buchannan Street. Alighting at the latter, I took the moving walkway to Queen Street, from where my journeys to the West Highlands are described in the next chapter.

CHAPTER THREE

WEST HIGHLANDS – IN SEARCH OF SNOW

Glasgow – Oban – Fort William – London

Other than the return from Arrochar and Tarbet after our *Maid of the Loch* cruise, my first journey on the West Highland Line had been for our holiday at Oban in 1973, when the trains were still locomotive hauled. The move to Sprinter operation is probably the biggest change on what many consider to be Britain's most scenic railway. My other trips have all been fairly recent, either visiting tidal islands or exploring Scotland after work meetings. I'd never been in winter so booked a February trip hoping to see the Highlands in snow.

Unlike Central and the two lower platforms at Queen Street, the seven upper Queen Street platforms accommodate only diesel trains, although plans recently announced to electrify the route to Edinburgh will bring wires into the station. Modern trains however have no difficulty negotiating the 1 in 42 gradient through the tunnel immediately outside the station, but until 1909 trains had been pulled by a rope attached to a stationary engine. Like Central however, Beeching's closure of a nearby terminus (Buchanan Street) means that Queen Street is pushed for capacity.

Separate trains used to run from Glasgow to Oban and Fort William, but Sprinter operation has allowed the more efficient operation of dividing at Crianlarich. With twenty eight passengers the Oban portion of the 12.21 was the busier. I'd booked an advance ticket for the bargain price of £9.40 for the 101 miles (it was £6.90 for a third the distance from Troon to Glasgow), but with all the reservations in one coach opted to sit in the other, which was almost empty. However, I soon questioned my choice, finding a lady nearby was exceeding the normal annoying sniffing, and snorting at regular intervals.

Joining the route I'd followed to Balloch the day before, we ran under the Erskine Bridge and along the banks of the Clyde. Dumbarton Hillfort, an ancient fortress guarding the Clyde, is the first spectacular landmark and a sign that we were leaving lowland Scotland. At Helensburgh the ferry to Gourock was crossing the Clyde, a journey that takes 40 minutes, compared to 2 hours by train and more than 2½ hours by bus. It was however due to close in two months time, Strathclyde Partnership for Transport deciding that it no longer merited subsidy.

Here we turned to the right, our single track line leaving the Clyde and heading into the hills. Climbing steeply above Gare Loch we looked down on the Faslane nuclear submarine base, then as the scenery started to get wilder, followed the slender Loch Long. From Arrochar & Tarbet the train runs above Loch Lomond and with no leaves on the trees we could see much more of the loch than just the glimpses possible in summer.

By now I was regretting my choice of carriage – the snorting lady had started talking! And why is it that people blessed with an annoying voice, feel the need both to use it at maximum volume and to spout total rubbish? The lady opposite her had joined the train at Dumbarton and was travelling back to her home on Mull after a scan at the hospital. She couldn't drive, so for her the train and ferry were a vital link, but must have regretted her selection of seat. Snorting lady found that they had a mutual acquaintance and must have told her a dozen times to 'tell Brian you met me'. Mull lady remained polite but snorting lady either failed to read or take heed of her obvious attempts at disinterest.

Ardlui is where north and southbound trains pass, the longer stop allowing smokers a chance to feed their habit. Snorting lady joined the handful of addicts on the platform, giving us a few minutes break, but soon returned at full volume. At Crianlarich more passengers got out to stretch legs, enjoy fresh mountain air, or pollute it, snorting lady joining the last group of course. I smiled at Mull lady, my comment 'having a quick rest' eliciting knowing raised eyebrows. For the rest of the journey she slept or perhaps feigned sleep, and I moved to the end of the carriage. Snorting lady was left with just the refreshment trolley lady to bellow at.

Oban used to be served by a line from Callander, which crossed the West Highland route at Crianlarich, where there were two stations. Beeching closed the eastern part of the line and trains switched to the current route from Glasgow, joining the old Callander and Oban railway via a sharp curve immediately after Crianlarich station.

From here the line heads west, through mountains, past little streams and tiny lochs. This was wild and remote – real Highland scenery. When discussing our most scenic railways the Oban line is often forgotten, but in many ways is just as spectacular as the more famous route to Fort William and Mallaig. Passing through Glen Lochy we reached Loch Awe, the ruined Kilchurn Castle atmospheric by the still waters of the third largest freshwater loch in Scotland. Two passengers joined at Loch Awe station, where an old carriage in West Highland Railway colours sits on an isolated length of track. Until recently it was used as a tea room and had been brought here by a ballast train in 1988. In a highly unusual operation, to save the cost of bringing a crane to this remote spot the main line was temporally severed and slued so the carriage could be shunted onto its own piece of track.

Passengers were joining and leaving at every station, the train a vital link for these isolated communities. A young lady with a bike had got on at Tyndrum, three alighted at Dalmally and five boarded at Taynuilt, from where we'd caught a boat up Loch Etive on our family holiday. Only Falls of Cruachan was deserted, its lack of lighting meaning that trains stop only in summer. Having closed in 1965, with the sort of initiative some claim only privatisation brings, it was reopened at a cost of just £10,000 in 1988. The platform was rebuilt by piling discarded concrete sleepers collected from linesides all over the Highlands, and the local council persuaded to build a path to the nearby Cruachan Visitors Centre.

It's hard to believe that Connel Ferry, the final stop before Oban, was once a busy junction with seventeen staff. The station at the head of Loch Etive retains the name 'Ferry', although this stopped running many years ago and the village is now known as just Connel. The branch to Ballachulish closed in 1966, but the impressive bridge over the loch remains. When built it was the second longest cantilever bridge in Europe and carried cars and pedestrians across in special trains. Later it was converted for use by cars or trains, although only one or the other could cross at a time, and when the railway closed the bridge switched to road use.

During the demolition of Connel Ferry signal box, contractors burning the wooden remains accidentally set fire to the track formation. Despite efforts to extinguish the fire, it continued to burn for several days, causing the embankment to crumble and smoke to issue from the trackbed. The Callander section of the line had closed a month early following a landslip and there were fears that damage from the fire might cause the loss of Oban's railway. As we will read about Ribblehead and Barmouth, infrastructure problems were used to try to justify closures, but fortunately common sense prevailed, retaining this vital link for both Oban and the Western Isles.

Known as 'Gateway to the Isles', ferries run from Oban to nine islands, and the boat from Mull was coming in as I walked along the waterfront to Kilchrenan House guesthouse. Deb and I stayed here in 1993, enjoying the fine views and breakfasts. On that holiday our only train journey was an evening trip to Dalmally, with a stroll along the River Orchy. I returned to Oban more recently, stopping a night before driving to Campbeltown to visit Davaar Island, and was pleased to be back again at one of my favourite Scottish towns. As the only place of any size for many miles and with ferries coming and going, Oban is always busy, but even in summer one doesn't have to go far to find tranquillity.

Our 1973 Oban holiday was perhaps most memorable for being thrown out of a bed and breakfast. After a few days staying with a Mrs McLoed, she suddenly announced that we'd have to leave. Apparently she was offended that my brother (aged five), had made disparaging comments about her dinners. Mum wanted to go home, but Dad wasn't going to have our holiday spoiled. The Tourist Information Office were quite horrified and managed to get us rooms with Mrs McDonald, a lovely lady whose welcome contrasted with the dour Mrs McLoed. She even kindly forwarded the notebook I left behind, which contained my log of the Flying Scotsman run that features in Chapter Seven.

It had started to rain almost as soon as I'd got off the train, but one of Oban's facilities that we'd found very useful on our childhood holiday has now gone – a glassworks by the harbour where we stood close to the furnaces to dry out from the rain. After wandering round the harbour and browsing an excellent selection of Scottish books in Waterstones, I took the advice of Colin at Kilchrenan House and had an early dinner at Piazza by the harbour. For early evening diners they charge the same as the time arriving, so sitting down at five to six I paid just £5.55 for a most enjoyable meal – a successful offer as there must have been more people here than the rest of Oban's restaurants put together.

A photo in their toilet showed the original station, a far grander affair than the two uncovered platforms which remain. These were built for the Ballachulish branch, but the train shed and original station building have been demolished, despite the latter being listed. Half a mile south of the station is one of our few remaining 'ticket platforms', where trains once halted for passengers' tickets to be checked. These were unpopular as they delayed arrival at the terminus, and were taken out of use when corridor trains made on-board collection possible.

Whilst guards now check tickets on Oban trains, those arriving at Glasgow have to negotiate automatic gates, the modern method of combating fare evasion, but often adding to journey times. Indeed on several occasions I've missed trains at Upminster because the gates invariably refuse to open for tickets to long distance destinations, although buying a ticket there is even worse. The days of experienced staff with knowledge of the railway network are gone and some struggle to sell any ticket that's off the C2C line. Although train journey times might be faster, hassles buying tickets, doors locked two minutes before departure, waiting for the guard to release them at stations and getting through the gates, can all add to the true travelling time.

Whilst on this theme, I must just tell you what annoys me on almost every journey back to Upminster. In the days of a guard on the train, they would check all was well before signalling to the driver to move off. Guards were however dispensed with to save money, although had they also done a bit of ticket checking, not just sat in the back cab, perhaps they'd have paid their way. So now the driver has to use a mirror to ensure it's safe to depart, but at Upminster the footbridge meant they couldn't put a mirror at the eight coach stopping point, so most busy trains have to halt at the end of the platform where the driver can use the twelve coach mirror. It may seem minor, but every day several thousand people have their journey extended by the extra thirty second walk, and every day some of those boarding at Upminster have to scamper along the platform, not expecting the train to stop at the far end.

It was still raining the next morning in Oban as I enjoyed breakfast in front of a real fire, watching the Lismore ferry glide across the misty harbour. The boat to Mull passed as I set out on a morning walk, two miles around the shore to Ganavan Bay – Oban's beach. We'd come here several times in 1973 and I was interested to see if it was still a family beach. It was a pleasant walk, albeit all on the road, especially once the rain ceased.

Thirty-eight years after we'd dug sandcastles and dammed streams, I instantly recognised the little bay, although there have been changes. The shelter where we'd sat to escape rain showers was gone, as was much of the sand at the top of the beach. This I was told gets washed away in winter storms but is replaced for the summer. The biggest change though was a collection of nineteen ugly white houses at the southern end of what was once a purely rural bay. A notice for 'Ganavan Sands' development said it was inspired by *'Natural Perfection'*, which indeed it was – until they built the apartments. In summer families still come to play on Ganavan Beach, and with highland cattle grazing yards away, sheep on the headland and views to Mull and Lismore across the sea, it's still a lovely spot – but why ever did they allow such ugly houses to be built here?

There were forty passengers on the 12.11 to Glasgow, with five more joining at Connel Ferry and four at Taynault. Swelled with walkers and tourists, in summer the trains are full, but all year round they provide a crucial service for West Highland residents. Part way through the Pass of Brander along the banks of Loch Awe we came to a stop, the guard and driver getting out and walking down the track. Here, under the steep slopes of Ben Cruachan, 'stone signals' protect the track. Mechanically linked to wires along the mountainside, the semaphore signals are tripped if a falling boulder breaks the wire, warning the driver of an obstruction on the line. Today it was a false alarm, the signal perhaps having been tripped by a sheep.

The system, which has been in use since 1882, has prevented many accidents, but failed to stop the derailment of an Oban-bound train in June 2010. On this occasion the 18.20 from Glasgow hit boulders which had fallen from below the wires, leaving one coach hanging over the embankment. A fire from leaking diesel was quickly put out and although eight were taken to hospital, none of the sixty passengers were seriously hurt.

Tyndrum, with a population of just 167, is the smallest place in UK to have two stations, one on the Oban line and one the Fort William. The Mallaig portion, to which we'd be joined at Crianlarich, could be seen running down the other side of the valley. We won the race and after watching the newly linked trains head off for Glasgow, I set out for a quick walk round the village. It didn't take long! There's one shop and a couple of hotels but not much to detain the visitor, although the village is an excellent base for mountain walking.

My parents had once spent 2½ hours on the station after arriving early in the morning on the sleeper. The refreshment room had opened at 9am, where they had breakfast and sat until the Oban train arrived. Today this was closed for the winter, but it's busy in summer providing welcome cups of tea for both train passengers and drivers. In 1973 there were no buffets or trolleys on the trains, and like many passengers Dad had hurried to the refreshment room to buy drinks when we stopped for a few minutes.

I was back in time to board the 14.21 to Fort William. The Oban portion left first, after which followed a moment of panic. I was just about to step aboard when the lights on the doors went out. Frantic pressing of the button and banging on the door had no effect and the train started to move. Visions of a six hour wait flashed before me, before a lady said not to worry – the guard had announced they'd be moving down the platform so the driver could change the points, and it was OK for passengers to wait on the platform. After my frantic banging I felt rather silly!

After running through Strath Fillan to Upper Tyndrum, the line heads north into the mountains, traversing a horseshoe curve that was built because there wasn't enough money for a viaduct. This is a rare line where most of the track is still jointed and we hear the clickety-clack of the wheels that used to accompany every train ride. As I used to in my childhood, I counted the joins to calculate the speed, one mile per hour for each length of track covered in 42 seconds. We were rattling along at 72mph.

After Bridge of Orchy we were on Rannoch Moor – a thousand foot high plateau surrounded by distant mountains – twenty miles of treeless peat bog with no roads. Many call the moor bleak or desolate, but with its myriad of little lochs I prefer to consider it a magical and awesome wilderness. To construct the route across this inhospitable terrain where traditional foundations would sink into the bogs, 19th century engineers floated the line on a mattress of tree roots, brushwood, earth and ash. There are no sheep or cattle here, just deer. Four stags looked up from nibbling the grass, thought for a moment, then decided to run away. Pools in the peat were frozen and thick slabs of ice partly covered the streams. It had been very cold here but the only snow was on the mountain tops. There was more snow in Essex than Scotland.

The moors are higher after Rannoch Station and Britain's only snow shelters protect the line. Avalanche fences are still in place, but with milder winters haven't been maintained. The line was however closed for two weeks in 2010 after four avalanches blocked the tracks near Bridge of Orchy.

1347 feet above sea level we stopped at Corrour, made famous in the film *Trainspotting* (which isn't about trains) and my favourite station in the whole of Britain. I came here once after a morning meeting in Glasgow, and found a perfect place – a railway station but no cars, a rough track but no road, a loch surrounded by mountains, wild moors and next to the station a single house offering B&B and meals. That afternoon I'd walked round the loch, enjoyed scampi & chips, then travelled back to Glasgow. One day I'll use the sleeper here, boarding the train on a London evening and getting off next morning in the wilds of Scotland at our highest main line station.

The station owes its existence to Sir John Stirling-Maxwell, the 10th Baronet of Pollock, who allowed the West Highland Railway Company to build the line across his land on the condition that they provided a station to serve his estate. Guests visiting for deer stalking and grouse shooting were conveyed from the station by horse-drawn carriage to the head of Loch Ossian, from where a small steamer took them to his shooting lodge. The estate still offers accommodation and the opportunity to shoot deer for those who enjoy killing wild animals, although now it's a Land Rover that meets the trains.

For some miles we ran along Loch Treig where mountains reflected in the still water, although with mist obscuring the summits today wasn't as spectacular as my last ride on the sleeper. Then with early morning sunshine and clear blue skies, the line was at its best. Descending back to sea level, the driver needed regular brake applications as we negotiated Monessie Gorge, where the railway perches on a ledge over the rocky canyon, with the fast flowing river and waterfalls below.

The West Highland Line seems to be a service people care about. All the stations are well maintained with the original buildings painted in green and white, although in mid winter they were sparsely used. There are no bus shelters here. In summer three even have tea rooms and Bridge of Orchy has a bunk house. Most of the train's twenty eight passengers were locals, but four students sitting near me were travelling for a weekend away and alighted at Spean Bridge. Last time I passed through here on the sleeper I observed a very small scale 'freight' operation – a lady giving the guard a tray of packets of hand made fudge to hand over to the steam train at Fort William, where they'd be sold to passengers en route to Mallaig.

The train reversed at Fort William, continuing to Mallaig on what many consider to be the most scenic of all our railways. We did the whole route once on the Jacobite steam train and I went as far as Arisaig, Britain's most westerly station, in search of tidal islands. It's a spectacular ride as the train passes beside lochs and sea, and over Glenfinnan Viaduct (which features in Harry Potter films, with Harry travelling over it both by steam train and flying Ford Anglia), but doesn't have quite the remote wildness of Rannoch Moor.

For many years Fort William was one of three British mainland towns that I'd only arrived at by water. The other two were Gosport, via the ferry from Portsmouth, and Dedham in Essex, which we'd rowed to from Flatford Mill on one of our childhood days out. The visit to Fort William was on our Oban holiday, aboard the *King George V*, a 1926 Clyde steamer in its penultimate year of service. Like the *Maid of the Loch*, I was fortunate to sail on this ship which belongs to a bygone era, and is said to have been our finest post war excursion steamer. Sadly she was destroyed by fire in 1981 while docked in Cardiff.

Today I had three hours until catching the sleeper back to London, but half of that would be in darkness. Despite its superb loch side location at the foot of Ben Nevis, the town itself is nothing special. An opportunity was lost when the railway station was moved back from the shore, but rather than open this up as the asset it should be, a dual carriageway was built between town and sea. Hence I headed the other way, on the Great Glen Way, along the banks of Loch Linnhe. I walked as far as Soldiers' Bridge, a footbridge over the River Lochy. It was named because it was built by the Royal Engineers on an exercise, and runs parallel to the bridge that takes the Mallaig line over the river. Constructed with cast iron pillars and castellated masonry towers, the railway bridge was designed to be sympathetic to the adjacent Inverlochy Castle. With dusk approaching I turned back after crossing the bridge, but after a twenty minute conversation with a man walking his dog (Skye), ended up negotiating the woods in the dark.

Fort William is an unattractive but civilised station, with ticket office, buffet, showers and possibly uniquely in the UK, self service left luggage lockers. Our few stations with left luggage facilities generally require bags to be searched or x-rayed, and it's refreshing that at least here Network Rail now takes a common sense view of the 'risk'. On an earlier visit I'd been less than happy at finding the lockers closed due to 'terrorist threat' and having to lug a heavy bag around.

Eight of us waited behind the barrier until at exactly the appointed time of 19.20, a man removed the tape and beckoned us onto the platform to board one of Britain's most famous trains. Known as 'The Deerstalker Express' on account of some of the more affluent types who have used it, the train is a true travel experience. In summer it's invariably fully booked, mostly with tourists, but having never used it in winter I was interested to see how many were travelling. The four coaches, two sleepers, a lounge car and a seated coach, are pulled by a powerful Class 67 locomotive. Capable of 125 miles per hour, it wasn't going to stretch its legs on this journey. These newer locomotives actually slowed the service down from the old Class 37s they replaced, their extra weight meaning greater speed restrictions on the bridges. I used the sleeper just a few weeks before the old locomotives were replaced and have to admit that their traditional shape and engine noise made for a more evocative ride than the quiet modern engines. On that occasion two enthusiasts were making the journey as a last chance to enjoy the Class 37, but the staff couldn't wait for the day they were replaced with something more reliable.

The lounge car on the Highland sleepers is a truly delightful experience. The menu includes a surprisingly large wine list, good choice of evening meals from chicken curry, cheeseburger and of course haggis, neeps & tatties, plus a new addition, some tempting deserts. Having had dinner in Fort William, I had room for just the chocolate pudding and custard, but was nearly tempted by the cheeseboard with grapes and oatcakes which has recently been restored to sleeper menus. Eleven passengers served by an attentive steward, with a quiet but friendly atmosphere – a little piece of Britishness trundling through the mountains.

In 1995 the train was nearly axed, but after a heated campaign and with some influential users, the government eventually agreed to continue the subsidy. Although far from paying its way, improved publicity (it has become a popular subject for travel journalists) has helped to fill the trains.

As we approached Roy Bridge the guard announced he was going to 'wave to Marjorie'. One of his colleagues, who was travelling to London to pick up her two young grandchildren, explained. Marjorie lives near the station and waves to all the trains – all eight that pass each day, except the sleeper on Thursday mornings when she goes shopping in town. She's always at her kitchen window, washing up as the train goes by. They think her plates must be wearing thin! Once someone was on the phone to her, but Marjorie said she'd have to go as the train was due and 'they like her to wave'. One day she didn't wave to the first train. The driver rang Fort William and asked them to look out on the next one. Again she didn't wave. Concerned by her absence, someone drove down in a car and found she wasn't well.

Just before the station there was Marjorie waving from her window. As we all waved back I wondered if somehow in the dark the driver had taken a wrong turning and taken us to the Island of Sodor. With a driver checking the track for landslides, rails moved to shunt a coach, trays of fudge and a waving old lady, the West Highland Line didn't seem far removed from the land of Thomas and co.

I retired to my bed at Crianlarich. Waking next morning I pulled up the blind. We were approaching Watford. Outside everything was white – I'd found the snow!

Post Script: Almost a year later I made another trip to Fort William, travelling on the sleeper from Euston. This time it was a wild and wintry journey. I pulled up the blind as dawn broke over Loch Lomond on a freezing Scottish morning. Suddenly there was a bang as the train juddered to a sudden stop – we had hit a tree. By the time I was dressed and leaning out the window, the guard and driver were trying to pull branches from under the locomotive. They wouldn't budge. A Network Rail man had to be summoned with a chainsaw. Fortunately we weren't far from Ardlui station and an hour after the collision we were free and trundling north again.

As we gained height the weather worsened. Gales of 100mph had been forecast for mountain tops, with wind chill down to -24°, and it was a wild run across Rannoch Moor. Sitting in a warm lounge car with breakfast, I didn't envy the man who got out at Corrour to go climbing in the blizzard. As we arrived at Fort William I half expected to find the Fat Controller thanking the engine for getting the train through in such weather, but to the superb ScotRail staff on the remarkable Highland Line these conditions are all in a day's work.

CHAPTER FOUR

OVER THE WATER TO KENT

Upminster – Aylesford – Stratford – Upminster

Not all our family outings involved half a dozen trains, a bus or a boat, and a long walk in the rain to see a pile of rocks. Sometimes it didn't rain. Today I set out to repeat the early 1970s trip that we remember as epitomising days out with the family – eight trains, a ferry, picnic in a railway station waiting room and a walk in continuous rain, all to see some prehistoric rocks – Kits Koty near Aylesford in Kent.

Our route to Kent involved train to Tilbury Riverside, the ferry to Gravesend, then more trains. It was a journey we did about once a year, but one I hadn't experienced since getting a car in 1979, even my father having to admit that the Dartford Tunnel was a quicker route to Kent.

Today didn't start well – C2C, the strangely named but usually efficient train operator, lost a train! Thirty-one passengers waited for the 9.18 to Grays, which the departure board showed as on time, but no train arrived. After a few minutes there was an announcement – '*Attention of customers on Platform Two, I'm trying to find out what's happened to your train*'. At least we had the rare sound of a real person on the public address, the automated announcements clearly unable to cope with a train having disappeared. As passengers shuffled feet or talked on mobiles there was still no news. C2C's computer seemed to think the train was running, but where was it? A lady told me this kept happening and she'd be late for work again. She worked in Costa's at Lakeside but fortunately her boss was understanding. Eventually we got another announcement – there had been problems earlier at Pitsea and the train wasn't coming. We'd have to wait for the 9.45. It was still a mystery why the computerised system hadn't known the train was cancelled, but showing the benefits of the old fashioned way, the real man at Upminster kept passengers informed, telling us that the 9.45 had just passed Dagenham and would be with us soon.

The excellent air conditioned Electrostar trains which were introduced in 2001, have revolutionised the London Tilbury & Southend route and proved to be the most reliable electric units in the country. The last of the old slam door units were withdrawn in 2003, making C2C the first train operator to replace its entire fleet. They are excellent trains, although today my journey through Essex countryside was marred by having to listen to the tinny sound of another man's music. Such is the lack of respect for C2C's Quiet Coaches that I've started avoiding them, finding the frustration of passengers sitting under a 'Quiet' sign, but blatantly playing music or talking on mobiles, even greater than the annoyance of the noise itself. Regular passengers will know that there's something magic about C2C's Quiet Coach signs – they are completely invisible to the residents of Barking.

Originally a through route from Romford, after the line was severed by the District Line, Upminster to Grays was run as a branch, with trains using bay platforms at both ends. In the days when my wife commuted to London, the tendency of those changing from the Grays line to push to the front to secure the best positions on the Fenchurch Street train, led to it being dubbed the 'Dragon Wagon'.

Trains on the single track route usually pass at Ockendon, once an attractive country station, but now mostly boarded up and scarred by an ugly concrete footbridge. The line gives pleasant views across the fields of Essex, the first countryside reached from London, Upminster being the start of the Green Belt. Chafford Hundred station was opened in 1993, serving the new town and Lakeside Shopping Centre, the large increase in passengers helping to transform the line from an hourly shuttle to half hourly service to London.

With no need to change at Grays (going out used to be OK but on the return we invariably had to run through the subway to catch the Upminster connection), I travelled through to Tilbury, sadly though not Tilbury Riverside, but Tilbury Town, a mile from the ferry terminal. Being on a spur off the main line, trains had to reverse at Riverside before continuing their journeys on to Southend, an operational difficulty that contributed to the station's demise.

Originally named Tilbury Fort, Tilbury Riverside station was opened in 1854, enabling the London Tilbury and Southend Railway to offer cheap fares via the ferry to Gravesend, then a 'seaside' resort, in competition with the South Eastern Railway's direct trains from London. Boat trains with restaurant cars used to run from St Pancras to connect with liners, but as planes replaced ships for international travel and the Dartford Tunnel reduced ferry usage, the station's days were numbered. What was once a hub of activity became a largely deserted outpost and to be honest closure was both inevitable and justified.

Tilbury Town and ferry are now linked by a bus, run by Clintona Coaches, who my wife used to drive for. Unfortunately it didn't bother to wait two minutes for my slightly late arriving train, leaving me a wait of 28 minutes for the next one.

The floating landing stage from which the ferry departs is now partly a car park and the old walkway to Tilbury Riverside Station, fenced off and derelict. The platforms and tracks were taken away and a metal wall erected along the open side of the station hall. The impressive station building, with a distinctive turret clock tower and weather vane on its roof, is Grade II listed, so fortunately couldn't be demolished. When passing on my *Essex Coast Walk* I wandered in, keen to see what had become of this historic building, which we used to pass through in my youth. In 2008 I wrote:

'*The old restaurant has now been refurbished as Tilbury Riverside Activity & Arts Centre and the cavernous main hall is a car park. With its high roof, history and atmosphere, this cathedral like interior through which so many travelled on their journeys around the world deserves more. It could be a museum, a concert hall, an exhibition centre, but a car park – No!*

The square brick-built ticket office, where returning boat passengers booked their tickets to London and beyond, still stands alone in the centre of the hall. Inside it has been gutted, but could easily be restored. The waiting rooms where those arriving from warmer climes sat awaiting their trains, are still open, empty and with radiators hanging off the wall, but again restorable. The gentlemen's toilet where my young brother once asked why there was a chocolate machine is still there, the sign in place but a fence preventing entry. I assume the 'chocolate machine' has long gone. The platform signs are still in place and a Network South East Poster from 1990 hangs on the station wall. What a pity that a more fitting use cannot be found for a building with such history, but also such potential.'

Four years later things were looking up. The 'Big Ocean Project' planned to turn the station into a National Migration Museum for 'Britain's Ellis Island'. Visitors would be able to follow the same walk the first post-war Caribbean immigrants did when they landed at Tilbury from Jamaica on the ship *Empire Windrush* in 1948, to see where the 'Ten Pound Poms' departed from for Australia and trace the journeys of many others who came through Tilbury in its glamorous heyday. The Port of Tilbury had pledged half of the £2.4 million required and it was hoped that the Heritage Lottery would provide the balance required to enable a fitting use to be found for this historic railway station.

My childhood memoires were of the ferry being a substantial vessel, with red seats facing inwards on the lower deck. Today the boat was rather more modest, the *Duchess M*, which was built in 1956 and originally served as one of the Portsmouth to Gosport ferries. After stints providing pleasure cruises on the Tyne and the Thames, she's been running between Tilbury and Gravesend since 2002. The ferries I remember from the 1960s carried up to 475 passengers, but *Duchess M* is licensed to carry just sixty, and there was plenty of room for the thirteen of us on the crossing. It would have been a tight fit one evening in August 2006 when more than ninety squeezed aboard, although after someone alerted the Port of London Authority the owners received a fine of £18,000.

As we pulled away from the jetty, I noted that there was no safety announcement telling us what to do should the vessel sink. Swim? I stood outside for the five minute voyage, which was an interesting experience, but an operation that seemed more the type one would encounter in some remote outpost, not the lowest public crossing of the Thames.

My only memory of Gravesend station, which I'd last used in the mid 1970s, was of the train indicator boards which were hung from hooks by station staff, and even then seemed to belong to an earlier era. These are long gone, replaced by the scrolling electric type, which give more information but less character.

There were plenty of spare seats on the 11.07 South Eastern train to Gillingham, although many were strewn with free *Metro* newspapers. The train clearly hadn't been cleaned when turned at Charing Cross and the toilet was a mess with paper everywhere. I was glad to have used it though, as the gents on Strood station was closed, a notice intriguingly informing intending customers that this was '*due to a leak*'.

After crossing the marshes by the banks of the Thames, immediately after Higham station the train passes through two tunnels with a gap of just 100 yards between them. These were once joined and originally carried the Thames Medway Canal, which ran from Gravesend to Strood. At 2¼ miles, it was the second longest canal tunnel in the UK and took five years to build. In 1830 it was closed for two months while the open air passing place was dug in the centre, and in 1844 the Gravesend and Rochester Railway laid its single track railway line through the tunnels.

In a bizarre arrangement trains and boats ran side by side, with the track partly on the tow path and partly on trestles over the water. Passengers were intrigued by the tunnels, which prompted them to open the carriage doors as trains passed through the bores. Consequently, during the first week of railway operation several carriages had doors torn off their hinges, and some passengers nearly lost their heads. Thereafter, on departure from Gravesend the doors on the side of the train nearest the tunnel wall were locked. Should the train break down, the only way out for passengers was through the unlocked door into the canal!

The arrangement continued for some years until the canal closed and a double track line was laid on its filled in bed. After a series of chalk falls, including a landslide which derailed a train in 1999, a 20mph speed restriction was imposed. It was thought that vibrations from the new Wainscot Bypass were harming the tunnel lining and in 2004 it was closed for a year for strengthening work.

The 11.35 from Strood to Maidstone was a nicer train, a '375' with seats arranged around tables. Three 'chavs' with the full gear of hoodies and baggy grey tracksuit bottoms decided that the whole coach would like to listen to their music, but turned it down a little when I asked. The Medway Valley Line isn't as scenic as it sounds. After the initial views across the estuary to Rochester Castle and cathedral, I saw more of the backs of rundown industrial units than the river, but there are some nice bits and the whole route probably looks better when the sun's shining.

The chavs got off at Halling and suddenly the journey seemed pleasant. The next stop, Snodland, is one of those very British place names that sounds slightly silly. Aylesford village is a few minutes walk from the station, over a 14th century bridge with a picturesque view across the river. The waterfront with the part Norman church behind, reflected in the rather muddy waters of the Medway, another view that was not at its best on a dull winter's day.

After buying a sandwich in the village's only remaining shop, I set off in search of the pile of rocks. An enjoyable walk of a couple of miles took me to the North Kent Way, and at the top of a hill just off the path were the rocks.

As piles of rocks go, Kit's Coty House, the remains of a megalithic long barrow, is reasonably impressive. Whilst it might make an interesting diversion on a countryside walk, there was little (more accurately nothing) to reward the child who'd been dragged here on trains, ferry and feet. I certainly don't recall sharing the views of Samuel Pepys who described them as, 'Three great stones standing upright and a great round one lying on them, of great bigness and I am mightily glad to have seen it'. Owned by English Heritage and open to visitors at 'any reasonable time' (when would be unreasonable I wondered?), a large cap stone is supported by three others. So yes, a pile of rocks. With no shelter from the rain, not even a picnic had been possible on our family visit, lunch having to wait for the station waiting room. Today however I enjoyed my sandwich with a fine vista across the Medway valley.

Like much of Kent though, the views are scarred with pockets of industry and the peace spoilt by a constant roar from motorways that criss-cross the county. With the M2 one side and the M20 the other, the Medway Valley is never quiet, yet it was the high speed rail line that caused such furore amongst the people of Kent. The Eurostars though pass with just a gentle whoosh, and are quieter and far less intrusive than the constant roar from the roads. There was similar outcry in Purfleet where I work, and extra sound barriers were installed alongside the line, but the high speed trains actually make less noise than the slower ones on the adjacent Southend line tracks.

I was back at Aylesford in time for the 14.39 to Strood and fortunately with no need for the station's waiting room, as this is now an Indian takeaway. The unusually tall and most attractive original station buildings remain, having been restored in the 1980s. Built of Kentish ragstone, gabled and highly decorated, and with windows which replicate those at Aylesford Priory, they are an outstanding example of how if the will is there, the unique character of a station can be maintained. After our family walk in the rain, Mum had draped our soaking wet coats over the heater, steam rising as they dried, a service the railway no longer provides in today's plastic shelter!

I shared a carriage with four lads in tracksuits talking about their night in the police cells and a man who thought we all wanted to hear music through his headphones. A few months earlier British Transport Police had been deployed on trains and stations to counter a spate of anti-social behaviour on the route. A numbers of warnings were issued for offences including spitting, smoking, fare evasion and possession of cannabis, but locals complained that after a couple of weeks the police disappeared and behaviour went back to normal. The Medway Valley Line may conjure images of tourists travelling serenely through scenic English countryside, but would perhaps be better named the chav valley line.

My return to Essex was under rather than on the Thames, my first trip on the high speed Class 395 'Javelin' trains that commenced operation in 2009. The common usage of the 'Javelin' name is in fact incorrect, the name officially only applying to their use for shuttling passengers between St Pancras and Stratford during the Olympics, but I hope it becomes accepted, a name being far more interesting than a number. Although capable of 140mph, they are generally limited to 125mph, unless running late, but have greatly reduced the journey time to London from many Kent stations. Some towns that aren't served by the new trains however lost out when the timetable was recast with four trains an hour using the high speed route, their service to London being reduced. With fares increased to help fund the new services, the *Daily Mail* was quick to pick up on commuters 'outrage'.

As I got off the Medway Line train a Javelin swept into Strood, its stylish curves looking a bit out of place on a mainly commuter railway. With a smart blue and grey interior and mix of comfortable seats, including a good number around tables, it seemed more like a long distance train, although lacks any catering. The ride was smooth, in fact I didn't even notice we'd started, and the toilet spotless. I was impressed. After a gentle run back through Gravesend, it took just ten minutes for the 16¾ miles from Ebbsfleet to Stratford International, an average of around 100mph.

It was announced, '*change at Stratford International for stations to East Anglia*', but I hadn't realised that it's some way from the main Stratford station. With no signs I wandered around for a few minutes and was unable to help a lost lady, before realising that the DLR stops at International and catching this to West Ham.

A quick change to C2C and I was soon back in Upminster. I'd got back an hour quicker than my journey out to Aylesford, but without the lost train and bus that wouldn't wait, both routes would have taken about the same. I'd experienced an interesting contrast in river crossings between a two year old train and a fifty-five year old boat, a nice walk in the Kent countryside and a pile of rocks. Other than newer trains and the loss of Tilbury Riverside, the journey out hadn't changed a great deal since my childhood travels. With the new high speed line and its Javelin trains, Stratford International and the DLR, the journey back was entirely new. What hadn't changed at all was the 4,000 year old pile of rocks!

CHAPTER FIVE

TO THE NORFOLK COAST

London – Norwich – Sheringham – Holt

As a young child I found a simple way to differentiate between two sets of grandparents. My father's parents once had a pond so were 'Grandma and Grandpa with the fish', as opposed to 'Grandma and Grandpa with the car'. For a few years in the mid 1960s my grandparents 'with the fish' lived near Norwich, although I recall little of our visits there. I have a vague memory of passing through Romford on an express train from Liverpool Street, and on other occasions of changing at Romford, Shenfield then Colchester to avoid travelling into London. Liverpool Street to Norwich on the Great Eastern Main Line was a journey I didn't make for about thirty years, but then became one of my favourite routes, travelling for work, football or with family.

In the 1970s Liverpool Street was a dark and dismal station, more reminiscent of the steam age, but extensive redevelopment completed in 1992 brought it up to modern standards. With a good selection of shops on two levels and a bright airy concourse, it's now one of our finest terminus stations. Other than a period when some Fenchurch Street line trains were started here, the only occasions I can recall using it in my youth were the boat train to Harwich on the way to camp with the Scouts in Holland in 1975, and three years later to Cambridge to watch West Ham. Both were diesel locomotive hauled trains with corridor coaches, but a lot has changed since then.

Today's journey was just a week after the Dutch company Abellio, under the name Greater Anglia, had taken over the franchise from National Express – the company who changed London to Norwich from being a special journey to a run of the mill trip. In 2008 National Express East Anglia received an award for its restaurants, boasted of the success on their website, then announced they were closing. No longer would we be able to enjoy Britain's best train catering – breakfast, lunch, dinner and even afternoon tea, as we watched East Anglian scenery passing by. National Express said that money had to be saved and that customers wanted smaller meals or snacks served at their seats, although this service soon disappeared too.

Essex Coast Walk starts by describing the delights of enjoying a full English breakfast on the way to a day's walking from Manningtree. Now all they offer is a limp microwaved bacon roll. With no catering other than the buffet, perhaps it's not surprising that despite it being only £8 more with an advance ticket, just five passengers chose the First Class coaches on the 9.30 to Norwich.

Shortly before completing the book, on another journey to Norwich I met a very helpful member of Greater Anglia's management. He told me that he too had been sad to see the restaurants go, but that as on other lines, they'd been scrapped simply for cost reasons. His view was that unless the government specify catering in the franchise agreement, operators will only provide what is commercially beneficial. On a short run such as London to Norwich he didn't believe that any sort of at seat meals could be cost effective, particularly given our change in dining habits and the number of food outlets on stations. I pointed out that East Midlands Trains and First Great Western provide hot meals on similar length journeys, but he couldn't see it returning on the Norwich line.

A lot of people complain about the Norwich trains, and the Mark Three coaches were a bit rattly and in need of sprucing up, but are basically sound. With plenty of tables, seats lining up with windows and locomotives rather than under-floor engines, these thirty year old coaches are far superior to many of our modern trains. Both the coaches and Class 90 electric locomotives used to run on Virgin's West Coast route, before being displaced by Pendolinos. They give the route an Inter City feel, unlike say Weymouth, which is a longer journey but seems just an extension of commuter services. Sadly there's now talk of replacing them with high density five coach units.

The stop at Stratford has been added in more recent years, with the station becoming an interchange for not only local trains and the Central Line, but the Jubilee Line, DLR and high speed trains to Kent. I had mixed feelings about the huge Olympic Park to the left of the station. The area is being regenerated, but like many fans, I strongly oppose West Ham moving from Upton Park to an athletics stadium.

After passing through the suburbs of East London and suburban Essex, the next stop was Chelmsford. For a few years alternate trains called at Shenfield, a useful interchange that I often used. The stopping pattern has changed quite a lot from all running non stop to Colchester, to at various times calls at Stratford, Shenfield, Ingatestone and Chelmsford. It's a difficult balance between the Inter City service to Norwich and the needs of commuters closer to London. The typical journey time of one hour fifty minutes with four stops is virtually unchanged from fifteen years ago, but the fastest of one hour forty-two minutes, seven minutes slower.

Trains now run half hourly, after doubling in frequency in 2000, and range from very full in the rush hours, to fairly quiet. Today it was about a third full, with around half the passengers making short journeys and half travelling longer distances. The guard came round before Colchester, with a smile for everyone as she checked our tickets. Llamas in a field just before Manningtree were something we wouldn't have seen years ago, but the station from where we started childhood family walks to Flatford Mill has changed very little.

The line's scenery isn't inspiring, but mostly rural as it travels through Suffolk and Norfolk. The most scenic bit is probably where it crosses the River Stour immediately after Manningtree. From here the cranes of Felixstowe Docks can be seen down the estuary. That Stoke Tunnel outside Ipswich station is the only one on the route, illustrates the flatness of East Anglia.

Two ladies boarding at Ipswich were travelling to Cromer to organise their mother's funeral. A sad journey for them. It was half term, and at Stowmarket and Diss groups of youngsters got on for a day out in Norwich. A slight delay due to signalling problems at Ipswich meant we were running seven minutes late, and the guard announced that she'd walk through the train to take numbers of passengers wanting to change for the Great

Yarmouth train, then see if she could get it held. I wished they'd done that when I was going to Looe. As it was we arrived with two minutes to spare, so she announced the platform, asking passengers to make their way there as quickly as possible. I wondered if in today's litigious society that would be grounds to sue if someone fell while hurrying.

As we did in the mid 1960s, I caught the train on the thirty mile branch to Sheringham. Known as the Bittern Line (no self respecting branch line is now without a name), as the Broads are one of the few areas where this very rare member of the heron family resides in England, the line's fortunes have improved in recent years. It is run as a Community Rail Partnership, one of more than fifty such arrangements across the country, where the train operator, local council, businesses and community work together on 'practical initiatives which lead to a more sustainable railway'. Support and publicity from the partnership has contributed to a tripling in the number of passengers and increase in services to nineteen a day.

The train was reasonably busy with all the local stations used. Salhouse, the first stop, is where we used to get out to visit my grandparents. On one of our visits, aged about six, I remember being invited into the signal box where the signalmen were cooking breakfast in a frying pan. In those more relaxed days I was allowed to pull the lever to change the signal. My sister also recalls the day, but for feeling slightly put out that as a girl she wasn't invited to work a lever. Perhaps she should count herself lucky that she wasn't expected to cook the breakfast! The goods siding and signal box are now long gone, but the village is luckier than many in Norfolk, having escaped Beeching's decimation of the county's railways.

At Hoveton and Wroxham (the two villages lie either side of the river) we crossed the River Bure on the bridge that seems to feature in almost all the line's publicity photographs. From here the Bure Valley Railway runs on the old Great Eastern route to Aylesham. Deb and I travelled on this narrow gauge line, which follows the meandering river, during a short holiday at Sheringham in 1991.

My only journey on the Bittern Line since the 1960s had been to Cromer, where I'd hired a car when checking out a tidal island. I didn't recall the route being particularly outstanding, so was surprised to read that it's been described as one of the fifty most scenic lines in the world. Other than running alongside the River Yare just after Norwich and a glimpse of the Broads at Wroxham, it was pleasant but not spectacular English scenery. Most notable were a succession of large churches, although it became slightly more hilly with a glimpse of the sea as we approached Cromer.

Here the train reverses, as we were leaving the old Great Eastern and continuing to Sheringham on the Midland and Great Northern Railway, which once ran east across Norfolk. Cromer used to have four stations and was originally the terminus of three separate railways, but is now yet another basic platform and shelter. For the eight minute ride on to Sheringham the scenery was more notable, with views of the North Sea.

Sheringham's single platform, which just fitted our two coach train, is the smallest terminus in the country. I hurried across the road to the town's original station, now home to the preserved North Norfolk Railway, where the 12.45 to Holt was waiting. This was a 'diesel railbus', a four wheeled lightweight railcar built in the 1950s for little-used lines. Cheap, but unreliable, they were withdrawn in the mid 1960s and most of the lines they worked closed by Beeching. With just a two minute connection, there was no time to buy a ticket and I received a minor telling off from the guard who had to write one out. A family of four were sitting at the front, where the large window gives a view of the track and driver, the younger boy who was five today, clutching a Thomas toy as he chatted away. A lady from Norwich University was taking publicity photos for the tourist office and these two lads made ideal material.

I got off at Weybourne, a delightfully preserved country station, where we passed a steam train heading back to Sheringham. Although it was out of season, a forty-five minute service was running and the line busy with families enjoying a half term day out. The railway has been used for filming a number of television programmes and Weybourne was the setting for *Dad's Army's* famous 'Royal Train' episode, when the platoon was soaked by spray from the water pick-up troughs as they lined up to salute the King's train. A display in the waiting room explained that the water actually came from fire brigade hoses on the track.

To complete my journey to Holt I boarded the next train, five coaches hauled by *Black Prince*, a steam locomotive built in Swindon as recently as 1959 and withdrawn by British Rail after just nine years service. In one of the many poor decisions in the history of our railways, nearly a thousand steam locomotives were built in the 1950s, then with the rush to modernise, scrapped and replaced by diesels which often proved unreliable. I'd expected to see a little tank engine, but this was a Standard Class 9F, one of the most powerful steam locomotives ever made in Britain, and intended for hauling heavy freight trains at high speed. It made an impressive sight as it approached Weybourne, trailing a huge plume of white steam.

The coaches were as I remember from early childhood journeys – a mixture of open carriages with tables and corridors with compartments, painted in the standard red used on many routes before everything became BR blue and white. The steam heating control in the compartment prompted memories of the days when steam used to leak from beneath the coaches, and trains seemed alive. It was on this type of coach that I have one of my earliest railway memories – a wheel tapper checking wheels in Plymouth station. At Holt there was another reminder of childhood travel; the bump when the engine reversed onto the train.

On the return journey I left the train at Weybourne, to walk the four miles *No, N. Norfolk Coast Path* along the coast path back to Sheringham. Part of the Peddars Way long distance path, it was a lovely walk on the grassy cliff top, high above shingle beaches. The train back to Norwich was a '156' Sprinter, much nicer than the '150' I'd come on. The guard announced that this was for Norwich, although that's where all the trains go. Unnecessary announcements were becoming a recurring observation on my travels. The one that annoys me most is on my local line; 'We welcome customers aboard this C2C *rail* service –'. Useful only for those passengers who might think they're on bus or perhaps a boat. The company only run trains, they don't use rail in their name, so what's the point?

The 18.00 to Liverpool Street was busy, although I had a table to myself, perhaps because no one wanted to smell the KFC I was eating. I did feel guilty polluting the train with dodgy food odour, but it was that or wait for the next one. If the train had provided a restaurant, or even a buffet that offered more hot choice than limp bacon rolls, soup or porridge, I'd gladly have used that. Across the aisle a man shared not food smells, but tinny music. He wasn't a youngster, the most common culprits, but a suited middle-aged man. Like a good number of others, he had a season ticket and got off at Ipswich. His place was taken by two students, who shared two ear pieces between them and their music with the rest of the coach.

At Colchester the train broke down. I thought it was odd when the air conditioning went off, and soon the guard announced there was a problem. A few minutes later we were told that the train had failed and all had to get off and join one on Platform Three. Just as everyone had squeezed on there was another announcement. They weren't able to move the broken down train, so ours couldn't get past. The following Norwich service was being held at Manningtree while the wires were checked, and we were now to proceed under the subway to Platform Two. As we all waited a train pulled in – heading for Norwich! Further announcement – please move to Platform One. With much muttering we all shuffled across and a stopping train soon arrived. When things go wrong passengers start talking and the regular travellers were at one – there may be a new operator but little changes on the Norwich line.

CHAPTER SIX

THE COTSWOLD LINE

London – Ledbury

In 1995 my parents moved from Essex to Ledbury, so a line that I'd only once used before became a regular trip. Leaving the London to Bristol route at Didcot, the Cotswold Line is the sort of journey I like best – comfortable trains, reasonable catering, pleasant views and a nice pace; neither too fast nor too slow.

The 10.42 from Paddington was one of the five HSTs which run each day to Hereford, with a couple of others turning back at Worcester. Three car Class 166 'Turbo Express' trains run additional services, but despite their name aren't really adequate for longer distances. They were soon to be replaced by the Class 180 Adelante trains, which had run on the line for several years until First Great Western dispensed with them in 2009 due to poor reliability.

Serving Oxford, and stopping at Slough for Windsor, on morning trains tourists make up a large proportion of passengers for the first part of the journey and as usual there was a mix of languages on the train. Sunday morning schedules allow slack in case of engineering work, which gave us a ten minute wait at Slough. For four American ladies this was fortunate, as after we'd been in the station for several minutes I heard them talking about Windsor. Had I not told them to get off and change here they'd have been carried on to Reading. I mentioned this to the guard who was rather surprised as he'd advised them to get off at the next stop just a few minutes before we reached Slough!

By cunningly booking a return to Worcester, the boundary for journeys with my Network Card (a third off), plus singles to and from Ledbury, I'd saved £12. This I put towards a £15 Weekend First upgrade, so enjoying the comfort of leather seats, a table and beyond Oxford, a whole coach to myself. The extra £3 I got back in a free drink, biscuits and crisps from the buffet.

Until recent years when fares became complicated, it was usually a simple matter of booking a single, day return, saver or open return. Now the plethora of tickets, often requiring advance purchase, means that fares range from very cheap to ridiculously expensive, and that often a knowledge of the system is needed to find the best deal. Euston to Manchester for example ranges from £12.50 each way to £308 anytime return (£441 First Class), but it is the higher prices that the media invariably quote when comparing train with plane. Air tickets however also show a huge range in cost depending on when you travel and book, but whilst this seems to be accepted, train passengers seem to think everyone should get the lowest fare.

My Sunday morning train was fairly quiet after Oxford, although the two evening trains pick up a new lot of passengers here and remain almost full well into the Cotswolds. Station car parks are full as commuters drive from outlying villages to catch the train to Oxford, Reading or London. The prosperity of the area is reflected by the high proportion who travel First Class, including a young schoolboy with a season ticket who I've twice seen boarding at Oxford and going to the buffet to collect a complimentary hot chocolate, before alighting at Charlbury.

A feature of the route is short platforms and on leaving Oxford the guard announced, 'Ladies and gentlemen. We've got a big train today and only small platforms on the Cotswold Line', then before each station told us which coaches would be opened. A while ago I'd seen a family miss the stop at Charlbury as they didn't get down the train in time. The guard explained that she'd made a clear announcement, but that they weren't the first to do it and certainly wouldn't be the last. In the days before 'health & safety' there was no central locking and passengers simply walked through the train. It was assumed that they wouldn't be stupid enough to leap out where there was no platform.

Hanborough, seven miles from Oxford, is the smallest station, with just two coaches fitting in the platform. A party of walkers got out here, perhaps heading for Blenheim Palace, birthplace of Winston Churchill, a couple of miles away. It was to Hanborough that Churchill made his last journey, the funeral train bringing his coffin for burial in the churchyard at Bladon on the edge of the Blenheim estate.

After once having to make do with an egg sandwich because the bacon baguettes had run out, I always get lunch early on the Cotswold Line, so wandered up to the buffet before Charlbury. As usual with First Great Western, the lady serving was friendly and on what is one of the quieter trains, seemed particularly pleased to have a customer. I enjoyed the baguette watching the scenery pass by. The hills are only gentle, but running through farmland, alongside rivers and Cotswold stone villages, this is typical English countryside.

In a short sighted move the track from Charlbury was singled in 1971, reducing the capacity of the line and meaning long stops and delays when trains passed. In 2011 Network Rail redoubled two sections and long closed platforms at Charlbury and Honeybourne were rebuilt. The latter now includes provision to serve the private Gloucestershire and Warwickshire Railway, which hopes to extend its steam operations from Cheltenham Racecourse and Toddington.

Honeybourne station had closed in 1969, but with new residential developments, some of which were related to nearby Long Lartin prison, it reopened in 1981. Pressure from the Cotswold Line Promotion Group was an important factor in the reopening, and in the increase in services from two or three a day to the current fourteen in each direction. Campaigning has led to a number of other significant improvements to the line, including retention of the Inter City trains which British Rail wanted to withdraw, citing the poor state of the track.

At Evesham we crossed the River Avon twice, once either side of the town, then ran through the Vale of Evesham, passing Pershore, another station where far more trains now stop. There are proposals to build a parkway station four miles before Worcester, where the line crosses the Birmingham to Bristol cross country route. This may replace Worcester Shrub Hill in the city, the only station where the whole train fits in the platform. Worcester Foregate Street, just half a mile down the line, is more centrally located, but has no parking. With an unusual track layout the station can be very confusing, as rather than different directions, the two platforms serve different routes.

Leaving Worcester the line runs high above the city on a sixty five arch brick viaduct, crossing the River Severn with views to the cathedral one way and racecourse the other. The original wooden bridge failed an inspection in 1859 and for nine months passengers had to alight from their train and walk across.

The spa town of Great Malvern also has two stations, Malvern Link and the historic Great Malvern. This was constructed in local stone following a French Gothic theme and most of the original remains, including many fine decorated pillars. The tea room is named after Lady Foley, who owned much of the land around Malvern and was a key sponsor in building the station. It was originally a private waiting room, where she could await her train without having to mix with members of the public. Lady Foley used to have a private station at Stoke Edith between Ledbury and Hereford, but only used this when travelling to Hereford, as she disliked tunnels, so had a carriage take her to Great Malvern if she was going to London.

Rising steeply above the town are the Malvern Hills. The original tunnel which took the line under the hills was prone to rock falls and the current one replaced it in 1926. The old abandoned bore was used to store torpedoes in World War Two. The next day we walked above the tunnel, the Malvern Hills being a regular outing from Ledbury. This eight mile ridge offers excellent walks, with views on a clear day to thirteen counties, including the Severn Valley to the east and Brecon Beacons to the west, plus of course trains passing far below.

After Colwall, another village fortunate to have an Inter City service to London, the train reaches Ledbury, where my parents were waiting. Another health & safety restriction means there's a delay in opening the doors. The tunnel just before the station is too narrow for the carriage doors to swing open, so the guard travels in the rear power car where he could operate the sliding exit door should an emergency evacuation be necessary. This however isn't a new issue. In the days of non corridor coaches passengers in compartments weren't allowed to travel through the tunnel, as they couldn't escape in the event of an emergency. Non corridor coaches could only pass through if passengers were transferred to a corridor coach, or in unavoidable circumstances, the guards van!

Two HSTs were passing at Ledbury, the only double track between Malvern tunnel and Hereford, a restriction which can cause delays, although these now seem less common. Longer turn rounds on London trains at Hereford, and Nottingham services now terminating at Birmingham, have both improved timekeeping.

First Great Western are yet to take advantage of the time saving opportunities resulting from track doubling between Oxford and Worcester, although easing the restrictions on passing places has improved punctuality. Indeed, at three hours five minutes, the fastest train to Hereford is twenty minutes slower than it was in 1996 (although making four more stops) and six minutes slower than 1985.

As well as the number of stops, motive power has a big effect on timings. Back in 1962, with ten intermediate stops compared to the current fifteen, the steam hauled Cathedrals Express took 3 hours 44 minutes to Hereford. My red book includes the log of our journey from Hereford in 1974, showing we took three hours twenty minutes, including adding extra coaches and a more powerful (Class 47) locomotive at Worcester. With better acceleration and the ability to run at 125mph between Paddington and Didcot, the journey time was reduced when HSTs took over the line. However, they were designed for long runs, not frequent stops, and the greater acceleration of the Turbo Trains means they are quicker between Cotswold Line stations. The Adelantes, with good acceleration, 125mph capability, and the comfort of long distance trains, are ideal for the line, other than the peak trains which require HST capacity.

It's a matter of debate as to whether the majority of passengers would rather see faster journey times, extra stops, or greater reliability that the timetables will be met. Mindful of financial penalties for lateness and keen to maximise passenger numbers, train operators now commonly choose to add stops and pad schedules, which extend journey times. The Cotswold Line is a prime example of slower services since privatisation.

CHAPTER SEVEN

HIGH SPEED TO EDINBURGH

London – Edinburgh – Dalmeny – Berwick – Alnmouth

For 149 years the north and southbound Flying Scotsman simultaneously left Kings Cross and Edinburgh around 10 o'clock every weekday morning. This was the most famous train in the world. Then in May 2011, with scant regard for history, East Coast Trains retimed the southbound train to leave Edinburgh at the ungodly hour of 5.40am. Worse still, it runs in just one direction, the northbound Flying Scotsman being no more. The locomotive has a new purple livery, but no guarantee that it will be used for the Flying Scotsman, and despite a policy to restore '*a touch of glamour and romance*', East Coast have sidelined a British institution.

The new train is fast, stopping only at Newcastle and taking just four hours to London, although I understand it is late more often than not. Compared to the ten and a half hours taken in 1862 (including a half hour stop at York for lunch), and the seven hours twenty minutes by the famous 4472 steam locomotive in 1938, this is indeed fast. However, it's only seven minutes quicker than when the line was electrified twenty five years ago and in the 1990s some trains were timetabled to take a fraction under the four hours.

Other than a holiday in Aberdeen when I was a toddler, my first journey to Scotland was on the Flying Scotsman in 1973, when we stayed at Edinburgh then Oban. Then we were hauled by *Royal Highland Fusilier,* one of the twenty-two Deltic diesel locomotives built in the early 1960s for high speed Edinburgh expresses. Most were scrapped when HSTs took over in 1978, but this is one of six to be preserved and still runs on heritage railways.

My trip to Edinburgh today was entirely free, and courtesy of reward points gained by buying tickets from East Coast, I was to travel First Class. With the 10.00 no longer the Flying Scotsman, I left an hour later, on the 11.00, which was scheduled to take 109 minutes for the non stop run to York, the average of 104 miles per hour making it one of the fastest runs in the country.

Arriving with time to spare I wandered round Kings Cross, stopping to watch the usual succession of tourists take photographs as they posed pushing Harry Potter's trolley into the wall on 'Platform 9¾'. The newly refurbished station was taking shape with a new concourse and bridge due to open a month later. It will be a big improvement on the cramped concourse and limited retail outlets, and hopefully will include somewhere passengers can sit down for a hot meal – something that's become more necessary since they stopped serving proper meals on most trains, but more of that later.

Settled in my comfortable seat, we pulled out right on time. Within two minutes I was offered tea or coffee. Three minutes later a trolley came round with cold drinks. At ten past eleven they brought lunch – four sandwiches, crisps and a piece of fruitcake. Alternatively I could have had a jacket potato with chilli, or some brie & cranberry wellington. Bar a biscuit after Newcastle, this ridiculously early lunch was the extent of East Coast's complimentary food service. A service that the company think is wonderful but not all customers feel the same about. Yes it's free, but personally I'd far rather have the option to buy what I want when I want rather than be given a few sandwiches at ten past eleven.

When British Rail handed over the route to GNER on privatisation there were sixty restaurants on the ninety seven Inter City trains to and from Kings Cross. GNER increased both the number of trains and restaurants, building a reputation for a quality service. I enjoyed many an excellent breakfast, lunch and dinner on a GNER train. National Express took over the franchise and decided to replace most restaurants with 'at seat dining'. On most trains there was still however a good choice of freshly cooked meals available at seat in First Class, or on a tray from the buffet for Standard Class. It didn't have the ambiance and conviviality of the restaurant, but the food was cheaper, still cooked by a chef and of excellent quality. The restaurants were expensive, although not excessively so for fine dining and silver service. They took up space on the trains and lost money, (although did that take account of the £200 plus business passengers were prepared to pay for First Class fares), so perhaps there was a case to reduce their number. The at seat dining was however an excellent compromise.

National Express refused to put further financial support into the East Coast operation and handed back the franchise, which is now run by the Department of Transport through East Coast Trains. East Coast decided that passengers don't want the choice to buy high quality meals on the train, but would prefer largely mediocre offerings for free. They still provide breakfasts and a few evening meals, but the latter with a choice of just two dishes and only on a handful of trains from Kings Cross. Standard Class passengers they decided don't want cooked meals at all, the options of cottage pie, lasagne and fish pie being removed from the buffet menus. Some suggested that this reduction in the buffet range was a cynical attempt to get more passengers to pay First Class fares, but whilst air is the main competitor to Scotland, they took away the high quality menu based hot meals that helped differentiate train from plane. East Coast said that more were travelling First Class, but neglected to mention their heavily discounted ticket offers that were perhaps more likely to have tempted passengers than a few free sandwiches.

So back to my journey north. Lunch finished and plates collected by 11.35, I settled down to enjoy the ride. It was a pleasant environment in First Class, although I'd have preferred not to be subjected to the regular phone calls of a loud American further down the coach. Most of us make the occasional call on the train, but some try to do it quietly, others don't!

For the first time for more than thirty years I logged the stations as we passed, comparing progress with the 1973 run in my little red book. We were through Peterborough in forty-five minutes compared to sixty behind the Deltic, and hardly slowed climbing Stoke Bank where travelling in the opposite direction Mallard had broken the world speed record. The 126mph fleetingly achieved in 1938 is just one mph more than the current line speed for much of the East Coast route. The Class 91 hauled 225 electric trains are actually capable of 140mph, but concerns over reading lineside signals at such speed means that only on the new high speed line to the Channel Tunnel, where there's in-cab signalling, can British trains exceed 125mph.

On the same track that Mallard achieved its record, a test run with a 225 set once reached 162mph.

Just before Retford we came to a halt. Two horses lifted their heads from munching grass to look up at the silver train stopped by their field. American man got on his phone again. The guard (East Coast seem to have gone back to the traditional name and dispensed with 'Train Manager') announced that there was a problem with the signals. Soon we slowly moved off, leaving the horses to enjoy lunch in peace. The guard told us we'd been delayed by seven minutes, but expected to make it up by Edinburgh.

By Doncaster we'd gained 21 minutes on the 1973 run, but the next station in my red book we wouldn't be seeing. Prior to 1983 Selby was on the East Coast Main Line, but when the National Coal Board started to exploit the huge reserves of the Selby coalfield, the line was diverted to avoid subsidence. The new section, which was funded by the NCB, was designed for 125mph and the first purpose built high speed railway in Britain.

We were 6 minutes late at York, where the minster can be seen to the right and the National Railway Museum to the left. The 44 miles from York to Darlington took exactly 26 minutes, an average of 102mph, compared to 32 minutes on our southbound 1973 journey. A note in my red book said 'continuous 100mph running', and the average of 82mph illustrated the performance of the Deltics. As a 12 year old I'd have been counting the beats or timing the mileposts, something that youngsters now would definitely view as 'sad'. The line here is flat, passing between the distant hills of the North York Moors and Dales, and ideally suited to high speed running. The definition of 'high speed' has of course changed over the years, and compared to much of Europe our 125mph expresses are positively pedestrian.

The railway passes on a hill to the north of Durham city centre, looking down on the cathedral and castle. The approach to Newcastle is also spectacular, crossing the Tyne with views of the many bridges in both directions. Our arrival in 2 hours 51 minutes was 45 minutes quicker than the non stop 1973 Flying Scotsman. In 1979 I'd done it in under three hours, again on the Flying Scotsman, then an HST, en route to see West Ham play at Newcastle. As usual a football special had been provided, but thanks to 'Persil Tickets', two for one vouchers with washing powder, many fans travelled as cheaply on the service train. It also had the advantage of avoiding escorts from the police, who hadn't yet realised not every supporter used the 'specials', something that some trouble makers took advantage of. It is from their mode of travel to away games that the West Ham hooligan group were named the 'Inter City Firm'.

Just outside Newcastle we passed the local station of Manors, where the police had escorted West Ham fans after the match. They made us all get on the special, but someone pulled the emergency cord at Newcastle and loads of us piled off and onto an Inter City. This was in the days when bad behaviour by football fans wasn't the rarity it is now, and we were delayed after a few broke into the buffet and police had to be called. Both policing and behaviour have changed considerably since these dark days of football hooliganism.

Although the southern part of the East Coast line is mostly unremarkable, as the train travels north the views improve markedly and the route from Newcastle to Edinburgh must be one of our most scenic main lines. There were occasional glimpses of the blue sea, then at Alnmouth the line runs close to the beach. Approaching Berwick there are spectacular views to Lindisfarne, with its castle and priory, then of the River Tweed as we crossed the magnificent Royal Border Bridge.

We left Berwick on time and were now running more than an hour ahead of the 1973 timings. This stretch is the most spectacular as the line runs on cliff tops high above rocky coves and beaches. The line is more curved here and there has been talk of introducing Pendolinos, whose tilting facility would reduce journey time, but at the expense of comfort. No thanks! Arrival at Edinburgh was at 15.16, eight minutes early and seventy three minutes faster than the 1973 run which had three less stops. Progress has been made.

Having spent many evenings in Edinburgh, I wanted to do something more specific than aimless wandering. After considering the walk up Arthur's Seat, the hill behind Holyrood Palace which we climbed on our 1973 holiday, or a train ride to the seaside at North Berwick, another of my post meeting jaunts, I decided to view the Forth Bridge. Once checked in at a hotel far enough from the centre to be both quiet and cheap, (with an intriguing note in the room requesting that the kettle was used only for boiling water – were they concerned that alternative liquids might be heated, or the kettle used for other purposes?), I returned to Waverley Station, boarding the 16.42 to Newcraighall.

I alighted at Dalmeny and walked down the path to the south bank of the Forth, coming out right under the famous bridge. And what an impressive sight it is. The huge steel structure, with gigantic 521 metre spans and containing 6½ million rivets, was completed in 1890 and must rank of one of the great feats of civilisation. Fifty seven men lost their lives during construction and at least eight more were saved by the rescue boats that were stationed under each cantilever. The more modern road bridge behind would look impressive in its own right, but alongside the magnificent spans of the railway bridge, seems a mere functional crossing. In 2011 a ten year project to cover the structure with three layers of epoxy coating was completed. Expected to last for 25 years, it will perhaps put an end to the famous expression to describe a never ending job. From underneath one gets a sense of the immense size of the bridge, the scale being illustrated each time a train crossed, looking like a toy far above.

I walked 1½ miles down the estuary to Hound Point, as I'd done en route to Cramond Island for *No Boat Required*, before turning back as darkness fell. Coming back the train was quiet, but a young lady on the phone sitting opposite had me intrigued as she told her friend that she was going to Stirling as she 'had to get away from him tonight'.

Next morning (after a slight delay as I'd taken my house rather than bedroom key down to breakfast and couldn't get back in) I explored a bit of Edinburgh I'd never visited before. Calton Hill, just south of the centre, has an eccentric collection of buildings and monuments. Most interesting are Nelson's Monument, a stone imitation of the admiral's telescope, and the National Monument, which was intended to be a replica of the Parthenon, but only the façade was completed. Its columns look rather out of place in a hill in Scotland. Even on a cloudy morning there were superb views across the city, with the foreground dominated by the ridged glass roof of Waverley Station. Covering an area of 25 acres it's the second largest station in Britain; (only Waterloo is larger). It's hard to believe that the valley where the railway runs through the city was once a fresh water loch, which was drained in the early 19th century.

Delayed by a hotel owner who thought I wanted to hear his views on bankers (I've got plenty of my own thanks), a couple who failed to understand the etiquette of letting someone in a hurry pass on the escalator, and inadequate signage on the station, I only just caught the 10.10 to Berwick. The train had come from Glasgow, whose cross country passengers now have to travel south via Edinburgh, and was going all the way to Penzance. Ian the Train Manager (not a guard today) introduced himself and welcomed us to the 'Class 211 Super Voyager', then Chris the Aussie trolley man listed the refreshments he'd been bringing down the train. Just three sandwiches I noted as he passed and no hot food for a journey of almost twelve hours. Of course no one goes all the way to Penzance, it's quicker, cheaper and more comfortable via London. As we arrived at Berwick, Ian reminded us to make sure we 'uplifted our luggage', a new variant on what always seems one of our less necessary announcements. A little absent minded I may be, but if I get on a train with a bag I'm still capable of leaving with it without the prompting of a nice man from the railways.

Last time I was at Berwick station I jumped into a waiting taxi and raced to Lindisfarne before the tide. I'd come on the sleeper to Edinburgh, which was late, missing the connection south and the only bus to the island before the causeway would be covered. We'd had a holiday at Berwick in 1974, staying across the river at Spittal, which wasn't as bad as it sounds! There's a nice sandy beach, and in its prime the promenade was packed with visitors. I don't recall seeing many other families and by the time we stayed it was probably already becoming a quiet sea front mainly frequented by dog walkers.

I spent my hour in Berwick walking along the banks of the Tweed and watching the occasional train cross the Royal Border Bridge. This twenty eight arched viaduct is one of our most spectacular railway structures, although the name is misleading, the Scottish border being three miles further north. When we walked here in 1974 we watched fisherman casting sweep nets for salmon, a traditional method that continues albeit it employing just two men compared to the seven hundred in 1953.

For the short hop to Alnmouth I joined the train which makes the longest journey of any in Britain: 8.20 from Aberdeen, arriving at Penzance at 21.42 – 13 hours and just a sandwich. My greeting on boarding was to hear a passenger swearing at the man with the refreshment trolley, who chose to ignore the outburst as other passengers tutted. Rather than catch a bus to Alnwick, where we'd holidayed in 1981 (another unusual choice?), in pleasant sunshine and unseasonable warmth I walked the mile to the village of Alnmouth. A sign outside the station to the village of Shilbottle was inevitably defaced with a slight modification to the first L. Perusing a choice of three pubs, two cafes and a hotel, I selected the Sun Inn where the welcome was friendly from both the landlady and two golden retrievers, and the lunch excellent.

After a walk along the beach, where we'd swum on our holiday, I returned to the station in good time for the 14.58 to London. There's still a working coal yard by the small station, something that used to be almost everywhere years ago, but are now quite rare and sadly no longer supplied by rail. Three o'clock came and went with no sign of the train. There was no indicator board or announcements. I asked the sole member of staff who told me there'd been 'problems down south' and it had just passed Berwick running thirty-one minutes late. Wandering along the platform I found a poster explaining that work had started to reopen the Aln Valley Railway to Alnmouth, hopefully restoring a link to yet another town that Beeching cut off from the railway system.

The train arrived thirty-five minutes late because of disruption resulting from a suicide at York in the morning. Most regular travellers will have been delayed by suicides, which have always happened on the railways, but now close the lines for longer as police carry out more extensive investigations. It is tragic for the victim and their family, but also traumatic for witnesses and the train drivers concerned. Some have never returned to work after the horror of being unable to do anything as someone jumped in front of their train.

The number of suicides on the railways remained fairly constant at around 200 for many years, but the financial crisis is thought to be the reason for a recent increase. There are initiatives to try to reduce the number, such as training staff to look out for persons who may be at risk and educating the media not to give details that might lead to copy cat attempts (suicides on the railways increased significantly after a newspaper report about the method as long ago as 1868). Some stations now display Samaritans posters at platform ends, but sadly so far these appear to have had little effect.

The guard told me that that as a result of the disruption the catering crew weren't joining until Newcastle, but going beyond his required duties, was fetching drinks for First Class passengers himself. At Newcastle the following London train overtook us, our lateness and extra stops making us the poor relation which they didn't want to delay another service. We left forty-four minutes late, a deficit that was exactly maintained to London. Soon the suited businessman on the opposite table gave up typing into his laptop and brought out a copy of *Viz*, the adult comic enjoyed openly by teenagers and others usually less overtly.

The complimentary offering was afternoon tea – two finger sandwiches, crisps and a scone with jam & cream. Whilst fine for mid afternoon, with the delay meaning I wouldn't be getting home until nearly 9 o'clock, this was an occasion when I would gladly have paid for a hot meal. I did manage to get an extra scone, but only because the train was quiet and they had lots left, as normally food portions are strictly controlled. Passengers who've complained have been told that as it's free they are not necessarily entitled to anything – fine, so give us back the choice to buy hot meals.

CHAPTER EIGHT

SOUTH WALES & ENGINEERING WORKS

London – Cardiff – Swansea – Carmarthen

I don't like getting up early. Actually I hate it. My wife isn't far from the truth when she says I only do it for West Ham. An early start was inevitable thanks to the twin powers who rule football, television and police, decreeing that kick off at Cardiff would be 12.45. The need to set my alarm at the ludicrous hour of 5.40am was thanks to engineering works in the Severn Tunnel, requiring diversion via Gloucester.

The 7.57 to Swansea was the first Inter City train out of Paddington and I'd never seen the station so quiet. Most of the few passengers milling around were laden with luggage and catching the Heathrow Express. It was strange to see the platforms empty and shops shut, although WH Smiths opened just in time for me to buy a Sunday paper.

The train was quiet too, both in numbers and sleepiness of passengers. People don't tend to talk much on early morning trains. Despite the small number of passengers, as often happens, the online booking system had told me that there were no forward facing seats available and would only book one looking backwards. I sat in one of the many unreserved forward seats wondering why we allow so much of our lives to be constrained by computers.

Normally, even with an early kick off there'd have been a good number of West Ham fans travelling, but for many plans were thwarted by a ridiculous arrangement imposed by South Wales Police. Visiting supporters were not sold tickets in advance, only vouchers to be exchanged for match tickets at West Cardiff Motorway Services. The aim was supposedly to keep away fans out of the city, although it appears that the imposition was not based on risk assessment, but part of a reciprocal agreement made earlier in the season when the Metropolitan Police imposed a similar restriction on Cardiff fans visiting Upton Park. I felt particularly sorry for a man with his two young sons who'd bought advance train tickets before the arrangement was announced, so was forced to pay the not inconsiderable cost of a taxi to and from the services. Like a number of others, I got round the restriction by simply buying a ticket in a home section of the ground, the police's draconian measure resulting in less segregation in the stadium.

With the Severn Tunnel closed we left the main line at Swindon, heading at a more sedate pace up single track line towards Kemble. As with the Cotswold Line, in a short sighted cost saving measure part of the route was singled in 1968, which now limits capacity and leads to long delays when incidents occur. Network Rail's plans to reinstate the second track where thwarted by the government in the guise of the Office of Rail Regulation in 2009, but two years later the Chancellor's Budget speech announced that funding would now be allocated, with the work to be competed by 2014.

Kemble is a pleasantly rural station and a small village to have a regular service to London, although most of the passengers drive from nearby Cirencester, a journey that could have been done by train until 1964. From here the line passes through the 'Golden Valley', a scenic if rather slow route along the River Frome to Stroud. Although not at its best in early morning rain (it was still only 9.30), it was a pleasant ride alongside the river and Stroudwater Canal.

Just before Stroud station the line passes the historic goods shed, which was built of local Cotswold limestone by Brunel in 1845, and is thought to be the oldest remaining wayside shed of its type. Reminding of the days when freight was carried between most stations on the network, large red letters on the side say, 'GWR STROUD STATION EXPRESS GOODS TRAIN SERVICES – DAY TRANSITS BETWEEN IMPORTANT TOWNS'. More recently mail and parcels were carried on passenger trains and my childhood journeys frequently had extended stops while sacks were unloaded from the guard's van. Early morning trains often had an extra van for newspapers, but bar a few dedicated mail trains, almost all such goods now travel by road or air.

Stonehouse, the next station, was for some years a regular destination for my business travels, until the company we dealt with went the way of so much British manufacturing and moved production to Europe.

At Gloucester the guard announced that the doors would not be released until the train came to a 'complete stop'. Leaving aside the impossibility of an incomplete stop, what is the point of this announcement which we often hear across the network? On a similar theme, why do Virgin's announcements refer to Euston as the '*final* destination'?

Gloucester station's claim to fame is arguably the longest platform in Britain. At 603 metres it is slightly shorter than Colchester, but as that's in two sections with a length in the middle where the track moves away from the platform, I don't think it counts.

The next section was new track to me and a very pleasant ride, running close to the River Severn. With the tide down a variety of bird life poked about in the mud. At Chepstow we crossed the River Wye with its steep muddy banks and looked up to the town's large Norman castle. There were good views of the two Severn road bridges, the older suspension bridge more impresive than the newer one that runs mostly on pillars.

After joining the main line we made a rare stop at Severn Tunnel Junction to pick up passengers from Bristol who'd come here on rail replacement coaches, then it was back on the normal route to Swansea. We had two childhood holidays using the South Wales Main Line, one to Mumbles and one to Tenby, but I recall nothing of either train journey. The first I remember was in the late 1970s, on a very long day trip with my father to the Central Wales Line. More of that in Chapter Ten. More latterly I've made fairly regular trips to Cardiff and Swansea, for work, West Ham and tidal islands, and my experience of First Great Western's service has invariably been good.

In 1979 I made an evening trip to Newport for a West Ham match, the 2:1 defeat, one of our all too frequent FA Cup exits to lower league clubs. Using Persil Tickets we travelled down on a fast Inter City, an HST stopping only at Bristol Parkway. As usual the club had chartered a locomotive hauled special train, but refused to allow supporters with British Rail tickets to board it after the match. If it hadn't been for the kindness of a ticket collector allowing us through another gate, we'd have had to wait until 2am for the Fishguard boat train. As it was we arrived in London just in time to catch the last train back to Upminster.

At Newport there are more bridges. The transporter bridge, one of only two in the UK, can be seen as the train crosses the River Usk. The Victorian stone railway bridge is somewhat more durable than the original wooden construction which was destroyed by fire when a heated bolt ignited preservative chemicals in the wood. Early railway bridges had their share of mishaps as engineering technology was stretched to and sometimes beyond the limit.

Cardiff is always a busy station, with little trains scampering off noisily to the valleys while HSTs glide sedately in and out, as if such hurried behaviour is beneath them. With announcements made in English and Welsh, and most trains making lots of stops, the public address is rarely quiet for long. When we visited for two play off finals and the FA Cup in succesive years, the city was alive. With extra service trains and charters running for both teams, trains had to queue to enter the station, and as we paused on the bridge before the platforms the sea of claret and blue on the streets below was a sight to behold. Today the centre was deserted and after a quick walk along the river by the Millenium Stadium, I headed off to Cardiff City Stadium, a mile or so west of the centre.

Back at Cardiff Central after a 2:0 win, I waited for the 15.40 to Swansea. Rather than return home I'd intended to revisit our two childhood holiday destinations, although as you'll see, only managed one. A two coach train to Ebbw Vale was full and standing in the next platform – good to see for a line that reopened in 2008. As is invaribaly the case, usage was soon far more than forecast, suggesting that it should have been reopened sooner, probably when the National Garden Exhibition was held in the town in 1992. It is good to see that the more enlightened governments in Wales and Scotland are reopening lines, putting the English Parliament to shame.

Mine was one of few English voices on the busy HST to Swansea, passengers mostly a mixture of those returning from a weekend away and an afternoon shopping in Cardiff. The run to Swansea is one of contrasting views to left and right. On one side the hills and valleys, bathed in afternoon sunshine, and on much of the other industry, the huge Port

Talbot steel works a welcome sign that we still have some heavy manufacturing left.

Crescent Guest House, where I spent the night, was the best accommodation I'd found so far. While most establishments claim to be friendly, this one really was. The owners Andy and Dena were keen not only to make sure everything I needed was provided, but also to chat. Often the advertised friendly welcome extends to a brief greeting, but here the owners were genuinely interested in their guests. It doesn't take a lot of effort to turn a reasonable overnight experience into an excellent one, and here I had the bonus of a bedroom that looked out across Swansea Bay. Many people don't realise that Swansea is on the coast, let alone how attractive the bay and beach are.

With dusk approaching I set out to walk the four miles along the front to Mumbles, where we'd holidayed in 1972. Other than a trip on the Central Wales Line, we spent most of the week on various beautiful beaches on the Gower. A couple of distinct memories are, arriving to find the flat was in a state (the blame was attributed to students who'd stayed the previous week) and my sister almost catching a conger eel from the pier (it fell off the line just as she hauled it up). Whilst it's always been a popular day trip destination, Mumbles remains a good holiday base for the Gower peninsula, with its fine beaches, scenery and walking.

It was a pleasant walk, first on the sandy beach, then following the route of the Mumbles Tramway – the world's first fare–paying passenger railway. After opening in 1807 with horse drawn wagons and carriages, the line's owners were keen to employ mechanical power and had close links with the foundry where Richard Trevithick was developing his steam locomotive. Confounding scientists who claimed that the use of steam engines for locomotion would be impossible, Trevithick's 'Penydarren' hauled ten tonnes of iron and seventy passengers along a nine mile route. The initial triumph though was frustrated by the relative weakness of the 19th century iron rails, which broke under its weight. Unable to use steam, the Mumbles railway experimented with other forms of traction, including attaching a sail to the carriage, which reduced the journey time but only if the wind was favourable!

Eventually steam was introduced, but a legal absurdity permitted two companies to operate services on the single track railway. One issued a court injunction to force the other to run exclusively horse-drawn services, while they used steam locomotives. The horse service had to leave a few minutes after the steam and apparently locomotive drivers frequently threw hot coals onto the track to upset the horse following.

The line's heyday was in the early 20th century, when with people packing every available space on double deck carriages, up to 1,800 were carried on each journey. The huge load restricted speed to 5mph and local children performed tricks and somersaults by the trackside, earning pennies thrown by passengers. A young boy was employed as lookout on the front of the locomotive and rung a bell if anything strayed onto the track. Passengers on the top deck were covered in smoke and smuts from the engine, but didn't complain about it making their 'Sunday best' clothes filthy, as it was believed that smoke killed germs!

After experimenting with battery power, overhead wires were put up in 1929 and the eleven electric trams were the largest in the UK. Five million passengers were carried in 1945, but by the 1950s sinister plans were being laid for the line's demise. It was now owned by a bus company, who favoured road transport and aimed to discourage use of the railway. Worn track was replaced in inadvisably short sections, leading to a bumpy ride, but rather than alienating passengers it endeared it to them more, the tram ride being known as the 'rock and roll to paradise'.

In 1958 however, to the dismay of the Swansea public, the owners announced the line's closure. A petition of 15,000 signatures was collected and a barrister hired to oppose the case in Parliament. He withdrew twelve hours before the hearing and with no time to properly brief his replacement, the proposal to dismantle the world's first and longest surviving railway was approved by Parliament. Within minutes of the final tram running on 5th January 1960, the track was being torn up. Had the line survived another ten years, by which time its value for both tourist and local traffic would have been properly appreciated, its future would probably have been secured. What a sad tale, which with technical difficulties, company wrangles and premature closure, has many echoes in the history of our railways and highlights lessons which should have been learned.

Feeling hungry at the end of my walk, what could be better than to find an

Italian restaurant right by the harbour? Refreshed and sustained I started to walk back, but soon succumbed to a bus that conveniently halted just as I passed the stop, and took me on a tour of residential Swansea on the way to a deserted and rather uninspiring city centre.

Next morning I was back at what the sign on the front still called Swansea High Street station, although has been known as simply Swansea since the city's Victoria station closed in the 1960s. All the other signs included the Welsh, Abertawe. (When I was back in Swansea two months later the station entrance was being renovated and the old sign had gone). My original plan had been to visit Tenby where we'd stayed in 1969, but major track renewals meant the line was closed all week. I had been back to Tenby fairly recently, attempting to visit St Catherine's Island and its Napoleonic Fort, but thwarted by an owner who doesn't welcome visitors. Unlike some of our childhood holiday destinations, Tenby I'd found to remain a delightful family resort, with sandy beaches that are still busy with children.

Without recourse to a rail replacement bus, today I could travel only as far as Carmarthen, the most scenic part of the route, running along the Loughor Estuary. Arriva Trains Wales' three coach '175' had come from Manchester, arriving spot on time and reversing at Swansea. These are excellent trains, with a pleasant blue and grey interior, and large windows giving a bright and airy feel. Unlike so many modern trains, the seat backs aren't too high and the ten tables per coach give passengers comfort and convenience, whilst adding to the roomy ambience. I'd far rather travel long distance in one of these than a Pendolino or Voyager.

As we climbed the steep gradient out of Swansea the guard came round asking if anyone wanted the three request stops. No one was alighting but two passengers joined at Gowerton, from where two years earlier I'd caught a bus onto the Gower on the way to Rhossili and Worm's Head. Two egrets stood impassive on the mud as we crossed the Loughor. These small white herons have only been living in the UK for the last twenty-five years, and are extending their range partly as a result of climate change. After Llanelli, where flowers in wooden tubs brightened up an otherwise dull station, we ran close to the sea, or more precisely a huge expanse of sand. At Ferryside, opposite Llansteffan with its Norman castle on the cliff, the line heads inland along the River Tywi. With no passengers joining we'd slowed but not stopped, although all these little stations made me want to get out and walk by the water. As we ran along the river bank towards Carmarthen a strange squeaking noise started. For a while I thought it was the train, which seemed odd as these are so smooth and quiet, but then realised it was a dog further down the coach!

I had only twenty minutes in Carmarthen, just time for a short walk along the river, before catching the same train back. The station has an unusual layout, with trains for Pembroke Dock, Fishguard and Milford Haven reversing here. Passengers walk across the track to access Platform Two. Fishguard was another line I'd used in 2010 for tidal island travelling, catching what was then the only daytime service. Starting from Cardiff, it was the only passenger train to use the Swansea avoiding line, saving having to reverse. This and the night train connect with ships to Ireland, but the service has recently been hugely improved by reopening of Goodwick station close the town, and an additional five trains funded by the Welsh Government.

Outside the station a gaggle of people waited for the bus which was calling at all stations to Pembroke Dock, and taking twenty minutes longer to Tenby than the train does. I decided that the failure to provide a train merited inclusion in my list of delays of over thirty minutes, and I suppose could have had its own category of more than a week late.

The train was returning to Manchester and was quite busy with a mix of local and longer distance travellers. Passengers joined at all the request stops, two elderly couples getting on at Kidwelly and predictably buying coffees from the trolley. In the last chapter I mentioned the adult comic *Viz*. Connoisseurs will be familiar with the Fat Slags, two Geordie girls who are – well let's say aptly named. At Llanelli their Welsh cousins got on – three loud, obese and not to put too finer point, obnoxious teenagers. They started by arguing with the guard, claiming he'd short changed them. He stood his ground – good for him. Then they put their music on. Not headphones but a mobile plonked on the table at full volume. Their language was, shall we say, not what one ought to expect from young ladies. What a contrast to the quiet elderly couples behind. No doubt comments were made when the girls got off at Swansea. With half an hour until the London train I wandered into the city, followed by loud mouthed bellowing – the Fat Slags were going shopping.

I'd paid a few pounds extra for a First Class advance ticket to Paddington and what a contrast – an oasis of calm with one of the best innovations on modern trains – a Travelling Chef. On twenty-eight First Great Western trains every day, while passengers sit back and enjoy the countryside, a chef works away in a tiny galley, producing superb breakfasts, snacks and lunches. My breakfast baguette, with bacon, sausage, egg and tomato, arrived on a china plate with metal cutlery. It even had a pile of mushrooms which weren't on the menu. Standard Class passengers can order the same freshly cooked food from the buffet and take it back to their seat in a box. What a contrast to the limp microwaved offerings that too often are the only hot choices. Sadly no other train operators have chosen to copy the Travelling Chef concept of freshly cooked hot food available to all passengers, and First Great Western have reduced the number of services it's on. Their franchise is soon due for renewal – I'd let them keep it purely on the basis of the wonderful Travelling Chef.

At Cardiff two gentlemen in smart suits sat at the table opposite. I gathered from their quiet conversation that they were politicians. MPs I think, but much as I'd have liked to ask so I could write about meeting someone famous, this isn't the done thing, especially in a First Class coach. In all my travelling I've only ever spoken to two vaguely famous people – 1970s West Ham and journeyman footballer Bill Green on a train to Fenchurch Street, and ex Liverpool player and inventor of the Predator boot, Australian Craig Johnston on a late evening service from Liverpool Street. Sadly I have to report that Mr Johnston was somewhat the worse for drink and made rather a fool of himself.

I realised that so far on my travels, other than in the lounge car of the Fort William sleeper, I hadn't had any interesting conversations on the trains. Over the years I've had the pleasure of meeting many interesting people and having enjoyable conversations on trains, but realised few of these had been recent. Maybe it's a reflection on society, but I'd suggest the reason is more train related. Restaurant cars often provided convivial discussion, but there are few of these left. The change in coach layout from tables to predominantly airline style seats with high seat backs tends to put people in their own little area, not sitting opposite, where most conversations start. Other than on the sleeper, the longest conversations on these travels had been at Upminster and Colchester when trains were delayed. Adversity leads to interaction between passengers and often this develops to conversation. Sadly it seems that another of the pleasures of rail travel is waning.

We arrived at Paddington three minutes late. It had taken 3 hours 7 minutes from Swansea, compared to the fastest timetabled service of 2 hours 58 minutes. Fifty years ago, when diesel had just replaced steam, the quickest was 3 hours 45 minutes, but it's slower now than when HSTs were introduced in the 1970s. The fastest journey twenty five years ago was 2 hours 43 minutes albeit it with two less stops than now. In 1986 trains ran non stop from London to Bristol Parkway in 65 minutes an average of 103mph. The quickest trains now stop twice but take an extra 18 minutes. The South Wales Main Line is another where journeys have become slower since privatisation.

CHAPTER NINE

HIGH SPEED TO THE NORTH WEST

London – Burnley – Windermere

Euston station was busy on a Saturday morning. There was a queue in WH Smiths, with just one person serving, and proceedings delayed by her having to ask every customer if they'd like to buy a huge bar of chocolate for a pound and each one politely declining. The 10.30 to Glasgow was half full, passenger numbers boosted by fellow West Ham fans on their way to Burnley.

I don't like Virgin's Pendolinos. They might be fast and look stylish, but for Standard Class passengers they're just not very nice to travel in. Seats are crammed in, with few tables, not all line up with windows, toilets have nasty chemical smells and the refreshments aren't much to write home about. Worst of all, like many passengers, I find the tilting which allows faster speeds around curves, means I can't read or work without a tendency to nausea. Journey times are reduced, but I'd rather take a bit longer and enjoy the ride.

The guard came round checking tickets, letting off a man behind me who had an advance ticket for the 9.30 train. There's no consistency in how passengers with advances for the wrong train are dealt with. Sometimes, like today, they just get a mild telling off, but others I've seen made to pay extra, although generally guards seem to find a cheaper option than the full single fare that announcements say will be charged.

The southern section of the West Coast Main Line runs through typically English countryside; pleasant rather than spectacular. On a sunny spring morning, with lambs in the fields, it was a nice ride, often alongside the

Grand Union Canal, the freight route to Birmingham before the railway was built. Shortly before Rugby the line runs parallel with another major transport artery, the M1 motorway. On our childhood journeys we used to enjoy this section as the train overtook cars, the occasional driver trying to keep up with the 100mph electric locomotive. This was once described as 'British Rail's best advert' and with the 125mph Pendolinos it's now an even better illustration of the relative speed of road and Inter City rail.

Shortly before Rugby the train passes through the 2,400 yard long Kilsby Tunnel, which cost the lives of 26 of the 1,250 navies who built what was then the world's longest railway tunnel. It was only necessary because landowners in Northampton forced Robert Stevenson to construct the line through Kilsby Ridge, the consequences of their opposition being that Northampton is on a loop so misses out on an Inter City service.

Ironically, a few days before my journey a colleague at work had cited Kilsby Tunnel as justifying his opposition to the HS2 high speed rail line. He'd been taken in by ill-informed locals in his Chiltern town, that the new line was only needed because of a tunnel south of Rugby that caused a bottleneck on the West Coast route. This was 'the only part of the line with two tracks' and 'local trains only allowed a few paths for Virgin'. Clearly both are rubbish, the other two tracks for slower trains run through Northampton. The wider, more polluting and noisier M40 was built with less opposition, but 180 years after Stevenson constructed his line to Birmingham, locals still object to railways in their 'back yards'.

Personally I think that new lines must be built, not just for the shorter journey times, but to provide capacity that is desperately needed, and to replace short haul flights. We must reduce air travel if we are to slow climate change, and fast electric trains between major cities in the UK and Europe are a far greener alternative. It is not environmentally sustainable for people to fly a few hundred miles and if these flights were scrapped there'd be space for long haul without need for new runways. Rather than prevaricating over HS2 and airport expansion, the government should push on with the former and scrap the latter.

It's an interesting comparison that the companies who appointed George Stevenson to build the London Birmingham railway did not form until late 1830, yet the line opened in 1838. After years of discussion, government approval was given for HS2 in January 2012, but it's not scheduled to open until 2026, almost twice the construction time as the current line – and that's with modern machinery, not the picks, shovels and wheelbarrows used by the Victorians.

Although we made a number of childhood journeys on the West Coast line, I can't recall any prior to electrification in 1967 and have no logs in my little red book. I do though remember my father congratulating the driver at Euston after a fast run from Rugby, our first trip behind an electric locomotive. Today we were through Milton Keynes in 30 minutes, a station that didn't exist until 1982, Inter City trains instead stopping at nearby Bletchley. The newly modelled station at Rugby was passed at full speed in 46 minutes, and Crewe reached in 86 minutes.

Just beyond Crewe station, in the sidings at Crewe Heritage Centre, can be seen the Advanced Passenger Train, British Rail's aborted attempt at a tilting train. Teething problems and bad publicity, some probably no more than typical journalistic British Rail bashing, led to the project being scrapped, but hindsight suggests that with more time and less political interference, the train could have been successful.

A four minutes early arrival at Warrington meant we'd done 182 miles in 100 minutes, an average of 109mph. They may not be the most comfortable trains, but Pendolinos are certainly fast, and with the many curves of the West Coast route tilting was the only way to achieve such journey times. As so often it's a matter of compromise, but although the body shell has to be smaller to facilitate tilting, it wasn't necessary to fit out the interior like an airliner.

It should be noted too that the faster times are often at the expense of intermediate stops. Passengers from stations between London and Crewe now have to change to reach Glasgow, and towns such as Nuneaton and Tamworth have virtually lost their Inter City service. I regularly travel to Stafford for work and now have less trains to choose from, but a very fast non stop 75 minute journey. But is that the journey time? With a ticket valid only on a specified train I have to leave longer to get to Euston in case of delays, and fewer trains often means a longer wait after my meeting. And it's a similar with fares. If booking a week or so ahead I can usually get a reasonably cheap advance ticket, but with meetings of unknown length, often end up spending time hanging around for the train I'm booked to return on. Sometimes I prefer London Midland's slow but cheap stopping service, where I can get a reasonably priced First Class ticket in an environment more conducive to working than Virgin's Pendolinos.

At Preston I got on the wrong train. There was no announcement that the 12.53 to York was late, so how was I to know that the train pulling into Platform Three was the 13.04 to Wigan? I sat on it for a minute then suddenly sensed something might not be right. A quick look at the indicator board showed I was on the wrong train – out I jumped and off it went. How close I was to heading to Wigan and perhaps missing kick off.

I first travelled on this part of the East Lancashire line in 1980 when watching West Ham at Blackburn and have been as far as Accrington several times for meetings. It's a pleasant ride, especially after Blackburn when the scenery becomes quite rural. The four coach '158' was busy and with the air conditioning out of order, very hot. The guard came round and unlocked the few small windows which open, but on a sunny spring day they weren't enough to make much difference. In the days before air conditioning trains often got very hot, although opening windows helped keep air flowing, but whilst it's a huge benefit when it works, when air conditioning is out of order poorly ventilated modern carriages can become stifling.

Burnley isn't a place many people visit without good reason. Mine was to Turf Moor and a rather disappointing 2:2 draw. With three stations and several options, West Ham fans were travelling by a variety of routes and at Burnley Manchester Road we had the rare sight of supporters waiting on both platforms to return to London – some via Leeds and some via Preston. The only other place I recall such a split was Wrexham, where half headed north to Chester and half south to return via Wolverhampton.

It was like returning to the 1970s on the 17.57 to Preston, with West Ham fans singing a repertoire of songs old and new. Annoying it may well have been to other travellers, and perhaps intimidating to a few, there was one huge difference from 1970s football travel – everything was good natured and there was not a hint of violence.

A stop outside the station meant we arrived eight minutes late, missing the Pendolino connection north, although a Birmingham to Edinburgh Virgin service wasn't too far behind. This diesel Super Voyager runs entirely under wires – not a good advert for electrification. They are similar to the standard Voyagers, but with tilting facility enabling faster cornering. Like Pendolinos, the Voyager coaches are tapered towards the roof to allow tilting, resulting in a less spacious interior than conventional coaches. At least these gain the speed advantage of tilting. Cross Country's Voyagers either have no tilting facility, or had the equipment removed so it can't be used even on the stretches of track set up for this, but passengers still have to put up with the claustrophobic interiors. To enhance my enjoyment of travelling by Voyager, a man was watching a film on his laptop with no ear phones, so the whole coach could hear – no less annoying than the singing football fans.

Oxenholme Lake District is one of our strangest station names. Although not actually in the National Park, the straightforward Oxenholme was altered to indicate that this is where to change for the Windermere branch. The village of Windermere itself owes its name to the railways, being known as Birthwaite until the branch line arrived in 1847.

A quirk resulting from privatisation means that the 11½ mile 'Lakes Line' branch through Kendal has 100mph trains that were designed for longer runs between the east and west coasts. The line is operated by TransPennine Express, who don't lease any of the lesser trains that would normally operate on a short branch. The seventeen passengers on the 19.37 to Windermere were hence able to enjoy the same pleasant surroundings of these bright air-conditioned Class 185 trains, with comfortable mauve seats, power points and tables, as those who travel from Manchester to Scotland or across the Pennines. It was quite an improvement from my last journeys on the line, when we stayed in Windermere on our honeymoon in 1982, or for our 1977 family holiday here, but passengers who have to endure Pacers (1980s railbuses) on much longer runs must wonder about the benefits of splitting up the railway system.

The train waited an extra minute for a slightly late London-bound train, the guard standing at the top of the subway to see if anyone was coming. Not for the first time I wondered why they didn't bother to do that when I went to Looe. With darkness now fallen, I had to wait for the return journey to enjoy the line's views, after spending a night in a hotel that could easily have been from our 1970s holidays. Mixed internet reviews and a cheap price had suggested my stay might be 'interesting', and whilst nothing was actually awful, I soon concluded that you get what you pay for. In this case, an eccentric proprietor, dull brown bedroom, toilet on the floor below and old style B&B quirks like a shower head and mirror that were positioned too low for anyone much over five foot.

Windermere 'village' is 1½ miles from the lake at Bowness, but there were no buses on either Saturday evening or Sunday. I walked down in the dark, just missing closing time at the chip shop and making do with a Coop cheese sandwich for a pound.

At 9.30 next morning Bowness was already starting to get busy. It was a beautiful day and the waterfront would soon be packed. Boats were lined up ready to take tourists on the lake, some to the Lakeside where the Lakeside and Haverthwaite Railway was having a Thomas Weekend on its 3½ mile line along the River Leven. What a shame this no longer runs through to Ulverston providing a through route to the southern lakes (thanks Dr Beeching).

A few yards away the National Trust owned Cockshott Point was peaceful; the lake picturesque with sun breaking through mist over its still water. As we did on our 1977 holiday, I walked to the chain ferry which crosses the lake to Far Sawrey. Then we'd walked on to Hill Top to see Beatrix Potter's house, although as a rebellious teenager I'd refused to go in and sat on the wall outside. Today I enjoyed a lovely walk along the lake's bank. As I sat on a fallen branch looking down to the still water, with the birds singing and sun shining through the trees, I thought, what a wonderful country we live in. And this isn't even the best part of the Lake District, but how much better than crowded Bowness.

I got a taxi back up the hill to Windermere station. Commenting to the driver on the number of people in Bowness, he said this was quiet. Next week was Easter and you would hardly see a blade of grass by the lake (well not unless you were prepared to walk a few yards). I'd noticed a lot of Chinese visitors and he said they come in the spring, then it's the Japanese, then Indians and Pakistanis, and in August rich Saudis arrive, escaping the heat in their country. The Lakes have always been busy, but we saw few foreigners here in 1977.

Like most of the branches I'd travelled on, Windermere station is just a single platform, the train shed having been replaced by a supermarket in 1986. The 12.58 to Oxenholme was quite busy and it was good to see a cleaner go through the train during its short turn round. Quite a few passengers were travelling long distance and six loud ladies with luggage waited on the platform, dithering whether to board as the seventh hadn't yet arrived. Having decided to wait, at the last minute they jumped on, their missing friend having to catch up, hopefully in time for their flight from Manchester.

The '185' gave a smooth and quiet ride on what is a scenic route through Lakeland hills. Oxenholme was busy with three trains in just a few minutes. Sunday afternoon, which used to be quiet, is now often the railways' busiest time of the week and 13.23 to Euston was quite full. I treated myself to a £15 Weekend First upgrade, which is particularly beneficial on Pendolinos, the lower seating density, all with tables and lining up with windows, making a much more pleasant and less claustrophobic environment.

Weekend catering isn't brilliant, but in the week First Class passengers receive complimentary food – the cooked breakfasts are good, lunch is just sandwiches, and 'dinner', which would be better described as a hot snack, is invariably disappointing. Only for breakfast does the food justify the restaurant symbol in the timetable. At least they dispensed with that awful Virgin Cola and now sell the real thing. Noting the limited food choice when travelling up, I'd bought some lunch in Windermere, including a pork pie, something famously stocked by British Rail buffets but now never seen on a train. Nor do they sell the large round fruit pies that I used to enjoy, even if half the contents usually ended up on my trousers. With Virgin it's no longer a buffet but a 'shop', although the only non refreshment items it appeared to stock were packs of playing cards and copies of *Hello* magazine.

Train buffets have evolved over the years and since privatisation vary considerably between operators. In many ways they've improved, with a wider range of hot drinks, although I miss that old machine that used to inject steam into the cup with a hiss, but always looked slightly dangerous. And in British Rail days they didn't insist that every item was carried back to your seat in a brown paper bag – for health & safety of course. It was on the West Coast Main Line that I once encountered the sort of jobsworth mentality that gave BR such a bad name.

On our honeymoon, Deb and I made a round trip from Windermere to Lancaster to Skipton, then over the Settle Carlisle line and back to Oxenholme. South of Carlisle we went to the buffet for toasted sandwiches. This was in the days when two staff worked the buffet and sandwiches were made to order. Deb wanted a cheese one, but although the menu only offered cheese and tomato, we assumed it would be no problem to have it made without the tomato. Oh yes it was. The man refused to make anything that wasn't exactly as on the menu. As the queue behind us grew and people looked on incredulously, he point blank refused to leave out the tomato. In the end we had no choice but to admit defeat. With today's 'customer service' hopefully one wouldn't see such inflexibility, but with the exception of East Coast's morning trains and First Great Western's travelling chef, neither is there any chance of buying a freshly made toasted sandwich.

CHAPTER TEN

HEART OF WALES LINE

London – Bristol – Swansea – Shrewsbury

This trip was a repeat of one I made with my father in the 1970s, soon after HSTs took over the Paddington to Swansea route. This time however, rather than a very long day with 472 miles travelling, I took a relaxing three days over the journey, making a slight diversion into Bristol to take in West Ham's match at City.

Diverting at Wootton Basset from the route covered in Chapter Eight, the line runs through Chippenham before climbing to Brunel's famous Box Tunnel, once the world's longest railway tunnel. According to legend the sun shines through the dead straight bore on 9th April, Brunel's birthday, although most sources suggest that he got his calculations slightly wrong and while it does shine through on a few days, its not normally 9th April. What he did get right though was the precise direction of the bores from each end, which when they met underground were just two inches out of alignment.

The run through Bath gives excellent views of the city, with its Georgian Royal Crescent and 15th century abbey church. Brunel's railway adds to the city's outstanding architecture, as it runs along castellated viaducts and twice crosses the River Avon. From here it's a short hop to Bristol, which we reached in an hour and forty minutes from London. This typical journey time is seven minutes slower than 1986 and only twenty minutes quicker than the fastest train in 1962. Then the Bristol Pullman and Bristolian, the latter hauled by *Warship* diesel locomotives which had recently taken over from steam, took two hours with just a stop at Bath. In the 1930s and 50s the trains were even faster, the steam hauled Bristolian taking one and three quarter hours non stop, just five minutes longer than today's HSTs. As with all our inter city routes, now there are far more trains, often with more stops and all taking roughly the same journey time. Previously one or two crack named expresses were often quicker than the rest.

London to Bristol is a journey I've made many times for work, enjoying a Travelling Chef breakfast until these were taken off most Bristol services. My first journey was in the mid 1960s when we travelled on the famous Blue Pullman. Just five sets were built of these fixed formation trains with diesel power cars at each end, two of which formed the Manchester Pullman from St Pancras. The remainder ran from Paddington to Birmingham, Swansea and Bristol, but all were withdrawn within just eleven years of being introduced.

West Ham's 1:1 draw was less than satisfactory, as was my hotel near Temple Meads station, where a weird noise kept me awake. Not the nearby trains, but a whistling sound like the wind, although the night was still and it was coming from inside the building. Strangely it stopped if I opened my door, but could be heard all along the corridor once the door was shut again, as I found at 2am when wandering round in pyjamas trying to find the source. If the lady on reception had seemed more concerned when I checked out in the morning, I might not have told you that it was the Ibis Hotel that I won't be staying at in future.

Temple Meads station is used by around 25,000 people each day and was busy with arriving commuters when I returned next morning. Platform numbers can be confusing, as there are eight tracks, but platforms numbered one to fifteen, and most rather than the usual A and B have a different number at each end. To further complicate matters, Platform Two isn't used for passenger trains and Platform Fourteen doesn't exist! The huge number of bikes on Platform One and regular comings and goings of cyclists illustrated a change from my youth, when it was mainly children who cycled and station racks held just a handful of bikes.

The 9.21 to Cardiff was surprisingly busy. As there were no ticket checks on the fifty-seven minute journey I can only conclude that the guard couldn't be bothered to walk through the two coach train. We went through Stapleton Road, where I once got off to watch West Ham play

Bristol Rovers at their old Eastville ground, then passed the Memorial Ground where they currently play, its two tall stands raised high against the suburban Bristol skyline. On our only visit here we'd walked from Montpelier on the Severn Beach line.

At Cardiff I changed to a First Great Western HST, preferring to wait a few minutes rather than board the very busy two coach Arriva Trains Wales train from Manchester. There was a Travelling Chef on board, but no announcement about this or the buffet. Sometimes I suspect that staff don't bother to advertise their service so they'll have less work to do, not thinking that poor sales may lead to catering cuts and job losses. Delays at signals outside Cardiff meant that arrival at Swansea was seven minutes late, although there was no explanation or apology. Mind you, I'd rather nothing than the impersonal automated announcements we get on C2C apologising for the 'delay and inconvenience it may cause' when the train is as little as three minutes late.

The Heart of Wales Line is one of Britain's great train rides. Leaving Swansea along the coastal route towards Carmarthen, it reverses at Llanelli and heads up into the Welsh hills. A look at the map and the size of the places it serves, shows the remoteness of this unique line from which you can see typical Wales – farmland, hills, mountains, beaches, castles, rivers, streams and an awful lot of sheep!

I'd travelled on it three times before. The first was on our Mumbles holiday, to Llanwrtyd Wells, where I was to stop tonight. At just under 4 hours it's a long haul from end to end, and an overnight stay would give me the chance to revisit one of our holiday excursions. The second was south from Craven Arms to Knighton when we'd stayed at Hereford, and the last the whole length of the line on the marathon round robin with my father. Then it was known as the Central Wales Line, before the change to the more romantic branding which helps sell it to tourists.

An eight coach HST in the adjacent platform made the single car '153' seem even smaller as it waited in Swansea station. Twenty five passengers were on board, several travelling all the way to Shrewsbury, presumably to enjoy the ride as it's almost an hour quicker via Hereford.

At Llanelli two lads ran across the bridge and jumped on board just as we were about to depart. With five hours until the next train I think I'd have left a bit more time. From here we joined the single track Heart of Wales Line. Travelling north east we followed the River Loughor, with low hills to our right. Most of the stations are requests but we stopped at the majority, and there was a steady turnover of passengers in our little train, with the total remaining around twenty. Several got out at Pontarddulais, where tulips bloomed in the station garden. There were once four platforms here and like most of the line's stations, sidings, a signal box and station master. Now just one is staffed. Many of the line's stations have though been adopted by local communities, who tend attractive gardens. The majority still have original buildings, although often not open for railway use, and there are few plastic shelters on the route.

Young calves in a field watched us pass unfazed, perhaps already used to the eight little trains which go by each day. In order to provide services for those wishing to spend a day in either Swansea or Shrewsbury, there are early and late trains from each end of the line, leaving only two at convenient times for the end to end traveller.

A goods train was waiting for us to clear Pantyffynnon, so that it could join the line from the Amman Valley branch. This was closed in 1988 after the Abernant Colliery was shut, but reopened in 2006 to serve Tairgwaith open cast mine. The Amman Valley Railway Society hope to run part of the route as a heritage steam line and there are longer term aspirations for light rail services on a 26 mile loop incorporating part of the Heart of Wales Line.

Eight passengers alighted at Ammanford, one of the busiest stops, with five more boarding, and I took the opportunity to move to a table. A man across the aisle had a case holding a strange looking apparatus with lots of wires and dials, which was connected to a probe stuck to the window – a definite case of 'suspicious activity' to report. He told me the equipment was to survey the 3G radio network, so Network Rail can find where the trains are, as at the moment they don't know.

We continued north at a sedate pace, slowing to 10mph for unguarded crossings. The train doesn't hurry, averaging just 29mph for 90 miles from Llanelli to Craven Arms, where it joins the main line from Hereford. At Llandeilo a silky grey cat on the station watched us arrive, then walked off along a wall, but looked back to observe our departure. He may have appeared nonchalant but I reckon he was a secret spotter. In summer a bus meets the trains here, taking visitors to various attractions, including the National Botanic Garden of Wales. Details of this and more information on the line are on the website of the Heart of Wales Travellers Association, an organisation which has done a great deal to promote and support this special railway line.

A few miles further north the line crosses the River Tywi on Glanrhyd Bridge, the scene of a tragic accident in 1987. In heavy floods the water swept away some of the supports and the bridge collapsed as a train crossed. Three passengers including a schoolboy, plus the driver, sadly drowned.

A taxi driver waved to the driver as we pulled into Llangadog, where an elderly lady got off with a large suitcase. As I've often found on rural transport, the majority of passengers were either youngsters or those of more mature years, with few between about twenty and sixty. For a while senior citizen pass holders from South Wales were permitted to travel free on the line, 23,000 doing so in twelve months. This works out at an average of about nine per train, but sometimes the number of pensioners going for free meant that other passengers had to stand. I've no objection to youngsters and the elderly getting subsidised travel, but I think they should pay something.

No one used Llanwrda, a tiny station with a little shelter and another lovely garden. It's hard to imagine that 10,000 tons of goods were handled here in 1923. So far the scenery had been pleasantly rural rather than outstanding, but soon after Llandovery we crossed the spectacular Cynghordy viaduct over the wide Bran Valley, one of the highlights of the line. From here we were climbing into the hills.

There's an interesting tale about the little halt of Cynghordy which we passed through without stopping. Many years ago a goat was due to be sent to Scotland to mate, but the station master couldn't sort out the right paperwork, so simply tethered the animal underneath the signal box. Her owner, who returned two weeks later to collect the goat, must have wondered why the trip had been unfruitful – and the goat was probably a bit disappointed too!

Perhaps the best views on the line are as the train climbs the one in sixty incline to Sugar Loaf Mountain, before plunging into a thousand yard tunnel. With just a couple of passengers a week, the tiny platform of Sugar Loaf Halt is the least used station in Wales. It was built for railway workers who lived in cottages by the line, and later used as a drop off point for banking engines, but remains open despite there being no village or even houses nearby. For complex reasons related to European funding zones, the platform has an electronic indicator screen, while busier stations further south don't.

As we descended to Llanwrtyd Wells, a shepherd and his dog were rounding up sheep on the hillside, a scene which could have been from a hundred years ago, but for the quad bike he was riding. The train waited a few minutes in the station and I chatted to the guard telling him this was my first ride on the line for thirty-five years. He agreed that not much had changed, adding that 'nor will it'. In many ways the Heart of Wales Line is still a journey from my youth.

With a population of just over 600, Llanwrtyd Wells claims to be the smallest town in Britain, yet as well as a railway station it retains a school, several shops, hotels and pubs – facilities that many larger villages have lost. The town has recently come to relative fame as a centre for unusual sports, including bog snorkelling and a man versus horse race. The World Alternative Games were due to be held here later in the year, featuring such events as worm charming, gravy wrestling, Pooh sticks and wife carrying, where the winner wins the weight of his spouse in beer.

After checking in to the excellent Bryncelyn Guest House, where the comfortable room and Lil's friendly welcome rivalled Swansea's Crescent for my best accommodation to date, I set off to walk into the hills. Our walk on the family's trip here had been enlivened by the company of Spot, a little dog who decided to join us. Today there was just me and hundreds of sheep with young lambs on the hill. Eight little lambs raised their heads above a grassy bank as I approached – what a great photo it would have been if only I'd taken the camera.

As I climbed the panorama constantly changed, with more and more hills and mountains revealing themselves on the horizon. When I stopped near the top the Brecon Beacons were visible in the distance, with the little town of Llanwrtyd Wells nestling in the valley. Although remote, the Heart of Wales scenery is more hills than mountains, and more farmland than wild moors. With so many scattered little communities its remoteness is different from the wilds of Scotland, but what is perhaps unique is the way the train connects these towns and villages, providing a link to the outside world, which from the top of Garn Dwad above Llanwrtyd Wells, seemed far far away.

Next morning I walked up the River Irfon, passing one of the spas that once brought visitors to take the foul tasting but supposedly curing waters. It's said that the 'benefits' of the sulphur spring waters were discovered by a Reverend Theophilus Evans in 1732, who suffered from scurvy and noticed a very healthy looking frog in a well. Reasoning that despite its foul smell the waters might have helped the frog, he drank some and found his scurvy cured. In 1972 the Dolycoed Wells were derelict, with sheep using them for shelter, but almost forty years later the buildings have been renovated as private houses. A man who was tending a roaring bonfire told me he was clearing the area around the spring, which was to be covered with a dome and opened to the public.

Several of the town's shops have recently closed, probably resulting from Tesco opening at Llandrindod Wells, half an hour away, but there's still a small chemist shop which looked little changed from the 1970s. Peter, the owner, told me a couple of stories about the railway. The first was of a local twelve year old boy who found a smoke bomb on a nearby army artillery range and let it off on the train. The train had to be evacuated, but the smoke was cleared then everyone got back on and the journey continued. These days the bomb squad would most likely have been called, the train taken out of service and the incident on *News at Ten*. The other was a couple who'd got on the wrong train, I think at Llandrindod Wells. At that time the passing loop was north of the station, so the guard flagged down a train going south, getting it to stop with the drivers' cab doors alongside each other. The couple walked through the cabs to change trains, a procedure which I'm sure isn't in the rule book and probably wouldn't happen today, although with the Heart of Wales Line you never know.

When visiting as a child, Llanwrtyd Wells had just been another place that we'd arrived at by train, gone for a walk, had a picnic and seen a bit of history. Aged eleven, I hadn't appreciated the beauty of the hills and history of the spas, but above all the remoteness of this little community. Of all the places I'd so far returned to, this was the one where I wanted to spend more time. It may be equalled by other little towns in Wales, but being in the middle of a wonderful railway line, Llanwrtyd Wells is a special place. I will be back!

The 11.05 to Shrewsbury passes a southbound service at Llanwrtyd Wells and for a few minutes the station was quite a hive of activity. Three passengers boarded to head north, with two getting off. The drivers and guards swapped trains, as crew return to their respective bases rather than travel the whole length of the line. With both trains stopping for a few minutes I got the driver's permission to take a photo from the foot crossing, something which certainly wouldn't be allowed on less relaxed railways.

One change since my previous journeys is that since 1986 traditional signals have been replaced by a system known as 'No Signalman Token Remote', in which the train crew insert a token into a mechanism in a little grey shed on each of the five stations with passing loops. The whole system is overseen by a signalman (or signaller as they are now more 'correctly' called) at Pantyffynnon. This operation completed, we departed Llanwrtyd, heading north through more delightful scenery. April was a good time to travel as I'm told that in summer vegetation obscures many of the views.

With most stations' request stops, the driver has to slow to look for boarding passengers, but if there are none only halts if told to by the guard. The guard from Swansea had told the one taking over to return to Shrewsbury that there was a passenger for Llangammarch Wells, but he couldn't find her. After calling out, he asked each of the fifteen passengers individually if they wanted Llangammarch, but none did. Eventually he found the lady, already by the front door ready to alight. Returning, he told the whole coach that he'd found the passenger and 'she's like my wife – hiding – well I wish she was'. The atmosphere on the Heart of Wales Line is rather different from most of our trains.

Two ladies with luggage joined the train at Builth Road, a station that's two miles from the small town of Builth Wells. Where it wasn't convenient to run the railway into a town the Victorians simply put a station at a more distant access point and added the 'Road' suffix. Two miles is nothing though – anyone arriving at the little station of Llanbister Road has a 5 ½ mile walk to the village. Although usually quiet, for a few days each year Builth Road is the busiest on the line, with special trains bringing visitors to the Royal Welsh Show. There actually used to be two stations here, one on the Mid-Wales Railway, an even more remote route that closed some years before Beeching could bring his axe down. The Heart of Wales Line was on his list to cull, but was saved by virtue of the remoteness of the communities it served and maybe more significantly, the six marginally constituencies it passed through.

There were eighteen passengers on board as we left Llandrindod Wells, another spa town, and the busiest intermediate station. It even has a privately run booking office and a glimpse into the waiting room showed an old fashioned weighing scale and sack barrow, that were common at the time of my childhood travels. A few miles further north we stopped at Dolau, the best kept station on the line, with a GWR seat and beautifully tended gardens. A plaque on the platform commemorates the Queen's visit by Royal Train in 2002 on her Golden Jubilee tour of Wales.

Soon we crossed the Grade II listed Knucklas Viaduct, one of the most beautiful in Britain, both for its setting and weathered stone construction with castellated towers at each end. The couple sitting opposite were however more concerned about discussing lunch than enjoying the views. Salad was one option mentioned, but looking at the size of them, perhaps it should have been the only one!

Five passengers were using Knighton station, which we'd come to in the 1970s to walk on Offa's Dyke. Unusually, rather than bring a picnic we ate out, having lunch in a grocer's shop, where the couple of dining tables seemed very much a secondary concern and the service incredibly slow. For some time I'd been hoping to visit Knighton with my brother, not for the slow lunch or country walk, but to the Subbuteo shop where we could have relived the many hours of childhood spent playing table football. Sadly though it closed down in 2010 and we were never able to make use of its teams and pitches. Both our collections of now forty year old players are however still in the loft and one day when no one's looking we'll get them out for a match.

As we left the hills and ran alongside the fast flowing River Teme, the little train was at last able to get a decent run – 61mph according to my count of the beats. I chatted to Jane the guard, agreeing how special this line is. At Craven Arms we joined the Marches Line from Newport, the double track and higher speed immediately different from the Heart of Wales. There was though one more highlight, the Shropshire Hills and the always inviting Long Mynd hill at Church Stretton, where on summer weekends shuttle buses take walkers from the station.

Arrival in Shrewsbury was two minutes early and waiting on the platform to meet me was my brother. Over lunch by the River Severn we discussed how lucky they are to live at the end of the lovely Heart of Wales railway and how remiss he had been to use it just once – to take his son to play Subbuteo! My enthusiasm seemed to have rubbed off, with a promise that they'd take a trip soon, but table football or not, I shall certainly return to this very special railway line.

CHAPTER ELEVEN

WREXHAM & SHROPSHIRE

Shrewsbury – Birmingham – Marylebone

The railway came to Shrewsbury in 1849. It remains an important junction with trains leaving to run on five different lines, but for nearly three years the service from Shrewsbury to London was the most enjoyable way to travel in England.

The several through trains a day run by BR was reduced to just one Virgin service, which I used a number of times when visiting my brother. Formed of comfortable Mark Three coaches and hauled by an electric locomotive, which was changed to a diesel at Wolverhampton, it was a pleasant way to travel. Then Virgin stopped the train and Shrewsbury lost its through service to London.

Privatisation was supposed to open up the railways to competition and in April 2008 a new company, Wrexham Shropshire and Marylebone Railway, started a service from Wrexham through Shrewsbury to London. This they hoped would exploit the gap in the market left by Virgin. It was no ordinary service but based on the principle of giving customers what they wanted, perhaps summarised by a paragraph in *No Boat Required*:

'Two weeks later I was at Marylebone station setting off for North Wales, travelling with the best train operator in Britain – Wrexham & Shropshire Railway. This little company offers all that is best about rail travel; a smooth and comfortable ride, quiet trains with locomotives not under floor engines, every seat at a table and lining up with large windows, cheap fares even if bought on the train, friendly staff who are only too pleased to help, and perhaps best of all, superb catering with a chef on every train.

My lamb shank would have graced a top restaurant. They are not always the quickest trains, but if I have time to spare I'll go out of my way to use them. This was to be a trip where the travel and scenery were as enjoyable as the islands.'

Rather than lease units, WSMR chose to use 1970s Mark Three coaches pulled by diesel locomotives, giving a quality of travel rarely enjoyed on more modern trains. To start with they even had to fix an engine to each end of the train, as the points that used to allow locomotives to run round their coaches in stations have nearly all gone. Costs were saved when they acquired DVTs (driving van trailers), which allowed the train to be driven from either end, but initial losses were still high. Service was however superb, with excellent complimentary hot meals for First Class passengers, even at weekends, and a proper buffet where Standard Class customers could order the meals and have them brought to their seat. For those not wanting a full meal, WSMR offered an excellent range of food and drink, including freshly cooked sausage or bacon rolls, which quickly became highly popular.

Fares were low, often just £10 single if booked in advance, and flexible tickets were much cheaper than Virgin's. Indeed they may have been too cheap. I almost felt guilty when my two sons and I could travel to Shrewsbury on a Family Railcard for less than £25 return. Occasionally we made it a treat and went First Class with a free cooked breakfast, still paying little more than Virgin's fare.

Initially a selection of mostly ex Virgin coaches were leased, but in 2009 WSMR introduced their own superbly refurbished stock. I happened to be at Wrexham the day the first set arrived and as the staff inspected it the pride in their own little railway was evident. With a pleasant grey interior, virtually every seat around tables and all lined up with windows, the best toilets on any British train and superb catering, this was travelling at its best. What it wasn't though was fast.

As a new operator WSMR had last pick of the timetabling paths and had to fit around other trains. The second morning train south, which I used to catch from Shrewsbury, would wait ten minutes at Birmingham International to let a Pendolino overtake, its passengers getting to London far quicker but in less comfort. The Chiltern Line it used to Marylebone wasn't fast and there were often hold ups at Banbury to let Cross Country go by, or behind local trains into London. Worst of all, with few paths through New Street, it took an age to get round Birmingham. Some services went from Leamington via Coventry, and others on a link line by Birmingham City's football ground, but all then headed off on a West Midlands tour through Tame Bridge Parkway, where they stopped although with little patronage. I used it a few times, changing to go on to Walsall, to Witton for Aston Villa v West Ham, or back to Birmingham – a slow but more pleasant journey than Virgin's Pendolinos.

Whilst I'd liked to have used WSMR's trains directly to Coventry, Birmingham or Wolverhampton, this wasn't possible. They either passed through without stopping, or halted but didn't unlock the doors. They did call at Wolverhampton, but only to pick up passengers heading north or set down going south. Once I asked the guard what would happen if I got out there having travelled from London and was told that if I was spotted by Virgin staff the company would be fined. The reason for this absurdity was a clause in Virgin's franchise agreement that prohibited any other company competing directly with their services. So privatisation, which was supposed to encourage competition, actually stifled it. Soon after WSMR started operating, Virgin commenced their own direct service from Wrexham to London, by the far quicker route via Crewe. Many questioned whether their sudden interest in serving Wrexham was entirely coincidental with the birth of a new operator.

Where they lost on speed WSMR gained on service, friendly staff, comfortable trains, excellent catering and reasonable fares. Typical of their employees' dedication was one journey when the buffet was flooded, but rather than close they moved stock to a table in the next coach and sold it from there. Usage grew and with better pathing and upgrade of the Chiltern route, journey times came down. The people of North Wales and Shropshire loved their very own railway and the friendly atmosphere on the trains, which contrasted to the hustle and bustle of changing at Birmingham. It was no accident that in the Spring 2010 National Passenger Survey by Passenger Focus, the independent rail watchdog, Wrexham & Shropshire scored a 99% satisfaction rating – the highest rating in the survey's history.

Wrexham & Shropshire's customer service extended to making every effort to avoid replacement buses, the easy but unpopular option other operators usually take during engineering work. Passengers dislike having to change into a bus, and many simply won't travel if the journey can't be completed by train. WSMR were prepared to find alternative routes and although journey times were extended, pasengers could travel in comfort. Several times at weekends we went from Shewsbury to London via Crewe and Birmingham, and once set out on tour of North London. From Marylebone the train headed towards Ruislip, then reversed, travelling south on the Greenford branch onto the Great Western Main Line. From here it ran almost into Paddington before taking the North London Line to Willesden, where it joined the West Coast Main Line to Birmingham and on to Shrewsbury. It must have cost a fortune in training drivers for the route or paying pilots from other companies, but this was the sort of service that made Wrexham & Shropshire so special.

After a chance meeting with Jo Philipps, the company's Marketing Executive, over dinner on the train, I started writing a book about Wrexham & Shropshire. It was to tell the story of this unique company, the staff who ran it and describe what could be seen as the train trundled through Shropshire and the West Midlands, then Leamington, Banbury, High Wycombe and into the historic Marylebone terminus. To write a piece about each town or village it served, I'd already made a few trips and on the 25th January 2011 was about to set out for another, when an email popped up on my screen:

'It is with great regret that we announce that Wrexham & Shropshire will stop operating trains on Friday 28th January'.

The company had cut one train a day when the recession started to reduce travel, but passenger numbers were picking up and it was thought to be heading for break even performance. I'd met Andy Hamilton, Wrexham & Shropshire's Managing Director, on the train a few months before, who was most upbeat about its prospects and agreed to an interview for the book. Chairman Adrian Shooter however told the BBC that *'there was no prospect of the business ever being profitable'*. Conspiracy theories abounded. Was the stock wanted elsewhere? Could it have been more profitable if a deal had been made with Arriva Trains Wales to serve Aberystwyth? Would the company have folded if it could have competed fairly with Virgin? And above all, could it be saved?

There were attempts to save the service, although not helped by the short notice of closure. A petition and Facebook campaign were launched, and local MPs raised the issue with Ministers. Less publicly, a group of interested parties in which I played a small part, got together to investigate the possibility of setting up a new company to run services. Options for leasing stock were explored but it soon became clear that without a large financial backer the idea was a non starter.

It was a sad day when I travelled south on the penultimate day of operation. The train was more full than usual, passenger numbers boosted by enthusiasts anxious for a last chance to ride this unique train. There was genuine sadness that such a customer friendly enterprise had failed and fingers pointed at Virgin for their part in the company's downfall. The last train was packed, with many a tear shed by staff and passengers alike. Television cameras were on the platform and the BBC played a recording of Train Manager Jane Meredith's final tearful announcement as her train pulled into Marylebone. This was the same Jane who I'd met on the Heart of Wales train from Llanwrtyd Wells, seeming very much at home on the friendly rural line.

Shortly after WSMR's closure it was announced that Chiltern Railways (who were owned by the same company) would be running locomotive hauled trains from Marylebone to Birmingham Moor Street, and soon WSMR stock appeared on the route. Debate continues as to whether it was finance or Chiltern's desire for the stock that resulted in the sudden demise of Wrexham & Shropshire. Whilst sad that WSMR is no more and that Shrewsbury no longer has a through service to London, it has however led to what has become the most enjoyable way to travel between England's two largest cities.

So returning to my journey home from Wales, which resumed after a huge lunch in The Armoury at Shrewsbury. With no through trains, it was back to catching a London Midland service then changing at Birmingham. The train was quite full, with more getting on at Telford, Shropshire's largest town. This route is well used and I've often seen people standing, not helped of course by London passengers no longer having through trains. Nor was the journey as pleasant, with the loud under floor engines of the four car '158', and two automated safety announcements after each stop.

Cosford station was temporarily closed, with the 1937 station buildings and wooden sleeper platforms being replaced. A station of unique character was to become ordinary. Wrexham & Shropshire used to stop here and so it was not entirely wasted, I shall quote from my aborted book:

'With its wooden platforms standing on stilts and two tiny shack like waiting rooms, Cosford station does not look like somewhere from where one can catch 'Inter City' trains to London. That there is no town or village of Cosford makes it seemingly even less likely that express trains should call here, however at less than a mile from Junction 3 of the M42 and with adjacent free car parking, Wrexham & Shropshire have recognised the station's park & ride potential. Indeed with machine gun carrying guards from RAF Cosford a few yards away, the company suggest that this is perhaps the safest station car park in the country!'

As the trolley came round I recalled our experience on the train back from Shrewsbury on the round robin Central Wales trip. This was in the days of secondary routes having British Rail's 'pork pie and sandwich' buffet, and the only hot food was soup. Unfortunately the steam machine had broken down and we declined the steward's offer of cold soup!

Another trip my father and I made using the line was from Wolverhampton to Ironbridge on the branch to Coalbrookdale. This had been closed to passengers in 1962, but was reopened with a special Sunday service for the summer of 1979, the bi-centenary of the bridge's construction. A temporary platform was built, with special fares available from around the country. The line is still open for freight but what a shame that this World Heritage Site, the birthplace of the industrial revolution, can't still be served by rail.

From Birmingham I naturally preferred the option of an old fashioned locomotive hauled train, so made the short walk to the superbly renovated Moor Street station and caught the 15.55 to Marylebone. Formed of five ex WSMR coaches hauled by a diesel engine, all painted in striking silver, Chiltern's branding for the new 'Mainline' service, this could have been a train from my youth.

For the payment of an additional ten pounds I travelled in the 'Business Zone', enjoying comfortable seats and complimentary drinks; as my notes record, such a civilised way to travel. Not that the Standard Class isn't comfortable, and with almost every seat at a table and lined up with nice big windows, far more so than Virgin's alternative.

The trains have a traditional buffet and Chiltern have revived the excellent WSMR sausage and bacon baps, but sadly don't offer the superb cooked meals that I'd often enjoyed to Shrewsbury. Furthermore, this isn't a slow option, the fastest Chiltern train taking ninety minutes to London, only six less than Virgin's average. Despite the huge sums spent on upgrading the route and new trains, Euston to Birmingham averages only eleven minutes less than the hour and thirty five average in 1976.

The Chiltern Line is a route I rarely used until the birth of Wrexham & Shropshire, but it's a nice ride through typically English scenery. I'm told that we went this way to Birmingham when a fast steam service was run from Paddington during the Euston line electrification, but my first memory of part of the route was from a special day out with my father in 1978. Then we'd travelled from Paddington to Stratford-upon-Avon on a vintage train organised by the Great Western Society, hauled by two steam locomotives – *Hinderton Hall* and *Cookham Manor*. This was my only experience of preserved main line steam and of the sort of enthusiastic clientele they attract!

A few weeks before completing this chapter I used Chiltern again to Birmingham, paying £50 for a flexible return ticket. A similar peak departure time and flexibility on Virgin would have cost £158. Should I have wanted to travel First Class, rather than the extra £10 each way on Chiltern, it would have been a total of £254 return. Of course cheaper advance tickets are often available, but I was travelling at a day's notice and was unsure of my return timing. My extra fifteen minutes journey time was easily justified by the greater comfort, let alone the huge cost saving.

On this train the coaches now had newly fitted automatic doors, to comply with disability legislation, with the added benefit of reducing station dwell times (when thoughtless passengers leave them open). The guard told me that it was hoped to bring in more locomotive hauled trains. His view was that Pendolinos were rubbish, looking like planes inside, and questioned the modern obsession of speed over comfort. With its recently reduced journey times, Chiltern were now providing both.

CHAPTER TWELVE

MYSTERY TRIP

London – ????

In the 1970s British Rail marketed a range of days out under the name 'Merrymakers'. Some, like the round robin we did on the Central Wales Line, were tickets on ordinary services, but others were excursions on special trains. My father and I went on several of each, including a trip to Betws-y-Coed and two mystery trips. The first mystery journey started at Euston and crossed to the Midland Main Line on the then freight only, but now closed, Northampton to Market Harborough line, eventually ending up at York. The second, which we went on in 1974 and is recorded in my red book, I set out to recreate today.

In 1974 our thirteen coach locomotive hauled train left St Pancras at 8.17. After picking up at Elstree, St Albans, Luton and Bedford, my log shows it arriving at Wellingborough at 9.51, and that here the engine was changed. My book records the engine number but I'd promised not to mention these; (OK it was 45077). Today I'd planned to catch an East Midlands Trains HST. I was however thwarted. The 1970s had returned to St Pancras. Train drivers were on strike!

One benefit of privatisation is that each train operator negotiates with its own staff, so strikes rarely affect the whole system. More enlightened attitudes and new legislation, mean that strikes in the UK are now far rarer than in my youth, and unless involving Network Rail staff such as signallers, generally they don't cripple the whole system. There is also more likely to be some sort of service operating, worked either by non striking staff or management. Today East Midlands Trains were running just one train an hour and I boarded the 10.30, calling at all major stations to Sheffield.

Sensibly this was formed of the longest train available, two five car Meridians coupled together.

With stylish livery and smart red seats, the Meridians look good inside and out, and are less cramped than the Voyagers on which they were based. Under-floor engines however cause noise and vibration, so where possible on my regular work trips to Leicester I choose a service using the quieter and more spacious HSTs. Staff too have told me that they prefer the older trains, and that I'm not the only passenger who will let a Meridian train leave and wait a few minutes for an HST.

There is one little annoyance with Meridians which I have to say is typical of the niggles which unnecessarily detract from enjoyment of modern train travel. The windows aren't that big and in First Class, curtains which can't be pulled back beyond the glass obscure the edges, reducing the view from seats. No doubt the designers put them in because they look nice, but with no thought to the passenger who wants to look out the window. Mind you it's not just trains where designers' ideas for aesthetics take precedence over practicality. I recently bought a new mobile phone. It looks nice but the shiny plastic it's made from is extremely slippery and I keep dropping it!

On my regular journeys to the East Midlands, if knowing roughly what time I'll be returning I try to book an Advance First Class ticket, which are often just a few pounds more than Standard Class. Sadly the excellent breakfasts are now available only on a few southbound trains, but bacon or sausage baguettes are still served at-seat and later in the day a range of very reasonably priced meals are available. I must make particular mention of Ross, one of the hosts on a recent journey from Nottingham, who told me he cooks a 'mean burger' and persuaded me to try it. Using an oven rather than microwave, he served up a beautifully presented and very tasty cheeseburger. My email thanking East Midlands Trains for providing a good meal received no reply.

As we left St Pancras it was announced that there would be, '*An at seat trolley service, with a wide variety of snacks and refreshment*'. Unfortunately buffets have been closed and a trolley provides the only refreshments for Standard Class passengers. This reached me six minutes after departure, its 'wide variety' including just a single sandwich.

Other than the mystery trip, the Midland Main Line wasn't a route we used as children. I didn't start travelling on it regularly until the late 1970s, when we caught locomotive hauled trains to Leicester and Nottingham for football, then later for work when HSTs had taken over. Services are now faster, with a top speed of 110mph, although with many restrictions from the curves which resulted from either landowners objecting to the line passing through their property, or Victorian engineers following contours to keep costs down. They are also more frequent and with the line almost self-contained, tend to be reliable – strikes permitting. Leicester, with three trains an hour, now has an excellent service, with trains going on to either Derby and Sheffield, or Nottingham.

Today's train, with its frequent stops, was slower than normal and unusually full. I shared my table with two business people on their way to a meeting at Kettering. The announcement for their stop wasn't made until we were pulling into the station and they left in a hurry. Just as we were drawing out I saw one of them running back and guessed that he'd forgotten something. Sure enough, under the seat was his bag. (Perhaps an earlier warning of the stop would have been more useful than the standard reminder to take all belongings.) I gave it to the guard as he passed by and with commendable efficiency, just six minutes later at Market Harborough a member of platform staff came aboard to collect it. He was pointed in the direction of the guard and presumably the bag put on the next train south.

After the initial pick ups, no further stops had been advertised for our mystery trip. Many routes and destinations were possible, with Trent Junction north of Loughborough (and just after East Midlands Parkway station that didn't exist then) the first major decision point. We'd stopped on the Trent Bridge here on the York mystery trip and the guard had come down the train telling everyone it was the Rhine! On the second trip the question was would we go north towards Nottingham and maybe on to Lincoln, or perhaps on the Erewash Valley line through Ilkeston, or west towards Derby? To replicate these options I'd planned to change at Leicester, but with the limited service today, remained on board, taking the route followed by the mystery trip towards Derby.

At Derby I could have changed for Crewe, Cross Country services, or the Derwent Valley Line to Matlock, but stayed on the train, heading towards

Sheffield as we had on the mystery trip. My red book shows us passing Chesterfield, but before Sheffield we'd branched west, on the scenic Hope Valley Line towards Manchester. Today I continued to the Steel City, where the strike meant almost an hour to wait as the East Midlands train to Liverpool was cancelled.

Sheffield, a city I've visited regularly for work and football, is a fine example of what happens when you build a huge out of town shopping centre. Since Meadowhall opened the city centre has lost shops and vitality, with for a place of its size, remarkably few places to eat. I spent my hour on the station, eating a pasty and observing a group of infant school children on a trip to the railway. As they watched trains come and go, a member of railway staff got drivers to hoot, and after asking the children for a song was given a rendition of 'God Save the Queen'.

The 14.11 TransPennine Express train to Manchester Airport (another station that didn't exist at the time of my mystery trip) was full, with a few passengers standing. The guard asked passengers to remove bags, feet and 'other body parts' from seats. A dog barked incessantly, its owner apologetic but unable to quieten it. The man opposite added to the din with loud music through his headphones, but turned it down when I asked. A lady told her friend on the phone, plus most of the coach, that she was, 'literally on the train'. It wasn't the best way to enjoy the Pennine scenery.

My most enjoyable journeys on the Hope Valley Line were in HSTs, when for a few years during upgrading of the West Coast route, through trains were run from St Pancras to Manchester. They were branded as 'Rio' services, after Rio Ferdinand who had recently been transferred across the Pennines from Leeds to Manchester United, and started his career with West Ham in London.

Soon after branching off the main line we entered the 3½ mile Totley Tunnel, which until construction of the HS1 tunnel under East London, was the second longest in England. This of course assumes we don't count tube lines, such as the 17¼ mile London Underground Northern Line tunnel from East Finchley to Morden, which was listed as the world's longest when I was a boy.

Trains emerge into the beautiful Hope Valley, where streams run by the track and hills rise invitingly on both sides. The village of Edale looked bleak in today's rain, but is often thronged with walkers, many who arrive by train for the Pennine Way which starts here. The powerful Class 185s give less time to enjoy the scenery than the locomotive hauled trains that used to run across the Pennines, and all too soon we were passing through Stockport and into Manchester.

My red book shows our mystery trip passing Manchester but today I had to change trains at Piccadilly. With its bright concourse this is one of our finest terminus stations, having been largely rebuilt for the 2002 Commonwealth Games. I never came to Manchester as a child, most of our travels as you may have noticed, heading to the coast. My first experience of the station, in 1985 for an FA Cup quarter final at Old Trafford, was somewhat less than welcoming. As I wrote in *Stand Up Sit Down*:

'Overhead line problems meant the trains were delayed arriving into Manchester. We were met by police with snarling dogs, held on leashes so their teeth were just inches from our genitals. One officer informed us quite openly that he hated "you Cockney bastards".'

My next train, a hot and noisy packed '150', was not a pleasure to travel in. It left from one of Piccadilly's two through platforms, which I've often used on the way to football, or when travelling to Preston via Manchester, taking advantage of the advance fares being cheaper than on the direct line from London. If time isn't important, a bit of ingenuity and flexibility can often find a far cheaper fare, and sometimes it isn't even necessary to get an alterative train, as split bookings can be less expensive than one ticket for the whole journey. And whilst on the subject of ticketing, I never book with *trainline.com*. They may advertise cheap tickets on TV, but the same fares can be bought through a host of other websites and most of these don't charge the booking fee that *trainline* do.

As our mystery trip had threaded its way through Manchester a host of destinations remained possibilities. As we approached Wigan there were still plenty of options. My clearest memory of the trip is waiting for some time at a red signal outside Wigan as 'Electric Scots' rushed by on the recently electrified line to Scotland. Rather than join the main line, we dropped down to Wigan Wallgate and now our destination was clear. Before proceeding though two Class 25 locomotives replaced our Class 45, which was presumably too heavy for the line ahead. Today I followed the same route, the 17½ mile, very flat and very straight line to Southport. In 1974 we'd taken 6¾ hours from St Pancras, including stopping twice to change engines. Today's journey had taken half an hour less, despite the strike and hour spent in Sheffield. In 1974 we'd had just fifty-four minutes in Southport before returning home via Crewe and Derby. This time I was staying overnight before heading further north.

David, owner of the Le Maitre guest house, seemed quite in awe of having an author staying, but rather surprised to find that unless you're a Bryson or Rowling, it's hard to make money from writing. Like many people I talk to, he was also surprised to find how little Amazon pay to writers and publishers.

After a mediocre carvery dinner in a restaurant where I was at least twenty years younger than every other diner, I set out to explore Southport. It's a strange town. Lord Street is one of the country's classic shopping streets, with a mix of independent and chain stores, impressive architecture and a touch of class. The sea front is some way from the town centre, beyond a large lake, and when the tide's down it can be another mile to the water. By the time I arrived the pier was closed and its ¾ mile long tramway had stopped running for the evening. This surprisingly modern battery powered articulated tram has been operating since 2005, and is the latest in a series of trams to have run here since 1863.

The Trans Pennine Trail starts at Southport and I followed this south for a short distance, before switching to a lovely path through salt marsh and sand dunes, which came out at Ainsdale. From here I caught a Merseyrail train for the three stops back to Southport. This was new track to me, my only previous use of this branch of Merseyrail being to Sandhills to catch the 'Soccerbus' to Anfield.

Southport station is yet another seaside terminus which has been much reduced in size, although still has six platforms serving two lines. Once there were thirteen and a far grander terminal building, which was replaced by a 1970s shopping centre. Recent renovation, including replacing the glass roof, has revived some of the character. Although the façade is plain,

Southport has been more fortunate than Morecambe a few miles further north, where the historic seafront station is now a pub and trains stop at a single uncovered platform.

With twice the number of coaches and less than half the number of passengers as my outward journey, the 10.24 to Manchester was a far more pleasant travelling experience. I alighted at Wigan Wallgate, a station retaining some character, and crossed the road to Wigan North Western, a station with none. When the West Coast Main Line was electrified many of its historic stations were replaced by bland new buildings, although those like Preston, Carlisle and Stoke, where the original survived, seem to function just as well as the new ones.

A short ride on a Pendolino, with few passengers and the luxury of a table to myself, took me to Preston. The trials and tribulations of my travels round the Cumbrian coast continue in the next chapter.

CHAPTER THIRTEEN

CUMBRIAN COAST

Preston – Seascale – Carlisle – Glasgow – Linlithgow

The Cumbrian Coast Railway, which runs close to the sea for much of its 120 miles from Lancaster to Carlisle, has been voted one of the two best hidden gems in the North of England. Ian Bevan, Managing Director of Northern Rail who launched the 2011 awards (which his company won), was quoted by the *News & Star* saying, '*We hope that by recognising them in this way we can highlight them to a wider audience and that many more people will be able to enjoy the great service and breath-taking views these network-wide winners have to offer*'. I was to find no argument about the quality of the views, but plenty to challenge Mr Bevan's statement as to the standard of service his company provides.

We travelled on the Cumbrian Coast Line just once in my childhood – our 1966 holiday at Seascale. My memories are hazy but two remain clear.

The first was travelling back from St Bees and the train breaking down. While other passengers sat in the hot train, the guard allowed us to play on the nearby beach until a freight train arrived and pushed us on to Seascale.

The second was on our journey home when we changed at Barrow. As we got off the DMU, the train in the next platform had a steam engine on the front. Both my sister and I still recall the excitement when we found this was the train that would be taking us on to Crewe. It was the last time I travelled on a standard gauge British Rail service train hauled by a steam locomotive.

More recently I'd used the southern part of the line three times when visiting tidal islands in Morecambe Bay. I wrote of the journey to Ulverston for a guided walk to Chapel Island in *No Boat Required*.

'It took little more than two hours for Virgin Trains' Pendolino to whisk me the 209 miles from London to Preston. (Don't tell Mr Branson though, but I actually preferred the old trains. The ones which rattled rather than swayed, where all the seats lined up with windows, most had tables and there were windows you could open should you wish – speed isn't everything). Changing to the Barrow train, I got my first glimpse of the sea just before Lancaster, then at Carnforth we branched off along the picturesque Furness Line. It was good to see that the charming little stations still had their original buildings, with hardly a concrete booking office or bus shelter waiting room amongst them. Much of the ride skirted the sea or salt marshes, as we passed through the villages of Arnside, Silverdale and the larger resort of Grange-over-Sands. I'd been advised to sit on the left and as the train passed over the 49 span Leven Viaduct, got my first view of Chapel Island, looking tiny in the wide expanse of sand and water.'

With the tide high as we crossed the viaduct, today there was no way anyone could have walked to the little tree covered island. It's hard to believe, but had things turned out differently it might have been possible to reach it by train. In 1837 George Stephenson was considering alternatives to the hilly route over Shap Fell, which the main West Coast line now follows. His idea was to take the railway from Lancaster to Morecambe (then known as Poulton), before proceeding across the sands to Humphrey Head on the Cartmell Peninsular, then cross the Leven Estuary to Furness. The line would have passed through Chapel Island, which he proposed as a station. Embankments would have been built on the sands, with the area inside of these reclaimed.

A year later the route across Morecambe Bay was surveyed by John Haughe, who put forward a more ambitious proposal to the Caledonian, West Cumberland and Furness Railway. Starting from each side of the bay piles would have been driven deep into the sand, using a machine mounted on wheels which would move forward as work progressed. Haughe considered that the work could be completed in 3½ years and that the embankments would require 10,453,785 tons of material. The Leven and Crake rivers would have been diverted, with tide-gates and bridges built to allow vessels to pass. He estimated that the total cost of this section of the line would be £434,131 9s 4d, but that at £23 per acre, the value of the 52,000 acres of reclaimed land would easily exceed this. The plan however was turned down by Parliament on the grounds of being too expensive and the costs underestimated. Both schemes were dropped and eventually the line on which I was travelling built from Carnforth to Ulverston.

My journey as far as Barrow today was on another of TransPennine Express's excellent Class 185 trains. This was running late and it seemed would arrive just after my connection was due to leave, although the guard expected that it would be held. I think the best way to tell you what happened is to reproduce my letter of complaint to Northern Rail:

Dear Sirs

I am writing to complain about Northern Rail's failure to hold the 13.31 service from Barrow to Carlisle on Wednesday 16th May, in order to allow passengers to connect from the late running TransPennine Express service from Manchester Airport.

Having travelled from London, I was changing to the TPE service at Preston, and on noting that this was running 22 minutes late went to the Customer Information Point to ask if the Carlisle train would be held at Barrow (it was due to depart Barrow 20 minutes after the TPE train's scheduled arrival). The information point was manned by Virgin staff who were unable to provide any meaningful assistance, simply looking up the scheduled time of departure from Barrow.

I spoke to the guard on the TPE train, who advised that he would speak to 'Barrow' after we had left Ulverston. The guard went through the train taking numbers and destinations of passengers intending to change to the Carlisle train. As we approached Barrow he made an announcement that passengers for the Carlisle train should go to the Customer Information Point at Barrow and it was clear that the train was not being held.

We arrived in Barrow at 13.33, two minutes after the Carlisle train was due to depart. The 12 passengers who wanted to change were understandably not happy to see that it had left. The lady from TPE was as helpful as she could be in the circumstances and taxis were arranged for those preferring to travel by road rather than wait for the next Northern Rail train at 14.54.

Having purchased a rail ticket I wished to travel by train, so waited for the next service. I noted the irony of passengers boarding taxis by a Northern Rail poster saying 'Enjoy the Cumbrian Coast by Train'.

As a result of the late arrival of the TPE service and Northern Rail's failure to hold the Carlisle train, I arrived at my destination of Seascale 84 minutes late. Whilst grateful for appropriate compensation (my ticket is enclosed), my main reason for writing is to ask why Northern Rail chose not to hold the Carlisle train for the 3 minutes it would have required to allow 12 passengers to make the change from the TPE service.

The following day I caught the 9.58 from Seascale to Carlisle, which was running approximately 20 minutes late. (The fact that there is no indicator board or Help Point at Seascale, so we had no idea when or if the train was going to arrive, is another matter which I suggest Northern Rail should deal with). The guard told me that there is some catch up time in the schedule, so he expected that some of the deficit would be made up. I note that the 13.31 is scheduled to take 16 minutes from Dalston to Carlisle, but that trains in the opposite direction take just 8 minutes, suggesting that there is a significant amount of recovery time built into your schedule.

The train arrived at Carlisle at 11.55 and as result I missed my booked connection to Glasgow. I noted though that the 11.55 Northern Rail train to Leeds was held for 3 minutes to allow passengers changing from the Barrow service to catch it.

Is it perhaps significant that you held the Leeds train on 17th to connect with your own late running service, but not the Carlisle train on 16th when a similar delay was due to TransPennine Express, who presumably will have to foot the bill for the taxis? (or pass this on to the company whose train broke down outside Manchester Piccadilly station causing the initial delay?).

I would be most grateful to hear Northern Rail's explanation as to why you chose to inconvenience 12 passengers at Barrow by refusing to hold your train for 3 minutes, and hopefully some assurance that in future you will take a more flexible stance to providing a service to your customers in such situations.

Yours sincerely

The first reply came from TransPennine Express, to whom Northern Rail had forwarded my letter. TPE apologised for the delay, which they said was due to a failed train in the Slade Lane area. As my journey was delayed by more than an hour they were able to offer compensation to the full value of my ticket, so please could I send the ticket. Having included it with my original letter to Northern Rail I sent a copy.

As I suspected, Northern Rail were leaving TPE to pay compensation to the passengers who were delayed by their decision not to hold the Carlisle train. TPE will no doubt have claimed from the company whose train broke down outside Manchester. They will perhaps pass it on to a maintenance contractor or component manufacturer and several steps down the line someone will have to foot the whole bill. Oh what a good idea it was to split British Rail into so many parts – well it was for the army of administrators, accountants and lawyers who make a fortune from the fragmented system.

The first paragraph of Northern's response, said '*I can understand your frustration at arriving at Carlisle to find your train had left on time*'. The second stated, '*I have carefully read your letter*'. Clearly not well enough though, as it was Barrow not Carlisle where I missed the connection. Perhaps I shouldn't be surprised. Once I wrote a letter of praise to Virgin Trains and received back a standard apology plus voucher for ten pounds!

I wrote again, pointing out a clause in the company's charter:

'*Northern will work with other train operators to provide a seamless national rail network*'.

The reply, whilst not answering my specific questions, said that they rarely hold connections in order not to delay passengers already on the train.

Meanwhile my correspondence with TPE continued. Having seen a copy of my ticket, they said it wasn't valid as it was dated a day before the delay. I wrote back explaining that I'd broken my journey overnight at Wigan. This they responded wasn't permitted. Regardless of whether the break of journey was permitted on the ticket, as I had arrived at Wigan after the last departure that would have allowed me to reach Seascale that night, I knew an overnight stop was allowed. I wrote back to TPE quoting National Rail

Conditions of Carriage Condition 16 which permit a break *'when you cannot reasonably complete your journey within one day.'*

TPE's reply again stated that my ticket wasn't valid for an overnight stop, unless this was as a result of disruption, but 'to resolve the matter' sent a voucher for £38.80, the value of the journey from Wigan to Seascale.

After taking further advice from the transport consultant and fares expert Barry Doe, I wrote once more, again referring to Condition 16. This time TPE said that the overnight stop regulation doesn't apply to passengers who simply have not allowed enough time to complete their journey. It does – otherwise how could one travel from say Penzance to Wick on one ticket?

Barry Doe used my experience in an article on break of journey in *Rail* magazine and raised the issue with ATOC, the Association of Train Operating Companies, who said that it would be discussed at a meeting on ticket conditions. Correspondence continued. My *sixth* letter to TPE was accompanied with a copy of Barry's article. TPE replied that they couldn't resolve the complaint and referred me to the independent watchdog, Passenger Focus. Ten weeks after writing and nine months after my journey, I had received just an acknowledgement from the watchdog.

Sadly this is not an isolated instance. Ticket regulations are far too complicated and there seems to be no consistency on when a break of journey is permitted. Even the various experts I'd consulted couldn't agree as to whether a break was permitted on my Seascale ticket. All though agreed that I could stop overnight if arriving at Wigan after the last connection to Seascale. The train companies don't seem to know themselves, so how can passengers possibly be expected to understand what is and isn't permitted

And so back to my journey. With typical Britishness most passengers were resigned rather than annoyed at missing the connection from Barrow, and regular travellers seemed used to such occurrences. After an hour in the town, where I was disappointed to find that the excellent Tourist Information Centre had been turned into a café with just a few racks of leaflets, I returned for the 14.54 to Carlisle. Repeated automated announcements were saying first that the train on Platform One was all stations to Carlisle, then immediately afterwards that the train on Platform One was not in service so please don't board it. Ignoring the latter instruction, I joined the surprisingly full single coach '153'. By the time we left there were forty nine passengers on board and few spare seats. All bar me appeared to be locals, and as I was to find, few tourists come this way. The guard came round checking tickets and noted on a scrap of paper that I wanted Seascale, one of many request stops.

Once finally on a train I wasn't to be disappointed by the scenery. The line is soon back by the sea, making a big loop round Duddon Sands to Millom. A few passengers got off at each stop and at Millom more than half the remainder alighted, with three school children getting on. At Silecroft we entered the Lake District National Park, with views to the fells on one side and the sea on the other. This was already a wonderful train ride and I hadn't yet got to the most spectacular bit.

The only places on this coast north of Barrow that I'd visited since 1966, were Maryport, a town with interesting industrial heritage which we drove to from Keswick, and Ravenglass. Deb and I had come here on the narrow gauge Ravenglass and Eskdale railway in 1982, after driving across the Hardknott Pass. Today one of the little steam trains was in the platform, waiting to climb seven miles to Dalegarth in the heart of the mountains. As so often on my travels I wished I had time to divert and explore.

I was the only passenger alighting at Seascale, which was probably the holiday destination I'd most wanted to return to. Not so much for the memories, but to find out why we stayed at a village a mile from Sellafield, that hardly anyone has even heard of.

In 1966 we'd paid 39 pounds and 9 shillings for a family of four staying eight nights at the Broombank Hotel (my father still has the bill). That had either closed or changed its name and I was surprised to find that the village now offers very little accommodation. The Bailey Ground Hotel, three minutes walk from the station, however proved to be an excellent choice. Run by the Mawson family, who refurbished the derelict building in 2008, it is a hotel with character. The family own the adjacent farm and I was rather surprised to come out of the bathroom and find a sheep looking in my bedroom window. Much of the restaurant food comes from the farm, with zero food miles, and it's no exaggeration to say that the fillet steak I enjoyed looking across the sea was probably the best I've ever tasted.

Kate Mawson told me that in 1966 Seascale would still have been quite popular, but with visitors declining. She said that the beach was once '*as busy as Blackpool*', with hundreds getting off trains and buses. Photos in the restaurant showed donkeys on the beach, a sandcastle competition and a steam train in the busy railway station. Today I'd walked for an hour along the beach and seen just one dog walker. As I watched from the restaurant enjoying my steak, it was again almost deserted – just two people flying kites and a lady walking with her little girl. Kate said no one comes here on holiday now and despite being the best beach in the area, there are few day visitors. A nice beach and a few interesting places to visit by train or bus was all we'd needed, but perhaps today's families expect more.

Her husband Ken lent me a book for the evening: *Seascale – The Village of Seascale the History and its People* by Neville Ramsden (1997). What a fascinating book it is. A section on the railway showed that in 1905 the village had eight trains a day each way, three of which ran through to London, the fastest taking seven hours ten minutes. Despite the high speed Pendolinos it still takes about five hours with a change at Carlisle or Preston. The current service is eleven trains a day, although none after 7pm, which thwarted my plan to walk up the coast and get a train back.

The book tells some interesting stories about Sellafield, the largest employer in West Cumbria, for whose workers several hundred homes were built in the village. After a fire at the plant in 1957, when radiation leaked in the worst nuclear accident in British history, reporters descended on the area looking for stories. Most had little understanding of the nuclear industry and certain local young men used to scour the papers to see which of their embellishments had taken the reporters' fancy. Having to wear lead lined underpants was considered one of their best! More seriously, the book explains that the cluster of childhood leukaemia found around the plant (sixteen in Seascale in forty years) had been found not to be caused by radioactivity. Instead it was related to the mass movement of people to a rural area, an effect seen at other locations, possibly due to a virus to which isolated communities had less immunity. (I should add though that not everyone accepts this theory.)

After dinner I walked the mile or so along a path by the railway line to Sellafield. The place is simply immense. Railway tracks run through locked gates and the sidings inside held a selection of locomotives and wagons. I took a few photos on my phone before continuing to Sellafield station, where they'd conveniently left the toilets open overnight. Many of the plant's workers commute by train, with morning and early evening services very busy. Until recently a locomotive hauled train had been run from Carlisle for workers. I'd hoped to travel on this experimental service but sadly it had ceased by my visit.

As I returned past the plant I took another couple of photos, but as I walked off a voice called me back. A policeman with machine gun over his shoulder was standing by the fence. *'Why was I taking photos?'* – *'An interest in railways and writing a book'*. *'Did I have any ID?'* – *'Yes'*. *'Can I see it?'* Just as I was about to pass my driving licence through the fence I had second thoughts. I wasn't going to have my name on the police computer. He wasn't happy that I'd declined. I'd taken the photos through a section of temporary fence and he decided that I might be a terrorist sizing the place up for an attack while the fence was under repair. That he hadn't stopped me when I'd taken the first photos (he and his mate were sitting in a car watching the fence) and that a terrorist might be more careful than to take pictures in front of two policemen, didn't seem to matter. Nor was my explanation accepted that I'd chosen the spot because the larger mesh made taking photos easier. To my protestation that there was no sign prohibiting photography, his response was that they were going to put these up soon, but I should have known anyway. How was I to know that it wasn't permitted to take photos of the trains, all of which can be seen on the public railway?

I thought of just walking off but that gun was rather big. After some minutes and with an impasse reached, I offered to delete the photos. That he seemed happy with but as I deleted them he noticed that one showed the bottom of the fence. This I'd taken of the ground by mistake, but now he had evidence of my 'suspicious activity'. If he'd been a very good policeman he might have noticed that the rest of the photos on the screen were of police dogs and officers outside Upton Park, taken at West Ham's last home game. These were for the Football Supporters' Federation monitoring of football policing, but had he noticed them I don't suppose I'd have been returning back by the railway line to Seascale quite so soon. But it wasn't quite over. As I walked back through the village a police car pulled up. *'Are you the person who was walking at Sellafield?'* – *'I have been for a walk past Sellafield.'* *'Are you going to let us have your name? – 'No!'*.

As I waited for the train the next morning I chatted to the only other passenger on the platform. Without an indicator board or public address we had no idea when, or indeed if, it would arrive, but she said this was common. There was a phone at the end of the opposite platform, but you're not allowed to cross the track and it's a five minutes walk round by road. If the train arrives in this time you'd miss it anyway.

I told the lady about my experience at Sellafield the previous evening and she told me a far sadder tale. She and her friend, both pensioners, enjoyed bird watching. One day her friend went along the coast to look at some young birds and was spotted using binoculars. The police took the lady into the plant and interviewed her, before accepting she wasn't a terrorist and letting her go. Not long afterwards, taxi driver Derrick Bird went on the rampage in Cumbria, killing twelve people. On one of the saddest days in the village's history, three died in Seascale, including the bird watcher Jane Robinson, who was shot yards from her home. Her friend told me that when they'd been needed to deal with the gunman, Sellafield's armed police had refused to come out to help.

Our train arrived twenty minutes late. The guard explained that there had been an electrical fault in the cab. To get on board, the lady I was talking to needed the single set of wooden steps which drivers have to line up with one of the doors when they stop. She told me that a 'Harrington Hump' had been promised. This low cost solution to the problem of many Victorian platforms being lower than modern trains, was first fitted at Harrington on the Cumbrian Coast line and is now being installed at various stations across the country. It took many complaints from users of Harrington, which apparently came to a head when a guard got off the train and couldn't get back on again, before something was done to help the large proportion of passengers who struggled with the step. Seascale's passengers and those who don't use the train because they can't get on it, await fitting of their hump.

From Seascale the gentler scenery of Lake District fells and sandy bays on the south of the line, is replaced by ruggedness as the train slowly threads

Night Riviera at Penzance (2012)

Liskeard Signal Box (2012)

The Author at Causeland (Looe Branch) (1977)

(Michael Caton)

Looe (2012)

Looe (1974)

(Michael Caton)

Oban (1973)

Oban (1993)

Oban (2012)

Fort William Sleeper north of Upper Tyndrum (2010)

Fort William Sleeper passes old snow fences in blizzard north of Corrour (2013)

Aylesford (2012)

'Javelin' crosses M25 viaduct by Thurrock Bridge (2012)

C2C near Ockendon (2011)

Liverpool Street (2012)

London to Norwich Express at Manningtree (2012)

North Norfolk Railway (2012)

Railbus at Weybourne (North Norfolk Railway) (2012))

Black Prince approaches Weybourne (North Norfolk Railway) (2012)

Voyager at Berwick – Aberdeen to Penzance – the longest journey of any train in Britain (2012)

Recently Electrified Euston (1966)

Highland Sleeper and Virgin Pendolino at Euston (2012)

'Class 47' enters Garsdale with Carlisle-bound train (1989)

Heart of Wales trains pass at Llanwrtyd Wells (2012)

Chiltern Trains 'Mainline' train at Birmingham Moor St (2012)

Seascale (1967)

Seascale (2012)

Cumbrian Coast train approaches Sellafield (2012)

DMU at Emerson Park just before electric trains took over Romford – Upminster (1986)

Emerson Park (2013)

Romford – Upminster DMU (1986)

Final DMU on Romford – Upminster Branch (1986)

Railbus at Braintree (1960)

Braintree (2013)

First Great Western HST at Cardiff (2012)

Deltic at Grosmont (North Yorkshire Moors Railway) (2012)

Merrymaker at Betsw-y-Coed (1974)

(Michael Caton)

Betsw-y-Coed (1960)

'158' Crosses Pont Brewit at Penryhndeudraeth (Cambrian Coast) (2010)

Cambrian Coast train at Dyffryn (with the author's pram in the foreground) (1961)

Barmouth Bridge (1961)

Barmouth Bridge (2012)

HST at Teignmouth (1985)

First Great Western HST Restaurant on Teignmouth Sea Wall (2012)

FGW 'Pacer' and Dartmoor Railway '205' at Okehampton (2012)

'Heritage' DMU at Corfe Castle (Swanage Railway) (2012)

Kings Cross (2012)

ScotRail '158' and snow fences at Forsinard (2012)

Altnabreac (2012)

Dent (1989)

Northern Rail '158' at Dent (2012)

Blea Moor (1989)

East Coast Trains pass at Newcastle (2012)

'City of Peterborough' approaches Peterborough Nene Valley (2012))

Rocher de Naye Mountain Railway (2012)

Italian local train at Pavia (2012)

German ICE at Brussels (2012)

its way between stony beaches and rocky cliffs. The line runs on the sea wall for most of the twenty five miles to Maryport, and only at St Bees Head and through the towns of Whitehaven and Workington, does it briefly leave the sea. Whilst not quite as picturesque as our most famous stretch of coastal railway from Exeter to Newton Abbot, this is wilder. The Irish Sea often crashes over the wall, making the single coach trains look lonely and vulnerable, but it's a lifeline to many who live in the towns and villages along the coast. It is debatable whether the line would have survived if it were not for Sellafield and the industry at Workington and Whitehaven, but without it this whole coastline would have been even more isolated.

I find it strange that a coast with lovely beaches, spectacular views, much history and close to the Lake District mountains, receives so few visitors. Perhaps both Northern Rail and the tourist authorities could learn from two posts on the *News & Star's* website in response to their story about the line winning the hidden gem award:

'It should also be noted that as scenic as the line is, its also one of the longest journeys in the country without any sort of buffet trolley and the last train north bound from Barrow is 17:30 and no Sunday service, making it extremely difficult to have any sort of day out for visitor. And also the trains are filthy.' – Elaine.

'If the bodies paid to promote Cumbrian tourism did their job properly – instead of putting ALL their eggs in the National Park basket – then it would simply be a 'gem' not a 'hidden gem'. Perhaps then, the length of the west coast of Cumbria wouldn't be dying the slow death it so obviously is.' – Chris

After Workington the train was virtually full, with most of the passengers travelling to Carlisle or beyond. At Aspatria, one of the few request stops we didn't call at, the driver slowed but didn't disturb two rabbits nibbling grass on the platform. The guard came round telling passengers for Leeds that their train would be held at Carlisle. It had been my original plan to catch this on the scenic route through Settle, but an urgent business meeting meant that instead I had to travel north to Glasgow. Taking just nine minutes from Dalston to Carlisle, compared to the sixteen timetabled, we made up time, arriving eighteen minutes late, at exactly the time the Leeds train was due out. Northern Rail held it for three minutes, allowing the good number of passengers changing to make the connection.

I'd missed the Pendolino for which I had an advance ticket, but a Virgin Voyager not far behind got me to Glasgow in time. The guard didn't bother to check tickets, so there was no need for me to explain why I wasn't on the booked train. One positive I did note was a spotlessly clean toilet, with tasteful pictures of flowers on the wall and a log on the wall to record checks by staff. Just a shame about the chemical smell, but it's hard to argue that modern retention toilets aren't an advance over those that dump their contents onto the track, sometimes spraying permanent way staff as they pass.

I'm usually sleeping when travelling between Carlisle and Glasgow, so it was a rare pleasure to enjoy the scenery on a daytime train. Contrasting with the coastal views of the East Coast route, this passes through the hills, valleys and moorland of the Southern Uplands, but both are an enjoyable end to a journey from London to Scotland.

As usual, after my meeting I looked for somewhere to spend the evening before getting the sleeper home. In pouring rain I caught the 18.15 from Glasgow Queen Street to Edinburgh, getting off at Linlithgow, a place I'd passed a few times and looked interesting.

When we first travelled on the line en route from Edinburgh to Oban in 1973, the trains had a diesel locomotive at each end, saving the time needed for a single engine to run round at the termini. Today's Class 170s provide a more frequent service, which is invariably busy, although with extra stops the fifty minute journey averages six minutes longer than 1976. With a train every fifteen minutes there's now no need to aim for a specific departure, another advantage of the greater frequency on our modern system.

It had been raining when I'd woken up at Seascale and hadn't stopped all day. By the time I'd walked 2½ miles round Linlithgow Loch I was somewhat wet. The ruined palace on the bank of the loch looked well worth a visit and I'd like to return when it's open. In better weather, one day I'll walk along the Union Canal and get the train back from Polmont.

At Glasgow Central I got told off. Passengers are supposed to be able to board the sleeper from 10pm, but staff rarely open the doors on time. At 10.20 I tried the door but it wouldn't budge. A rather scary attendant appeared and told me a little crossly that trying to open the doors when the orange lock light is on pulls them off the catch. Suitably admonished, I settled into my berth and climbed into bed. As I did it rocked violently. It hadn't been properly fitted into the recess on the wall. Pyjamas off, clothes back on and bag repacked, I went to find the attendant. Her inspection confirmed the fault and another berth had to be found. Whether her lack of an apology was normal, or a result of me being a naughty boy with the coach door, I've no idea.

Whilst most sleeper staff are extremely helpful and give the impression that they love the job, occasionally on the Glasgow train I've found one who might be better employed where a friendly attitude to the public is less important. On this train, as well as late boarding and opening of the lounge car, I have on a number of times been told to leave my berth at Euston well before the advertised 8am. On one occasion I was hassled to hurry several times and eventually told that I must get off immediately as the train was about to leave for the sidings. On alighting I found that there wasn't even a locomotive on the front!

Postscript

Three months after writing and ten months after my journey, I received a phone call from Passenger Focus. After discussion with ATOC it had been confirmed that my ticket was indeed valid to stop overnight in Wigan. TransPennine Express had reluctantly agreed that they were wrong and I was to expect a letter from them shortly. The letter duly arrived. It stated, *'you were not permitted to break your journey in the fashion you did'*. Despite being told by Passenger Focus, The Association of Train Operating Companies and ticketing experts, TransPennine Express simply refused to accept that they were wrong. It seems that the company's Customer Relations Department works on an unusual premise – the customer is always wrong.

CHAPTER FOURTEEN

THE ESSEX COAST

Upminster – Romford – Burnham-on-Crouch – Walton-on-the-Naze – Clacton – Harwich

As children, the 3 ½ mile branch from Upminster to Romford was our own little railway and every diesel multiple unit we encountered round the country was 'a train like our Romford train'. It was a journey we made often, invariably sitting at the front, watching the driver through the cab window. Sometimes we were invited inside and would chat to the driver.

When I started work I'd catch the 7.20 every morning, getting off at Emerson Park, the only intermediate station, then waiting for a bus to Harold Hill. The train was never late; the bus often was. As I set off for a trip to the Essex coast, I considered what has changed in my fifty years of using our own little known branch line.

Services still run half hourly, with a stop at Emerson Park, which in my childhood days was known as Emerson Park Halt and was a charming little station with gas lamps. Officially it is no longer a 'Halt', although signs erected by National Express a few years ago still welcome passengers to 'Emerson Park Halt'. It is now unstaffed, with the station building where a single member of staff sold and collected tickets, recently demolished. The train still runs largely between the ends of long back gardens, with trees and hedges giving an unexpectedly rural appearance for a railway inside Greater London.

The Upminster end is virtually unaltered since the dead end Platform Six was built in 1957, soon after DMUs had replaced steam haulage. Locally the line is still referred to as the 'Push and Pull', from the days when a steam locomotive pulled the train one way and pushed it the other. One little oddity at Upminster is a half installed set of points, which were intended to link the line with the London Underground Depot, so District Line trains could be diesel hauled to Ilford Depot for refurbishment. The point-work was never completed as the refurbishment was transferred to Wakefield, with transfers carried out by road.

At Romford the long siding to a coal yard has gone, with houses built on the yard, but the bay platform is little changed. The old waiting room and blocked off staircase that we used to look down as children have been removed. These were part of the London Tilbury and Southend station, which was separate to the main station on the Liverpool Street line. The footbridge, which was later built to link them, remains as the only access to the Upminster platform, its wooden floor over which I've often run to catch a train, now covered with tarmac.

The major change to the railway is that no longer do two or three car Diesel Multiple Units, the 'trains like our Romford train', run up and down, but it's now electric with the service provided by various four car units. Often these are nicer than those running on longer lines, having carpets and First Class sections (which anyone can use). The journey is no quicker, partly because of the line's 30mph limit, and partly because their faster acceleration is negated by the frustratingly slow approaches to the terminal stations required by the modern TPWS safety system. In fact having been eight minutes on every train for at least forty years, the December 2012 timetable increased all journeys to nine minutes. The reason I'm told is that today's driving techniques mean eight minutes can't be achieved, a consequence of which is that the extra morning rush hour service now can't be fitted into the timetable. Progress?

In my fifty years of travelling the line has never run on Sundays, as the majority of passengers are commuters, school children and shoppers, although with increased leisure travel and shops open seven days, there is perhaps now a case for a service. Trains finish earlier in the evening now, the last departure from Romford being 19.42, whereas in the late 1970s I could catch the 21.10 after evening college.

We are however very lucky that trains run at all, as in the 1960s the line survived two attempts to close it. Those of us who still travel on it owe a debt to the small band of people who fought to save the line, led I'm proud to say by my father who set up and chaired the Romford – Upminster Branch Line Users' Association.

Beeching put forward lines for closure based purely on economics, but ignoring social need. I remember much talk about the 'Cooper Brothers Formula', a sort of 1960s railway equivalent to cricket's Duckworth Lewis method, which costed each line. The formula was derived by accountants and failed to consider the loss of income from passengers who with no local trains would not use rail for long distance journeys, or of hardship caused by withdrawal of services. It was based on the 'total replacement cost' rather than the 'marginal' savings that would be made if the line closed. British Rail didn't want the line, the local council considered it doomed, but twice well presented evidence from local users swayed Public Inquiries to recommend reprieve.

The line's long term future was finally secured by electrification in 1986. On the last day of diesel operation British Rail brought out a green 'heritage' unit and travel was free. My father and I joined the final train to Romford, with most of the fifty or so passengers there just for the historic ride. Detonators were placed on the track and we left Upminster to a hail of bangs. Part way to Emerson Park the train halted. There had been one objector to electrification, a man whose garden backed onto to railway and it was here that we'd stopped. Out got the driver, a regular on the line and quite a character. More detonators were laid and as we restarted to a hail of bangs, our driver saluted in 'honour' of the man who didn't want electric trains at the bottom of his garden!

As well as 'our Romford train', for this chapter I've travelled on some of the Essex branches that I'd been on as a child, and again thirty years later for coastal walks. With the longest coastline of any English county, Essex is fortunate that this is still served by six railway lines, although several others are long gone.

The north bank of the Thames estuary is served by the London Tilbury and Southend line, which we used to catch to Southend, usually then riding on the train along the world's longest pier. More often though we got off at the quieter Leigh or Chalkwell, often walking along the sea wall and returning from further down the line. Having already mentioned C2C, all I shall add is that this is one of the successes since privatisation, with more comfortable, frequent and reliable trains.

The Liverpool Street line to Southend Victoria we rarely used beyond Wickford, but some of my coast walks started or ended at Hockley and Rochford. The two routes from Southend to London were one of the rare opportunities for privatisation to allow competition – so why did the government award both franchises to National Express?

Moving northwards, the next line to the coast is the more rural Southminster branch, which runs along the River Crouch to the Dengie Peninsular, one of the most remote stretches of coast in England. Indeed, the fourteen miles from Burnham-on-Crouch to St Peter-on-the-Wall chapel near Bradwell is the longest stretch of English coastline without any kind of settlement. A trip to the yachting town of Burnham-on-Crouch, one stop before Southminster, was a regular childhood day out and later an easy way to get close to the Crouch Valley for coastal walking. It was this that I planned to do today.

On our childhood journeys we used to change at Romford for a Southend train, then at Wickford for the Southminster branch. Now some Southminster trains run through from Liverpool Street (as they did pre 1960s), but today engineering work meant they were starting at Shenfield, to where I caught the regular 'Metro' service. As we trundled over the M25, up Brentwood Bank and dithered into Shenfield, I wondered how many times I've spent this short journey repeatedly checking my watch to see if I'll make a connection.

When changing here I've often been frustrated by another of modern rail travel's little annoyances. The first thing you need to do on arriving at a station is check the indicator to know the platform of your train. At Romford, Shenfield and other stations on the Greater Anglia lines, the displays alternate. Half the time they show train times and the other half a notice, usually either about future engineering or 'security'. It may seem insignificant, but the wait for platform numbers to appear can be enough to miss a train.

At Wickford we left the Southend line for one of Essex's rural branches. Tickets were promptly checked and I sat back looking for glimpses of the 'sea'. With the line set back from the Crouch, the water is mostly out of sight, but every so often a sail appears, seemingly gliding across the fields. The village of Battlesbridge, the first stop, is at the river's tidal limit and was once a busy little port shipping flour and hay to London. Now its mill is a popular antiques centre, but despite the sign on the station, I doubt that many customers arrive by train.

Our childhood journeys were on 'a train like our Romford train', but this line was also electrified in 1986. The railway has retained all six stations on its 16½ mile route, although most are unrecognisable from former years. A photograph of Woodham Ferrers in *Branch Line to Southminster* (Dennis Swindale 2008) shows a turntable, sidings, double track and a bridge linking the platforms. A branch from here to Maldon was closed during World War Two but never reopened and now just a single track serves one platform. It is however the busiest station on the line, thanks to the new town which grew up in the 1960s & 70s.

The unusual situation of the heaviest traffic being on the first five miles of the branch wasn't helpful when closure was muted, however the line was never formally threatened, probably because it was required to carry waste from Bradwell nuclear power station. This ceased after decommissioning, ending one of our more unusual timetable quirks, as I wrote when using Southminster in *Essex Coast Walk*:

'Just outside the station is a crane gantry over a short section of track, surrounded by a high security fence. This is used to transfer loads of nuclear waste from Bradwell Power Station to the train used to take them to Sellafield for reprocessing. It runs once a week, but the time is kept secret for security reasons. I can however tell you that there's normally an hourly service from Southminster, but that the timetable shows that on Thursdays the 13.17 doesn't run, leaving the line clear. Why it is kept clear I cannot say.'

After my recent experience in Cumbria, it's probably a good thing I hadn't tried to take a photograph.

Today I alighted at North Fambridge, the mid point of the line and the only remaining passing loop. Until 2007 the station had been simply Fambridge, but as the ferry to South Fambridge closed around 1950 and it's a fifteen mile walk via Battlesbridge, a change of name was probably overdue.

It takes the train ten minutes for the six miles to Burnham-on-Crouch, stopping at the village of Althorne on the way. A leisurely and enjoyable walk of about nine miles along the river bank took me four hours, stopping by the water to eat lunch. The tide rose higher than I'd ever seen it, almost engulfing Bridgemarsh Island near Althorne. Essex has a rapidly changing coast and it's hard to believe that before the sea broke through the walls, the island was inhabited and once held a brick works linked to the jetty by a tramway.

Burnham waterfront was busy with people going about their boating business, strolling by the river, or simply watching the world go by. As I arrived at the station a group of baseball cap wearing teenagers departed, one disdainfully tossing his empty bottle onto the track. Before condemning them too much perhaps you should read the opening paragraph from Chapter Sixteen of *Essex Coast Walk*.

'It made my blood boil. As the Southminster train pulled out of Shenfield station the platform attendant nonchalantly kicked a polystyrene cup onto the track. There was a bin a few yards away but this man, an employee of the railway, chose to litter the track. I gave him a hard 'Paddington Bear' stare and vowed to write a letter (but never got round to it).'

My next trip took me on the 'Sunshine Coast Line' to the resorts of Walton-on-the-Naze and Clacton. The Class 360 electric unit that I boarded at Shenfield gave a comfortable and remarkably quiet ride up the Great Eastern Main Line. Unlike those we travelled on as children, there was no buffet or even a trolley, but these are excellent trains.

After passing through the centre of Chelmsford, with views of the river and cricket ground, we stopped at Witham, from where a branch runs to Braintree. Of my journey along the line in 1960 I recall nothing – it was a few months before I was born! My parents had travelled on a diesel railbus, Braintree being the only line where they were regularly used that escaped closure. What would the infamous doctor say if he knew that it was now electrified with a through service to London?

Fifty three years later I went back to Braintree to take a photograph to compare with my father's from 1960. It was a pleasant run through rural Essex, with the views enhanced by a covering of snow. The main station building remains, but now with just one platform. Deb came with me and was pleased to make acquaintance of the station cat, who kept her occupied while her husband went about the embarrassing business of photographing trains!

What a shame though that the other end of the branch, from Witham to Maldon, closed in 1964, leaving this growing town without a railway. The line was originally built as double track, but one was lifted as long ago as the Crimean War, when it was sold to the War Office. The railway's six viaducts were constructed economically using timber (one still remains), however the station at Maldon was a far grander affair than necessary, as one of the railway's financiers was the local Member of Parliament and extended the employment of the railway workers to improve his chances of re-election.

After leaving the main line at Colchester, we were soon alongside the River Colne approaching the attractive town of Wivenhoe. The highly scenic branch along the river to Brightlingsea was another that I travelled on just before Beeching's axe fell, closure partly justified by the cost of maintaining the swing bridge over Alresford Creek. The trackbed now makes a very pleasant walk along the estuary.

Trains used to divide at Thorpe-le-Soken, but now run through to Clacton, with a connecting stopping train from Colchester taking passengers to Walton-on-the-Naze. I say connecting, but my experiences when walking the coast were variable. Clacton trains were then calling at Romford but as I wrote in *Essex Coast Walk*, the journeys didn't always go smoothly.

'On hearing an announcement on Romford station that the Clacton train was running late, I enquired in the office as to whether the Walton-on-the-Naze connection would be held at Thorpe-le-Soken. The answer was, yes it's only an hourly service, so should wait. Arriving at Thorpe-le-Soken 14 minutes late, there was however no Walton train opposite. As about fifteen of us stood hopefully on the platform, a man appeared from the booking office and directed us to the waiting room, advising that the next train was not for another 45 minutes. Apparently the decisions are made in London and while he would have liked to have held the connection, or to have organised a replacement bus, local staff are no longer permitted to use their initiative. Responding to my comment that I would write a letter to

One Railway, he assured me that they would take no notice. He'd worked there for forty years and they don't listen to him.

After initial minor mutterings of discontent, the other passengers settled themselves silently in the waiting room, resigned to the delay. I completed my token protest, a complaint he had clearly heard many times before, then walked into the village to determine if there was a bus to Kirby-le-Soken. There is. It runs at 8 minutes past every other hour. This was however the hour it wasn't running. I returned to the station. Here I found a notice explaining that Walton connections are held for up to 12 minutes, meaning that as the indicator showed that the next Clacton train was running 13 minutes late, slavish adherence to the policy would soon deposit another group of dissatisfied passengers on Thorpe-le-Soken station.'

And returning home after walking to Walton:

'The train left 5 minutes late. They don't hold London connections at Thorpe-le-Soken, so allowed the fast train to depart one minute before mine arrived. I therefore missed the last train from Romford to Upminster and for the want of this one minute had to travel via London, arriving home 1½ hours late. Needless to say I wrote a letter.'

Today there were no such problems. The Walton train was waiting in the platform. As we headed through rural Essex I chatted to a man who'd come from Harlow to walk on the coast. Essex we agreed, is a county that far exceeds its reputation.

Frinton, the penultimate stop, is a town that in many ways was defined by the railway. Its residents are some of the most traditional in the country, for many years fiercely resisting the opening of both a pub and chip shop. After a three year battle the council granted a licence and the Lock & Barrel eventually opened in September 2000. The pub was packed, but the Secretary of the Residents Association famously stated that this was, *'the worst day in Frinton since the Luftwaffe beat up the town in 1944'*, a remark which found its way into the Times Book of Quotations.

There is only one road into the town and that crosses the railway by the station. Residents refer to the town 'inside the gates' that symbolically kept the riff raff out, and were horrified when Network Rail announced that when the line was resignalled the 19th century wooden gates would be replaced by automatic barriers. The gates featured in a BBC documentary, which Terry Allen the town's Mayor told, '*Paris has its Eiffel Tower, London has Tower Bridge and in Frinton we have the gates. All over the world people talk about them. They are the symbol of Frinton.*' At the prospect of losing them he later added '*It's like taking the university out of Oxford*'. A three year battle ended at 2am on 18th April 2009, when Network Rail engineers removed the gates under cover of darkness, the day before campaigners planned a final protest.

Walton-on-the-Naze is another seaside terminus which now has just one platform, although the original Great Eastern building remains as residential accommodation. It's just a short walk down the hill to the pier, the third longest in England. As a child I recall riding on the little train that used to run along the pier, but closed down in the 1970s.

It's an easy walk from Walton to Clacton, with a paved path on the sea wall all the way. After the exclusive Frinton Golf Club however I diverted inland a little, walking through Holland Haven Nature Reserve, before rounding the headland and towards Clacton Pier. This was one of those walks where the landmark looked about a mile away, but after half an hour's walking didn't seem any closer. Eventually I reached Clacton and what a contrast to Frinton. Exclusive isn't a word you'd use here!

With four platforms and its original large buildings, Clacton station looks as if it should be served by more than the hourly London trains which are the only off peak activity. Gone are the days of holiday trains arriving from across the country, although on sunny weekends there are still a good number of day trippers. With an eighty six minute journey to London (five minutes quicker than 1976), commuters are now the line's main users.

Automatic barriers haven't yet reached here and today I had the rare experience of my ticket being checked by a real person manning a gate. In all my travels only at Clacton, Euston and Glasgow Central did I see what we used to call a ticket collector – I wished I'd asked him what his modern title was. It was to my benefit though because he happily let me board with a return from Walton-on-the-Naze, rather than have to buy a single back to Thorpe-le-Soken. Such discretion is beyond the capabilities of a computer driven gate.

My final Essex branch line was the 'Mayflower Line' to the historic port of Harwich. I caught a Norwich train from Stratford, boarding at Platform 10A, which confusingly isn't part of Platform 10. A few weeks earlier I'd been back to Sheringham to visit a friend and along with several passengers had to rush through the subway from Platform 10 at the last minute. I'd met a member of Greater Anglia's management on the train, who explained that the platform had been recently reopened, but it was hard to renumber the whole station as it's used by several different operators. He said he'd bring it up with the appropriate people. I sent an email to Customer Services, which also mentioned the very hot water in the Sheringham train toilet that scalded my hand. They didn't reply. I checked today and there was still no notice on Platform 10 advising passengers that this wasn't 10A. Running a railway is hugely complex, but there's no excuse for not putting the simple things right.

Manningtree, the junction for Harwich, is a proper country railway station, still with its original buildings. Etched windows on the Norwich-bound platform show 'General Waiting Room' and 'Ladies Waiting Room', although only the former remains in use, the fairer sex now having to share with us gentleman. Nowadays one wouldn't expect such separation, but it was common in Victorian times and I recall seeing ladies only compartments on trains to Fenchurch Street.

On Platform Two is one of our best station buffets. More a pub than a buffet, customers sit up to a bar on stools to enjoy good food and drink. It's open late in the evening and used by locals as well as train travellers. What a refreshing change from the catering chains that now inhabit most of our larger railway stations.

I joined the four coach train for Harwich, which leaves every hour from the bay platform. It's quite a busy little line and perhaps the most scenic in Essex, although I haven't travelled on the most rural branch to Sudbury. Mistley, the first stop, is a historic village which used to have an extensive malting industry, for which the railway provided several sidings. It is still a small port and two ships were berthed at the quay. A steep horse drawn incline once linked this to the main railway.

Beyond Mistley the line runs above the Stour Estuary, with superb views across the water to Suffolk. Bird life abounds and this is another of our picturesque, but lesser known stretches of coastal railway. I left the train at Wrabness, the most rural of the line's stations, although like most of our country stations it once had sidings, a signal box and coal yard. In World War Two one of the sidings was extended to the riverside to accommodate a large rail-mounted gun.

In bright sunshine I repeated one of my favourite sections of Essex Coast Walk; along the river bank, through gentle countryside and ending on the trackbed of the original railway into Harwich. The line was diverted to serve Harwich and Parkeston Quay, which was built on reclaimed land by the Great Eastern Railway in 1883. Passenger ships still run to the Netherlands and Sweden, although far fewer people pass through the station than in the days when boat trains of up to twelve coaches ran from London and the North. There is still a boat train from Liverpool Street, connecting with the ferry to Hoek van Holland. It remained locomotive hauled for a while after electrification, but today's old electric units which stop frequently hardly compare to the grand trains of previous generations.

The station is now less romantically named Harwich International and the fine brick-built building which once held a hotel, used for offices. There is far less freight carried on by rail but extensive sidings remain, albeit covered in weeds. Today just a single diesel locomotive stood lonely on the tracks, waiting hopefully for a train to pull. Walking past the oil terminal west of the station I had however been pleased to see a long line of tank wagons in a siding, each one of which would otherwise had meant yet another lorry on the roads.

The town of Harwich has a fine nautical history and many buildings of both interest and beauty. It is from the *Mayflower*, which set sail from Harwich for America in 1620, that the railway takes its name. Like most of our branch line termini, Harwich Town station is a shadow of its former self. Overgrown and rusting sidings lie idle, but once handled the arrival or departure of a train ferry with thirty six wagons every six hours, day and night. The train ferry terminal, where wagons were shunted onto the decks of ferries bound for Zeebrugge, closed in 1987, but the wharf with its ramp that rises and falls with the water to allow the railway to connect with the ship, is now a listed building.

Reflecting on my journeys on Essex branch lines as I returned home, I concluded that other than electrification and rolling stock, comparatively little has altered since the late 1960s. It was in the late 50s and early 60s that our rural railways changed so much, with the stations losing staff, platforms and goods yards, diesel replacing steam and widespread car ownership meaning many no longer used their local railway. In recent years though improved services and Community Rail Partnerships have helped to reduce the decline, with many rural lines across the country now carrying greatly increased passengers numbers.

CHAPTER FIFTEEN

THREE YORKSHIRE RESORTS

London – Whitby – Scarborough – Bridlington

My earliest memories that I can date are from our 1964 holiday to Whitby, when I was three. On this trip I've retraced our journey, travelled back by a roundabout route to Scarborough where we had a family holiday with our boys in 2002, then gone south to Bridlington where I've been many times on business.

King Cross's bright new concourse that was almost finished when I went to Edinburgh, was now open – and what an improvement it is. Flows of arriving and departing passengers are largely separated, with the often congested area in front of the departure board now just for people getting off the trains, while those waiting to board use the stunning new western concourse. With a vast steel and glass lattice-work roof, (Europe's largest single-span station structure), this is modern architecture to be proud of. One by one our major stations are being modernised, making travelling easier for the increasing numbers of passengers, but unlike the 1960s Euston disaster, sympathetically blending new and old.

On a July Monday morning the 10.00 to Aberdeen was almost fully booked. I'd like to have booked a seat, but East Coast's inflexible computer system would allow me to reserve only on the 10.30 with a Bridlington ticket, which allowed just nine minutes to change at York. As the station's designated 'minimum connection time' is eight minutes the computer allows only the later train, but with my plans for the day dependent on getting the Scarborough connection, I didn't want to risk missing it. Fortunately, in the Quiet Coach right at the front of the HST I found a table seat that was booked only from Newcastle to Montrose, one of many which I noted had reservations on Scotland's east coast. As part of a customer consultation Transport Scotland had recently suggested stopping cross border services beyond Edinburgh, but clearly there is a demand, and many people simply won't travel if they have to change.

An on time arrival after a non stop journey averaging 102mph gave me fifty minutes in York – time for a very quick look in the National Railway Museum. First port of call was the workshop to see if Flying Scotsman was back from boiler repairs. Yes it was, so I could tell Ben, my young nephew who loves trains, that the engine had returned home. Then some nostalgia from my youth; *Western Fusilier*, one of the iconic diesel engines that took us on so many journeys to Devon, and a look at some old British Rail posters with slogans from the 1970s – '*See a friend this weekend*' and '*Inter City makes the going easy*'.

In 1964 Whitby was served by three railways; from York via Pickering, Scarborough and Middlesbrough (a fourth to Saltburn had closed in 1958). The Beeching Report however recommended closing all three. Faced with advice that closure of the Middlesbrough line would cause 'grave hardship', the Government reprieved this, but the 'severe hardship' resulting from loss of the other two routes wasn't enough to save them. Tomorrow I would travel on the Esk Valley Line from Middlesbrough, but today left York on the 12.41 to Scarborough, the same way we'd gone nearly fifty years ago.

The three coach TransPennine Express was full and with some persuasion an elderly man accepted my reserved seat. Many passengers had luggage, travelling by train to the seaside as we used to. In these days of mass car ownership it's easy to forget that the railways still play an important role in taking people on holiday. The Whitby line had branched off at Malton, so it was here that I alighted. The gentleman (for that's what he was) to whom I'd given a seat tapped me as I walked past, saying thank you again.

With no train, I caught a bus for the eight miles to the interesting market town of Pickering. I'd have liked a look around but needed to continue my journey north. When Beeching closed the line in 1965 he could hardly have envisaged that just eight years later trains would be running from Pickering again – not by British Rail, but the privately run North Yorkshire Moors Railway (NYMR). The combination of the line's beautiful scenery and the steam locomotives that British Rail had so hastily discarded, has turned a little used railway into a major tourist attraction, now carrying over 200,000 passengers a year. One wonders how many more of the 6,000 miles of railway closed in the 1960s could have been saved with the sort of commitment and initiative displayed by the preservation movement and modern Community Rail Partnerships?

NYMR purchased only the most spectacular section of the line, and although British Rail trains continued to run as far as Malton, and from Grosmont to Whitby, the less scenic six miles south of Pickering closed. The possibility of reopening has often been discussed, and was adopted as a policy objective by North Yorkshire County Council, but considerable engineering work would be required as houses and a new road have been built on the trackbed at Pickering. For the foreseeable future the gap has to be bridged by taxi or Coastliner's double decker buses.

In 1964 it had been a steam train that took us from York to Whitby, but ironically today NYMR were using mostly diesel traction. The 1960 built Class 24 locomotive that hauled our six mostly compartment coaches was however very much of my childhood era. More than a hundred and fifty were built at the railway towns of Crewe, Derby and Darlington, and mainly used on freight and secondary passenger routes, such as the Scottish highland lines. As the number of people who travelled in the steam era diminishes, preserved lines are increasingly finding a nostalgia interest in diesel locomotives, although it's not always to the satisfaction of some visitors who expect a steam train.

As we climbed through the wooded valley alongside the Pickering Beck, the guard came into my compartment to check tickets. We chatted for a while. He originated from Essex, living most of his life just a few miles from Upminster, before retiring to Yorkshire. With the trains and scenery, he wouldn't want to be anywhere else. He told me that the line was built by George Stevenson and was one of the world's first railways, with trains originally pulled by horses.

We passed a steam train at Levisham, where an elderly couple got off carrying shopping bags. It was good to see the line providing a service to locals as well as tourists. Levisham and the request stop of Newtondale Halt provide access to Newtondale Forest, which has recently been closed to cars, allowing peace for walkers and wildlife. Beyond here the train runs across open moorland before stopping at Goathland, a much filmed station that appears as Hogsmeade in Harry Potter and Aidensfield in the TV series *Heartbeat*, which was filmed in the village. The line's final 3½ miles are beside the Musk Esk, a fast flowing upland stream, as it descends to the terminus of Grosmont. Here I was to change train, but not to 'National Rail' but another NYMR train running on Network Rail tracks. In a very rare but eminently sensible arrangement, in summer months Whitby's four services from Middlesbrough are augmented by others run by NYMR.

It was a fine train that pulled into Grosmont to take me on to Whitby. Six dark red coaches hauled by *Royal Scots Grey*, one of the six surviving Deltic diesel locomotives that were the fastest of their day. Completed in 1961, *Royal Scots Grey* was the first production Deltic and the most powerful locomotive in the world. In 1964 a Deltic would have hauled similar red coaches to York, where we'd changed to a steam train. Today the huge engine that once raced up and down the east coast at 100mph, pootled alongside the picturesque River Esk, bringing trade to the town and photographers to the lineside. The locomotive was on a short visit to NYMR and seemed to be impressing tourists as well as enthusiasts who'd come to film or ride behind it.

I didn't see Whitby at its best. Steady rain fell all evening and my plan for a good walk along the cliffs had to be curtailed. Rather than a quick takeaway fish and chips, I enjoyed a more leisurely meal in a harbourside restaurant. The 'Whitby scampi' was excellent even if there's some doubt whether it was actually landed or just processed here. I chatted to two ladies on the next table. One came from Ledbury and knew my parents' house. It didn't take long for 'small world' to be uttered.

Venturing out into the rain, I climbed the 199 steps to Whitby Abbey on the east cliff. I remember coming here when I was three and asking my father why the abbey was broken. '*The King broke it,*' he told me. Henry VIII was indeed responsible for the abbey's closure, although centuries of wind and rain, plus German naval shelling in 1914, have contributed to the ruin that stands romantically above the town.

Just slugs, assorted snails and darting swallows kept me company as I walked along the cliff to Saltwick Bay. Far below two men were pulling a net from the sea – a simple method of fishing that's little changed for centuries – even millennia. Conscious of having a work meeting the next day and having brought only one pair of shoes, an increasingly muddy path forced me to turn back. Nevertheless I was wet through by the time I got back to my hotel.

I chatted to the proprietor over breakfast. Like many resorts, the coming of the railway was a catalyst for its expansion, but despite the limited service and indirect route, he said they still get visitors by train. One quite wealthy couple stay every year, enjoying leaving their car in London and travelling about by train and bus. I didn't agree with his belief that the Esk Valley Line will eventually close. He thought the choice to keep this of the three routes had been correct at the time, as it had more settlements and school children, but now the Scarborough line would be more useful. We travelled on this scenic route through Robin Hood's Bay in 1964, a year before it closed. There were attempts to preserve it as a private railway, but costs were too great and the trackbed is now part of the national cycle network.

Whitby is a proper seaside town, with a nice balance between locals and tourists. Its relatively remote position means that fewer day trippers venture here than Scarborough or Bridlington down the coast, and it retains an active shipping industry, albeit far smaller than in years gone by. With narrow streets rising each side of the Esk it is a picturesque and interesting town. Lacking the brashness of Scarborough, Whitby is probably less of a family holiday destination, but suited our needs back in 1964 and is somewhere I'd like to return to for a longer stay.

On a warm and sunny morning I arrived in good time for the 8.50 to Middlesbrough. The two car '156' that pulled in looked surprisingly full and I counted fifty-one school children alighting. This is a railway line that serves a crucial social need. Sixteen adults and one excited little girl boarded. They were going to Redcar and she informed us all every time we passed a cow, horse, duck or rabbit!

An illustration of Whitby's isolation is that it's the only branch line in England, Wales or Scotland that can't be reached in just one change from London. Just four trains a day make their way along the Esk, criss-crossing the river over a series of bridges. The most impressive bridge however we went under – the dramatic red brick Larpool Viaduct that once carried the

Scarborough line 120 feet above the river. One or two passengers joined at every stop, with the odd one getting off. The line isn't just used by end to end travellers but is a lifeline to the small villages it passes through. At Glaisdale the guard helped a lady in a wheelchair. Potatoes grew on a disused platform at Lealholm. Three walkers alighted at Commondale, where we were now on heather covered open moor. The train isn't fast, averaging just 24mph for the thirty five miles to Middlesbrough, but it wouldn't be right to hurry through such scenery.

At Battersby the train stops for ten minutes before reversing and heading back towards Whitby, then diverging northwards. It was the first stop that no one got on or off, but with just a handful of houses nearby the station doesn't get much use. The tracks continue westwards, although the guard couldn't remember where to, but said they're used for the occasional shunting movement. They are the remains of a line to Northallerton that closed as long ago as 1954.

I had six minutes in Middlesbrough. It was long enough. The Tees Valley Line to Darlington isn't our most scenic, and in a '142' Pacer, nor was it the most comfortable. These 'buses on rails' have only four wheels and are known as 'nodding donkeys' for their tendency to bounce along the track. The two coach train was almost full, one poor man travelling back to see his family in Norwich after his grandfather had died in the night. He'd hoped to get to see him a few days earlier but couldn't raise the £109 fare. Advance fares may be cheaper but they don't suit all circumstances.

My advance ticket to York had cost £14, but the shorter TransPennine Express route from Middlesbrough to Northallerton was almost double the price. When I'd looked at booking from York to Whitby the cheapest fare East Coast's computer initially offered was £27, but entering 'not via Darlington' showed a ticket on the more direct route for just £12.70. How many times are people overcharged by lack of information and the complexities of our rail fares?

From Eaglescliffe the line follows the route of the original Stockton and Darlington Railway, the world's first commercial steam passenger railway. Whilst Middlesbrough no longer has any direct trains to London, the small town of Eaglescliffe has four a day. Matching some of the enterprise shown by their Victorian railway forefathers, the 'open access' operator Grand

Central Railway runs four trains a day to Sunderland, stopping at a number of towns that would never have expected direct Inter City services to London. We once used it for an FA Cup match at Hartlepool, with Grand Central's five car HST virtually filled by West Ham fans.

Our bouncing Pacer positively raced through Teesside Airport station, which has the surprising distinction of being the least used in Britain. That just two trains a week call here, and those simply to avoid the procedures required to close it, explain the low usage. In October 2009, Alex Neilson, stationmaster of nearby Chester-le-Street, organised an outing here to raise the station's profile. Twenty-six people arrived by train, boosting the usage figures for the year. In the whole of the following year, with no special outing, just eighteen passengers were counted as alighting or boarding. Mr Nelson hoped to persuade the authorities to improve the airport's rail service and move the station closer than the current fifteen minute walk to the terminal.

With wide platforms, red brick walls and three huge arched roofs supported by ornate pillars, Darlington is an impressive station. Its design has something of a continental flavour. On my last visit, en route to Middlesbrough, I'd been stopped by a policeman who insisted on searching my rucksack under the terrorism legislation that seems to be used as an excuse for random searching. To my question as to whether I looked like a terrorist, he replied that I could be 'animal rights'. Had I not have changed from business attire before travelling from Glasgow, I very much doubt that I'd have been troubled.

Today's annoyance was down to our modern railway system – having to watch an East Coast train leave and wait for Cross Country's Voyager on which my ticket was valid. True to form, the whole coach smelled of toilet chemical and the trolley came by with its regulation three sandwiches.

In 1964 we'd travelled 22 miles from Whitby for a day out in Scarborough. Beeching's closure of the coastal and Pickering lines meant it was taking me all morning for 136 miles via Darlington and York. (I could have reduced this by eight but for twice the fare on TPE.) Hence from York I repeated yesterday's journey to Malton.

A particularly cheerful guard checked tickets and told passengers times for return trains or Bridlington connections. Approaching Malton he made a special announcement – the two passengers travelling to London should alight here and catch the train back to York. Two Chinese ladies got off. I once made a similar error at Brussels, when I ran up the steps, jumped into a train, the doors shut, and as it set off realised I was heading the wrong way. The guard spoke no English but understood that with a ticket for Amsterdam I was on the wrong train. Like the Chinese tourists, I got off at the first stop and made my way back.

Scarborough is a traditional British seaside resort with donkey rides, candy floss, slot machines and chips – lots of chips! In 2002 we'd stayed opposite the South Cliff Lift, Britain's first funicular railway, which fascinated our two year old son. Now a teenager, he wasn't a bit interested when I told him I'd ridden it today – his concern was that I'd embarrass him in the book!

Like Blackpool, Torquay and Newquay, Scarborough is big enough for a car not to be necessary for a week's holiday and as I'd seen on the trains from York, the railway remains important to the town's tourist trade. The station retains its original Victorian buildings and with trains running long distances there's still an air of importance about the place. Every summer steam trains come here from York, but part of its history was lost with removal of an eleven semaphore signal gantry in 2010. The station does however hold a record – the continuous seat backing onto the wall on Platform One, is at 152 yards, the longest in the world.

The Yorkshire Coast Line to Hull is a busy railway, serving some quite isolated communities, although only once does it give a glimpse of the sea. Unusually for Yorkshire, the route is generally flat and the views nothing special. The single track line to Bridlington has fewer trains, and with jointed track and wooden sleepers, seems more of a rural branch than the busier section further south. This afternoon the 14.54 from Scarborough was almost full, with passengers alighting at all the intermediate stops.

Filey station merits comment, having an overall roof which was once common in East Yorkshire. The listed building dating from 1846 seems apt for a town that in many ways seems a place that time forgot, but for many is the nicest resort on this section of Yorkshire's coast.

Bridlington is a smaller version of Scarborough, even having North and South beaches either side of the harbour. I've been coming here several times a year on business for about twenty years, experiencing all four seasons and weather from hot sunshine to wild North Sea gales. Rain today again curtailed my walk along the cliffs.

My stays in Bridlington follow a regular routine. Arrive by train late afternoon, check in at the seafront Expanse Hotel, walk along the cliffs, meeting over dinner and again at our customer's factory in Carnaby next morning. Sadly Carnaby station, three miles from Bridlington, closed in 1970, so I have to use a taxi. I say meeting over dinner, but it's more two friends who've known each other through glue for thirty years, putting the world to rights. Sharing similar views on business, the environment and the state of football, Simon and I are invariably the last to leave the dining room as we pontificate on the modern world.

The Expanse Hotel was a fitting setting to look back at what has changed from our youth, as in many ways it seems stuck in the 1970s – but all the better for it. The restaurant has moved on from Brown Windsor soup and prawn cocktail, but steering clear of modern poncy food, offers a selection of good wholesome British roasts, steak and fish, with proper hot puddings served with custard. It suits the clientele, the majority of whom are well over retirement age and cluster round the entrance waiting for the dining room to open. Rooms are unfussy but comfortable, with beds adequate rather than the ridiculously wide ones that modern hotels seem to think they have to provide, and televisions mostly old style with just five channels. Reception is neither particularly efficient nor overly friendly, although I'm told that this may just be the natural Yorkshire way. With views across the beach and the roar of the North Sea through the window, it is though a hotel I'd choose over a modern identikit chain any day.

Bridlington has one of our most unspoiled railway stations, with the brick-built 1912 concourse retaining many of its original features. In summer it's a mass of colour with floral displays provided by the owner of the station buffet. One of only three original buffets left in Britain, it has been renovated to former glory and filled with railway memorabilia. With good food and a range of real ales, it's well worth a visit.

The two car '158' was full with chatter of Yorkshire ladies on their way to Hull. More joined at Natterton, Driffield and Hutton Cranswick, and after Beverley we were virtually full. The half hourly service is a fairly recent improvement and seems to have helped attract more passengers to the line.

A large sign welcoming visitors to 'New Hull' suggests a city which knows it has an image problem. The city has improved in recent years, not least the station, which is light and airy, and as Hull Paragon Interchange, is now conveniently joined to a large bus station. Redevelopment has been sympathetic, retaining the station's interesting architecture, including the wood panelled booking office which is now occupied by WH Smiths. I've stayed at the Victorian station hotel several times, although would advise against a room looking over the concourse unless you want to be woken by announcements of early morning trains to Doncaster, Beverley and London.

For many years Hull just had one through train a day to London – the Hull Executive, which replaced the Hull Pullman in 1978. I used to catch it from London, enjoying dinner as I travelled. Then changes in ticket restrictions meant that 'Saver' tickets weren't valid and unless I could book in advance and knew when I'd be returning, a prohibitively expensive full fare had to be purchased. In 2001 however, Hull gained a new and cheaper direct service to London. Hull Trains was born.

Our first 'open access' operator, the company carries 750,000 passengers a year on its ninety services a week. The staff of over a hundred were mostly recruited from Hull and the surrounding area, adding to the family feel and customer orientated business. Like Wrexham & Shropshire, Hull Trains has become much appreciated by locals and has brought new visitors to the area. The company though hasn't been without its difficulties, mostly related to problems with rolling stock, not helped by taking over the unreliable Adelante trains that First Great Western had discarded. Hull Trains seem to have resolved the problems, but as I waited for the 12.30 to Kings Cross all was not well.

The train pulled into the station in good time, passengers alighted and the doors were closed. The train was announced but the doors remained locked. Two men in orange overalls appeared. 12.30 came and went. A man from Hull Trains walked down the platform, talking to each group of waiting passengers, and telling us that there was a problem with the doors but it should be fixed in fifteen minutes. Another suited man appeared, the Engineering Operations Manager, joining the concerned huddle of staff by the driver's cab. One of the orange men appeared, shaking his head. It didn't look good. Managers talked into their mobiles and the fitter returned to the train. Every effort was clearly being made to run the train and keep passengers informed. In BR days communication was often poor, but in simpler times before computers and automatic doors, there was less to go wrong. If a locomotive broke down there was usually another around that could replace it. Suddenly all the doors opened. The problem had been fixed and we could board.

Sarah our 'on board manager' greeted us and introduced Pat, Tracy and Amy, our 'on board team'. Within minutes we were passing under the Humber Bridge and running along the river bank on one of our less celebrated scenic stretches of coastal railway. Northern's trains from Hull to Doncaster go through Goole, but we went via Selby, giving the town a link to London that was virtually lost when the East Coast line was diverted. A swing bridge just north of the station takes the line over the River Ouse, where ships still retain priority over trains.

I wandered down to the buffet, returning with a microwaved cheese and ham panini that tasted better than its limpness suggested. Sitting at a table in the Quiet Coach this was a very pleasant way to travel. Hull Train's staff give the impression that they enjoy their work and want to provide a good service. There was a friendly tone to all the announcements and the bright Adelante trains add to the enjoyable ambiance of travel. Hull Trains has been a success of privatisation.

From Doncaster it was almost constant 125mph running, the five coach Adelante matching the performance of East Coast's electric trains. Indeed until recently Hull Trains had the fastest train in Britain. In 1938 around 120 trains averaged at least than 60mph and five over 70mph. In 2011 a study by the Rail Performance Society looked at all 228 trains that averaged over 100mph for part of their journey and found that Hull Trains' 7.20 from Kings Cross topped the list, averaging 111mph for the 77.7 miles from Stevenage to Grantham. Weekday trains have now lost the Stevenage stop and the best run on Sundays averages a mere 108mph.

Despite a slow approach to the terminus, we took just 64 minutes for the 105¼ miles from Grantham to London. At Kings Cross I thanked the driver. With a little smile he agreed it had been a good run. I think he'd enjoyed it too!

CHAPTER SIXTEEN

NORTH WALES CIRCULAR

Cardiff – Llandudno – Porthmadog – Shrewsbury

I've had more holidays in North Wales than anywhere except Devon – three at Llandudno and four on the Cambrian Coast. This was a round trip through all the resorts, including a ride on the Ffestiniog narrow gauge steam line, and starting from Cardiff on one of our most unusual trains.

Originally known as '*Y Geralt Gymro – Gerald of Wales*', after the 12th century Welsh poet and preacher, but now less romantically as the '*Premier Service*', a locomotive hauled train runs from Holyhead to Cardiff each weekday morning, returning late afternoon. Funded by the Welsh Assembly Government to provide a high quality link between the north and south, it has become one of our more controversial trains. The amount of subsidy seems to be kept secret for 'commercial confidentiality' and some suggest that it may be influenced by Assembly members who use the train to Cardiff. Railway staff have been heard to refer to it as '*The Royal Train*' and when I visited Wrexham & Shropshire's office to discuss my proposed book, they talked of passengers changing from '*Grumpy Gerald*'.

Travelling up the Marches Line from Newport, we called at Cwmbran and Abergavenny, but then ran non stop to Shrewsbury, strangely skipping the city of Hereford. Timings may be the official reason but many suspect it's geography – Hereford is in England.

In many ways the train is a relic from my youth, with Mark Two coaches that were built between 1964 and 1975. Their distinctive sound as the brakes are applied reminded me of many childhood journeys. The first time I used it the locomotive was a Class 57, originating from the 1960s, but these have now been replaced by much more recent Class 67s. Seats are all around tables and half of the rear coach is the guard's van, a rare sight on today's railway. Doors have pull down windows and I spent part of the journey standing by an open window, enjoying the feel of warm air rushing past my face – a rare pleasure on today's trains.

Keen to sample the complimentary three course dinner, I joined five other passengers in First Class. Two were business people returning home, and three ex railway employees enjoying an evening run to Shrewsbury, which they do once a year on what one said was, *'the best train in Britain'*. Tables were nicely set with white cloths and menus printed in Welsh and English. The 16.15 departure is a bit early for dinner but orders were taken after we left the London line at Newport, heading north through pleasant scenery. A sunny July evening was perfect for travel, the countryside looking its best as the sun fell.

There was a delay at Cwmbran as a disabled passenger boarded and a ramp had to be found. He'd phoned Arriva Trains Wales to book assistance but no one had told the train crew. By Abergavenny I was eating my starter, a tapas platter with 'continental meats'. As we rattled through Hereford the main course of lamb had arrived. It was OK but not nearly as good as the duck I'd had last time. The dessert of fresh strawberries with clotted cream was however excellent. Staff were friendly and efficient, but overall dinner didn't match First Great Western's. I wrote on the comments card, *'Enjoyable but personally I would prefer larger portions of more simple food'*.

At Ludlow we saw the castle and racecourse. Stokesay Castle at Craven Arms would have made a great photograph reflected in the lake. We came here from Hereford in 1974, getting a lift back to Ludlow from a couple who saw us waiting at the bus stop. Trains were locomotive hauled then, but far fewer than the '175s' that now nip up and down the line. The section from here to Shrewsbury I'd covered in a rather smaller train on my Heart of Wales journey.

Outside Shrewsbury's new football ground three teenagers greeted us, but with a somewhat ruder wave than are usually directed at trains. Now we headed further into England, to Crewe, although shortly after my journey the train was to be retimed, departing two hours later and going on the shorter route via Wrexham. The new schedule would also include a stop at Hereford.

An American joined us, enjoying an unexpected free dinner. He was travelling to Bangor. The steward told me that few passengers go all the way to Holyhead. The last time I'd been on this stretch was taking the boys to Llandudno in 2003. Deb had driven but on a summer Saturday the boys and I preferred the train to a long car journey on busy roads. Mind you the '175' from Crewe wasn't too pleasant – absolutely packed until hordes got off at Rhyl. Today's four coach train was still well filled, at least two sitting at each table.

At Shotton we crossed the Wrexham to Bidstone 'Borderlands Line', which I used a couple of times linking with Wrexham and Shropshire for a cheap and enjoyable, but slow route to Merseyside. At Flint we were back in Wales and alongside the Dee Estuary. Hilbre Island, where I'd walked from West Kirby for *No Boat Required,* could be seen across the water. Prestatyn and Rhyl are two resorts that have recently gained investment after being badly run down, but the sad state of Colwyn Bay's pier could be seen from the train.

Arrival at Llandudno Junction is scheduled two minutes after a Manchester train leaves for Llandudno. We'd been slowed by signals as we followed behind, but it doesn't wait to make the connection, perhaps understandably as I was the only one changing. As *Gerald of Wales* departed it struck me that the once everyday sight of the rear of a coach with its red tail light disappearing into the distance, is now rare, as virtually all modern trains can be driven from each end. With forty minutes to wait I walked along Conwy Bridge, before completing the short run to Llandudno.

With its curved promenade and a pier at one end, Llandudno reminds me of Torquay. Lined with elegant hotels, it's an attractive seafront, with the limestone Great Orme headland rising behind the town. On each of our holidays here we've enjoyed the trip to the summit on Britain's longest cable hauled tramway. Opened in 1902, the ride on the blue and white tramcars which rattle along the street and across the cliff, is a unique experience.

As dusk fell I walked to the pier, then back along the promenade to find the flat where we'd stayed with the boys. Although its beach is nothing special, Llandudno is an excellent base for family holidays, with nearby castles, steam trains and the lovely sands of Anglesey. I remember the stays with the boys and in 1975 with my parents, as two of our best family holidays. Like Torquay, out of season the town is kept going by more elderly people on coach holidays, but it was surprising to find that even in the school holidays the majority of visitors seemed to be of more mature years. When I walked back to the sea next morning most of the larger hotels had coaches outside, with grey haired guests waiting to board. There were children about and a sandcastle competition advertised, but Llandudno seems to be another seaside town where the average age of visitors has considerably increased since the 1970s.

My guesthouse displayed plenty of 1970s eccentricities. I was greeted with surprise – they'd forgotten that I'd arranged to check in later than the 7pm limit and thought I wasn't coming. The information folder listed a string of rules. The bed squeaked every time I moved. The shower was one of those specially manufactured for bed and breakfast accommodation, where water alternates from scalding to freezing. The bathroom was so small that any person of above average girth would struggle to turn round, let alone sit on the toilet. The owners struggled to cope; the wife, a friendly round lady who cooked a good breakfast but got my order wrong, and her husband, quiet and slightly flustered. I mentioned the shower and aware of the breakfast mistake, they wanted to give me ten pounds off. I declined; this was a proper British seaside guesthouse with quirks but no pretensions. I liked it.

Llandudno station is a sad sight. All that remains of the once grand frontage and extensive glass canopy, is a small covered waiting area and booking office. The platforms are open to the elements and an air of desolation pervades. How different it must have been in the 19th century when carriages met trains, drawing up on the road that still separates the two main platforms. As I waited a tabby cat walked down the platform. Across the tracks a seagull stood impassively. For a minute cat and bird stared at each other, then as the train approached the cat jumped onto the track. Seagull was gone before he reached the other side.

My last journey along the twenty seven mile Conwy Valley Line was on a February morning, returning from a tidal island at Porthmadog, when I'd joined just a handful of locals. Today, with a change to the Ffestiniog Railway, I was doing the same journey in reverse.

The two coach 10.22 to Blaenau Ffestiniog was well filled, mostly with tourists. Deganwy, the first stop, once had a busy quay where slate was brought by train and loaded onto coastal steamers, the main purpose for building the railway from Blaenau Ffestiniog. Today it's a quiet village, beautifully situated opposite Conwy Castle on the river's estuary. A family with two young boys boarded here. As they looked for a table to sit together, a fat man reading his Kindle sat resolutely hogging one for himself.

From Llandudno Junction the picturesque ride continued alongside the gradually narrowing River Conwy, with low mist hanging on the hills either side. With the tide low a variety of birds pottered about on the mud and a heron stood still on the water's edge. Fat man started to play a noisy game on his phone.

Passengers were joining at every stop. At Tal-y-Cafyn there was a beautifully tended garden on the disused platform and a sign with the old station name that was changed in 1974; Tal-y-Cafyn and Eglwysbach, a stiff challenge in Welsh pronunciation. The driver picked up a new token at North Llanrwyst, the signalman walking down the steps from his traditional box accompanied by his dog, who wagged his tail vigorously as the two men chatted. The station here has the only passing loop on the line and the disused, but well preserved buildings, an almost ecclesiastical appearance.

By Llanrwyst, the small town's second station which is nearer to the centre and opened in 1989, I could bear the constant bleeping from fat man's phone no longer. I asked him to turn it down. He switched it off without a word of either complaint or apology, then spent the rest of the journey staring blankly forward.

The impressive station at Betws-y-Coed was busy with passengers alighting and tourists using the shops and cafes that have sympathetically taken over the station buildings. Opposite, where there was once another platform, is a small railway centre where I took the boys on Kieron's fourth birthday – in the days he still liked trains! When Dad and I came here on a Merrymaker trip in the mid 1970s, an eight coach diesel multiple unit had met the London train at Llandudno Junction, bringing a sudden influx of visitors to the town.

From here the scenery becomes more rugged, climbing through the Lledr Valley with mountains either side. The Conwy Valley Line is one of our most scenic railways, probably more so than the more celebrated Ffestiniog. Perched on a hill in front of Moel Siabod mountain, Dolwddelan Castle is perhaps the most dramatically sited of all the Welsh castles and gives one of our most spectacular views from a railway. We walked here from Dolwddelan station in 1975.

A 2 ½ mile tunnel, the longest in Wales and the longest with just one track in the UK, takes the line under Moel Dyrnogydd. It is dead straight and travelling in the front of a DMU in 1975 we'd watched the pin prick of light gradually grow as we progressed deep under the mountain. The train emerges into a world of slate – layers upon layers of grey stone precariously covering the mountainsides, hanging over the train as though threatening to plummet onto the rails.

Passing through the remains of the old station, our journey ended at the joint station with the Ffestiniog Railway, that opened in 1982. The interchange between gauges in a mountain environment has parallels with Switzerland, but the surreal views here were not quite the same. It is no accident that the map shows a yellow line around Blaenau Ffestiniog, indicating that it's excluded from Snowdonia National Park. Hemmed in by the mountains and huge piles of slate, it is a grey and often depressing place. Like Princetown on Dartmoor and Buxton in the Peak District, it seems to rain here more days than not. In fact with an annual rainfall of seventy nine inches Blaenau Ffestiniog is Britain's second wettest town (Fort William is the wettest). With just light drizzle, today was one of the drier days that I've been here.

Crossing the platform, I boarded the eight coach narrow gauge Ffestiniog train – one of the 'Great Little Trains of Wales'. Where once slate trains ran by gravity to the docks at Porthmadog, now tourists are pulled by steam engines, most of which used to drag the empty trucks back up the line. It was hard to believe that our locomotive, *Merddin Emrys*, was built as long ago as 1879. Running through forests and along mountain sides, by fast flowing streams and serene lakes, in tunnels and around horseshoe bends, and climbing over 700 feet on a 13½ mile journey, it is a spectacular ride.

At Tanygrisiau we had to wait fifteen minutes to pass a late running train. The lady from the buffet took cups of tea to the driver and fireman. Soon a puff of steam appeared at the far end of the Llyn Ystradau reservoir, then disappeared into a cutting as the little train ran behind the hydro electric power station. This section of track hadn't been built when we first visited the Ffestiniog in 1971. The line had been severed by the reservoir when the power station opened, but over thirteen years largely volunteer labour constructed the 'Great Deviation' around the reservoir, allowing trains to once again reach Blaenau. To gain height the only complete spiral on Britain's railways was built from Ddualt station, reaching the 310 yard Moelwyn Tunnel, which was constructed by a team led by three Cornish tin miners.

Tokens exchanged, we set off over the level crossing. A family waved, their young lad jumping back as the engine whistled. Part of the old alignment could be seen as we passed the end of the lake, the drop in height from the new line illustrating the huge task achieved by the 1970s 'deviationists'. Ddualt is now a request stop on the wildest section of the line, but in 1971 had been the temporary terminus. Then we'd travelled on the partly built new line in a diesel hauled shuttle train.

The busy scene at Tan-y-bwlch, the main intermediate station, was one unique to Wales – two narrow gauge steam trains passing on packed platforms in a wooded Snowdonian valley. It was hard to believe that all these people were travelling on trains with rails less than two feet apart.

After Minffordd, where there's an interchange with the Cambrian Coast Line, and Boston Lodge where we changed driver and fireman, the train crosses the Cobb, a man-made stone causeway over the Glaslyn estuary. To the left is a small tidal island, Cei Ballast. Once just a sandbank, it was formed by ballast that was dumped from ships returning to collect slate from Porthmadog Harbour and with stone from all around the world, is a unique geological site.

The bustling town of Porthmadog is served by no less than four railways.

The Ffestiniog's station is shared by the highly scenic Welsh Highland Railway, which runs twenty five miles over the foothills of Snowdon to Caernarfon. After restoration in sections the full route opened in 2011, providing a useful link across Wales, although British Rail's Caernarfon to Bangor line remains closed, leaving a nine mile gap to the main system. We travelled on the Welsh Highland in August 2003, which happened to be the day Prince Charles was officially opening the line. We saw his train but not the prince.

In 1980 we'd taken the short ride on what was then the Welsh Highland Railway, but after a fall out between groups, became the Welsh Highland Heritage Railway. This runs just a mile to Pen-y-Mount, where it meets the longer line, but with no intersection between the two. As I waited on Porthmadog station for the 14.56 to Pwllheli, a taxi driver came over saying that it was running fifteen minutes late, so I took the opportunity to wander over to the Heritage station. With good fortune I happened to glance up as the Pwllheli train passed – bang on time. A quick dash got me back just in time. Taxi drivers don't know everything.

In *No Boat Required* I wrote that the train ride along the Cambrian Coast is a journey everyone should do once in their lifetime – a spectacular ride through beautiful scenery that few seem to know is there. Then I'd travelled from Machynlleth to Porthmadog, but today I was going a little further north – to Criccieth where we'd holidayed in 1971. This was the first time I'd been back, but unlike some of the places I've returned to, there was no feeling of familiarity.

The station is now an unstaffed halt and the passing loop has long gone, but the main building remains and is decorated with attractive murals depicting marine themes. My short stay gave time for only a quick feel of the town, but I liked it very much. A quiet family seaside resort, hugely attractive with its two beaches overlooked by a 13th century castle. Adding Criccieth to the list of places to one day return to, I departed south towards Barmouth.

My offer to pay for the earlier journey from Porthmadog when the guard hadn't come round was refused, as it was 'the railway's fault'. He thought the previous guard must have either run out of change or battery on his ticket machine, as it had been a busy day. Quite a crowd were waiting to join at Porthmadog. A couple sat opposite me, the lady saying she preferred to travel backwards as 'it's safer'. I assured her that the chance of us bumping into anything was pretty remote.

At Penrhyndeudraeth a wooden bridge crosses the River Dwyryd. This is shared with light road traffic but buses have to make an eight mile detour, a factor that helped reprieve the line when it was put up for closure in 1971. The coast's geography meant that it was impractical to run a bus service in the railway's place. Closure would have caused considerable hardship to those living on the Cambrian Coast and resulted in loss of tourism. An Action Group fought the proposal, with a special train running to London for a protest march to Downing Street, which my father joined at Euston. During our Criccieth holiday he visited the leader of the action group to discuss the railway, although quite what the man thought of two children accompanying him carrying buckets of lug worms for fishing into his office, I've no idea!

Beyond the bridge is the request stop of Llandecwyn, one of a number of very small halts on the line. British Rail tried to close it in the 1990s but were refused permission. As we'd travelled up and down the line in 1971 we often came across a young railway enthusiast who appeared to be making it his mission to use all the request stops. We called him 'Master Halt'. On one occasion when the train stopped to pick up a single passenger he was greeted by the guard saying 'not you again'!

On our Criccieth holiday we walked from Llandecwyn to Llyn Tecwyn, a small lake a couple of miles away, and more recently I came here from Talsarnau, the next stop, via the tidal island of Ynys Gifftan. Beyond the island the Italianate village of Portmerion can be seen as the train heads towards Harlech, where the line nestles under the Edwardian castle.

Last time I'd been through here Harlech had been busy with school children, but today it was holidaymakers who packed the train. Almost every seat was taken, but this was nothing yet. A lady with her young daughter joined me, taking refuge from the other coach where the air conditioning had failed. Their family were staying at Tal-y-Bont and travelling to different places on the line each day. With so much to see on the Cambrian Coast and narrow gauge lines that run into the mountains, a car just isn't necessary here.

The line moves slightly inland at Pensarn, where a girl got on, buying a return to Tywyn. This is a line used all year round by locals as well as tourists. Dyffryn, a few miles south, was where I had my first holiday at the age of six months, when the railway was still steam. What a lovely setting with miles of sandy beach to the right and mountains to the left. My father's family holidayed here during the war, the coastguard instructing them on pacing a safe distance from a mine before they could play on the beach. Later the owner of the holiday bungalow where they stayed sent a postcard advising that *the risk of hospital has gone*', his cryptic message letting them know that the beach was now safe, but without risking the Germans finding out.

Barmouth station was packed with passengers waiting to join. I was glad to be getting off and waited to watch whether everyone would fit on. It was touch and go, but with the guard's help the last family and their pushchair were somehow squeezed in. It was as crammed as a commuter train into London. What a shame for the many passengers who'd come up here for a day out on the first sunny day for weeks. Will they choose the train next time? Unbeknown to me, my niece joined the train at Aberdovey where she'd been with friends from Shrewsbury. She said it was an awful journey with passengers packed in, no air-conditioning and hardly any windows that opened.

Once a ship building town, Barmouth is now very much a holiday resort, and particularly popular with West Midlands folk. Nestled between mountains and a long sandy beach, and at the mouth of the beautiful Mawddach Estuary, it's a resort for all ages. We stayed here in 1965, arriving on a through train from London, and again in 1980, when having just passed my test, I drove, leaving a day early to watch West Ham in the Charity Shield at Wembley.

One of my few memories of 1965 is being slightly scared of the place where we stayed. My guesthouse today was equally memorable. It was one of those following the recent trend of filling the room with artefacts to pretend it's Victorian. The room was comfortable, if rather oddly decorated, but I'd rather they'd put the effort into better fitting windows to stop noise from the road, bathroom fittings that didn't require a degree in plumbing to operate, and simple facilities like a bar of soap, glass and information folder in the room. There weren't even any fire instructions. The beautifully typed breakfast menu let itself down with the spelling of 'porage', but the food was good. Fortunately I arrived on time. The other couple staying came down half an hour before they'd booked breakfast and with a mild telling off were told they'd have to wait as the husband had gone to the market. On checking out it was my turn to step out of line, my proffered credit card being greeted by, 'we don't take cards', uttered without a hint of apology. There were no signs but apparently I should have noticed when booking. I won't be returning.

The highlight of a visit to Barmouth is the half mile walk along the longest wooden trestle bridge in Europe, which takes the railway over the Mawddach Estuary. With views of the Rhinog mountains north of the river, the massive Cadr Idris to the south and the sublime estuary itself, this must be one of the most beautiful stretches of railway in Britain. For the sum of ninety pence one can walk on the path beside the track, enjoying superb views up the river.

In 1980 damage to timber supports caused by toredo marine worms resulted in closure of the bridge and threatened the line's future. Ten years earlier this might have been its death knell, but after repairs costing £2 million the bridge was reopened six months later. For some years locomotives weren't allowed to cross, resulting in an end of freight on the line, most of which served an explosives factory at Penrhyndeudraeth.

At the end of the bridge is Morfa Mawddach station, formerly Barmouth Junction. The triangular platform, which was still in place when we came here in 1980, is now overgrown and just a single request platform remains. It is however reasonably well used with people parking here and taking the train over the bridge to Barmouth, avoiding the twelve mile drive via Dolgellau. Until 1965 it was the junction for the highly scenic Barmouth – Ruabon line, two sections of which now have heritage trains – narrow gauge steam trains along Bala Lake and standard gauge from Llangollen to Carrog.

I walked about three miles along the old line, which now forms the Mawddach Trail for walkers and cyclists. It is a wonderful walk, which has been made easier since a storm washed away most of the ballast. That in 1961 I came along here in a steam train, is one of the more graphic illustrations of the changes in our railways. In 1961 there were 17,830 miles of track. In 2012 there are 10,072.

As I crossed Barmouth Bridge on another busy '158' next morning, a puff of smoke appeared behind the dunes. This was the Fairbourne Railway, a two mile miniature railway that was originally a tramway built to carry building materials for construction of the village, but has taken tourists to the beach since conversion to steam in 1916. A ferry links the terminus at Penrhyn Point with Barmouth, the two modes of transport heavily reliant on each other for trade. The line's heyday was in the 1960s and 70s, since when foreign holidays and competition from the increasing number of narrow gauge lines, has cut passenger numbers. Following the death in 2011 of its major benefactor, Professor Tony Atkinson, who covered its annual shortfall, a crisis fund was launched to ensure the railway's future.

Our family travelled on the miniature railway on most of our Cambrian holidays, but it is my brother who has used it most recently, not as a tourist but on a specially run educational field trip train. With much of interest to geographers on this coast, he brings students from Shrewsbury Sixth Form College here each year, and arranged for the Fairbourne Railway to run a special train, stopping at intervals for the students to get off and view the sand dunes.

A dramatic incident involving the Fairbourne Railway is one of my few memories from our 1965 holiday. The story could have come from Thomas the Tank Engine, but it could also have been a tragedy. We were sitting on the train waiting to leave for Fairbourne when two children were spotted being carried out to sea on inflatables. Shouts failed to attract attention so the engine driver repeatedly sounded his whistle. His whistling alerted a boatman who went down the river and rescued the children.

Today holidaymakers plus several locals with shopping alighted from the Cambrian Coast train and a party of Girl Guides on their way to Cardiff joined our busy train. From Fairbourne the line runs on a ledge under the cliffs, passing through a rock shelter which protects the train. Twice before this was built steam locomotives fell to the beach with loss of their crew. Just before Llwyngwril someone spotted a porpoise. The whole coach turned their heads as three or four leaped from the sea. What a magnificent sight from this wonderful railway. Lots of families were enjoying the ride as we rattled along the cliff top, but surely many more would if only they considered such a holiday (and if there was room on the trains for them – the four car '158' that we waited to pass at Tywyn was virtually full).

Aberdovey is the line's more upmarket resort and even has two stations. When I'd travelled northwards for *No Boat Required* a large group of youngsters from the nearby Outward Bound Centre had joined the train at Penhelig, just east of the town. In another hugely scenic section, the track winds its way along the Dovey Estuary. On the opposite bank a train from Aberystwyth, which would soon be joined with ours, was making its way towards Dovey Junction where the lines meet. We arrived together and the three waiting passengers had a choice of train. They picked ours.

As we departed side by side the guard announced, '*As we head on a collision course, look out to the left for the ospreys' nest, Monty and Nora stars of BBC Springwatch*'. Neither bird was at home in their huge nest at the top of a pole just thirty yards from the railway – and the Aberystwyth train was held back – we didn't crash!

The two trains were attached at Machynlleth, where more Guides from Aberystwyth joined those in my coach. Also changing portions was a well stocked refreshment trolley from which I bought a chicken sandwich, the choice of four exceeding Cross Country's standard three!

After the wonders of the Cambrian Coast, the Cambrian Main Line to Shrewsbury seemed a bit of an anti-climax. It's scenic ride through hills and wooded valleys, but doesn't match the spectacular coastal line. Over decades journey times have been accelerated far more than on the coast, partly due to line upgrades and partly as far more of the smaller stations closed. Accidents of geography mean that tiny settlements on the branch have kept a train service, while larger places on the main line go without.

I had greatly enjoyed my circular trip around North Wales, rekindling memories of childhood travels and prompting a desire to return again to so many places on the way. Other than more modern diesel multiple units, it is an area of our railways where not a great deal has changed since the late 1960s. The trains seem well used in both summer and winter, with perhaps the biggest problem being inadequate capacity for all those who wish to ride the superb Cambrian Coast railway.

CHAPTER SEVENTEEN

NEWTON ABBOT NEWTON ABBOT

Upminster – Torquay

'*Newton Abbot, Newton Abbot*', would be the first sound we'd hear as we arrived to see our much loved grandparents (the ones with the car). A real man on the clear public address telling arriving passengers where they were and those departing where the train was going: '*The train at Platform Two is for Torre, Torquay and Paignton*'. I still can't pass through the station without saying '*Newton Abbot, Newton Abbot*' to myself. We'd run along the platform and into the arms of Grandma and Grandpa, blurting out news of the journey before Mum and Dad caught us up. Our twice yearly stays in Devon have given me some of my best childhood memories and made the run from Paddington the main line I remember most. Forty years on I set out to see what has changed.

The day didn't get off to the best start. A downpour meant I arrived at Upminster station thoroughly soaked. I thought the rain was stopping so didn't bother with the bus. With trains to London every ten minutes, rather than three an hour with a thirty minute gap, no longer do we have to hurry for a specific train.

The ride to Fenchurch Street has changed both in quality of train and views from the window. Today's air conditioned Electrostars are a marked improvement in comfort and reliability, but their potential for reducing journey times has been limited by the line speed, extra stop at West Ham and safety requirements of a slow approach to Fenchurch Street. The factories we used to pass are gone, as are the cranes of the docks, replaced by the tall buildings of London's new commercial centre. The city's skyline has gained the Gherkin, Shard, Nat West Tower and Dome. The Post

Office Tower, once Britain's tallest building and new when I looked across London as a child, no longer stands above everything else.

Since 1999 most trains have stopped at West Ham, providing a link to the Jubilee Line and a convenient route to South London. More recently the Docklands Light Railway has taken over the end section of the North London Line to Woolwich, making West Ham an increasingly important interchange station. Limehouse too links with the DLR, bringing far more passengers than the few who used what was formerly Stepney East, a dingy station with wooden platforms.

Fenchurch Street, the first station to have been built inside the City of London, has been upgraded to a bright modern terminus. It's still not linked to the Underground, the Fleet Line that was planned to come here in the 1970s, being modified to run south of the Thames as the Jubilee. Unusually amongst London termini, the public address is provided by a real person, often Susan Gibbs, who after being 'the voice of Fenchurch Street' for twelve years received the MBE for 'services to public transport'. A major improvement is that the Crosswall entrance, which provides a short walk to Tower Hill, is now always open rather than just in peak hours. Usually we had to walk the long way round, Mum shepherding the children while Dad struggled with heavy cases. No one had thought of attaching wheels and a handle to pull them with, and every so often Dad would stop to rest or change hands. Occasionally for holidays we'd send a large case on in advance, a service that seems to belong to an era even before our childhood travels.

We never walked to Aldgate, which took no longer but wasn't considered an interchange. Some years ago I had protracted correspondence with London Transport as to why the barrier gates wouldn't open for tickets to Upminster, but their answer was that the computer didn't allow it. That it was often quicker to walk from Aldgate than travel via Tower Hill and that computers only do what a person programmes them to do, didn't seem to have crossed their mind.

At Tower Hill Dad had to queue for tickets, as British Rail tickets didn't include the Underground. Whilst through tickets now cover crossing London, advance fares are often only available from major stations, so today I had to pay separately to Paddington. With Oyster Cards though, there's no need to queue. We always waited for the Circle Line, but from Aldgate there's the option of a Metropolitan with a change further down the line. What a contrast the new Metropolitan Line trains are with the undergrounds of my youth. Gone are the guard and smoking carriages, but new is air conditioning and 'Sonia', the recorded announcement that 'gets *on yer* nerves'.

On a summer Saturday Paddington was busy with holidaymakers loaded with luggage, clustering around two banks of electronic screens – functional but less romantic than the old clapper board departure board that faced passengers emerging from the tube. The station is much lighter though and with many more places to shop. Who would have envisaged a Marks & Spencer's on Paddington Station?

The platform for the 12.33 to Paignton was announced only five minutes before departure. Confusion reigned as we boarded – the seat reservations said Cardiff and Swansea. An announcement, '*Would the Train Manager please contact the driver*', didn't bode well, but just four minutes late we pulled out of Paddington.

Today I was on an HST. Other than the sleeper, all the trains from Paddington to Devon are HSTs. So are all the trains to Bristol, Cardiff and Swansea. Gone is the variety that added to the excitement of a train journey for a young lad. Dad and I would walk to the front to watch the engine back onto the train. Usually it was a '*Western*', initially in iconic maroon livery, then later in British Rail blue. Occasionally in the early days we had a '*Warship*', a less powerful locomotive that was not much faster than the steam engines they replaced. More latterly we'd sometimes have a Class 47 (which Dad always called a *Brush Sulzer*), or a Class 50 – powerful locomotives that were displaced from Crewe to Glasgow trains after electrification. When very young I travelled behind steam and once was allowed onto the footplate of a locomotive in Paddington station, but sadly I don't recall it at all.

The *Westerns*, each of which was named, were synonymous with the route to Cornwall at a time when travel probably had more in common with the steam era than with our modern express trains. No longer do we see the engine that brought coaches into Paddington follow the train out of the platform as it returned for its next duty. The sidings just outside Paddington where locomotives once waited for their trains are long gone, but the fixed formation HSTs with a power car at each end allow far quicker turn rounds.

The fastest stretch of the route is from London to Reading, part of Brunel's railway to Bristol. This is the only part where HSTs reach their maximum 125mph speed. The line is both straight and flat, although in parallels with our new high speed lines, the engineers didn't get it all their own way. Brunel had wanted to build the railway past the village of Sonning, but local objections forced him to take it through a deep cutting. Like so many railway structures, it is hard to comprehend that the 60 foot deep Sonning Cutting was dug by hand, with around 25,000 cubic yards of spoil a week removed in wheelbarrows and horse drawn carts.

The approach to Reading has been a bottleneck for many years, particularly westbound where all trains on the fast line have to stop at Platform One. Work on major redevelopment to reduce congestion and increase capacity was well underway, but not planned for completion until 2015, when a viaduct to the west of the station will take the fast lines over the slow tracks. The improvement is long overdue, and I have often wondered, what is the point of powering 36 miles from Paddington only to wait at signals outside the station?

It is remarkable how little of the view from the window has changed since the 1960s. The line to Devon still runs through typical rural England and makes pleasant viewing all the way. Probably the biggest change is at Reading. Suttons Seeds, whose extensive premises announced the approach to the town, moved down the line to Torquay in 1976, being replaced by modern commercial buildings that now line both sides of the railway. Huntley & Palmers' biscuit factory shut the same year and the famous trolleybuses, that I recall seeing from the train, were withdrawn in 1968.

The locomotive hauled trains of my childhood had a mix of compartment coaches and open seating around tables. Seats could be booked but it was rare that my parents considered the cost necessary, and although trains were busy I don't ever recall us having to stand. If possible we'd get a compartment, spreading out at each stop to deter others entering. This was perhaps the only occasion when parents were happy to tolerate bad behaviour, fighting children putting off other passengers and keeping the compartment for ourselves. Usually I was very well behaved on trains, happy to look out of the window and record times of the run. My sister often wasn't! Mum would keep us occupied playing I-Spy or paper games, often writing down everything we could see beginning with a certain letter.

Originally HSTs had mostly table seats, but First Great Western have refurbished their sets, although sadly not for the better. To provide extra capacity for commuters from the Thames Valley each coach now has just two tables, an arrangement totally unsuited to family travel. For some time one coach was designated a 'Family Coach', but this has now been replaced by the 'Entertainment Coach' with TV screens in seat backs. This includes a display of the train speed and progress along the route, something that would have kept me occupied for hours.

Mum always made a picnic, but we had to wait. *'Not until Taunton,'* was her way of breaking up the journey, but we never understood why we couldn't have it sooner. Often there were no buffets on the train, just restaurants, and with no public address a steward would come down the train, opening all the compartment doors announcing *'last call for lunch'*. Although without the choice and high quality of more modern dining cars, it was too expensive for us. Huge silver pots of tea or coffee would be brought through the train, but for us children it was just warm squash from home. No cans of Coke then. For reasons best known to them, today's train operators don't like to use 'buffet' and have branded them with a range of names from shop, to bar to café. First Great Western's was an 'Express Café'. The young lady serving was bright and friendly and I enjoyed a bacon baguette as we headed west.

The races were on at Newbury, the first time I'd seen the racecourse in action in the many times I'd been by. I did use Newbury Racecourse station a couple of times to visit a customer for work – another who found it strange that I'd come by train. Our stop at Newbury was extended while the guard (sorry Train Manager) helped an elderly lady get on with a walking frame. There may no longer be porters on the platforms, but if arranged in advance all our railways are very willing to provide personal help to elderly or disabled travellers.

From Newbury it's a scenic ride alongside the Kennet and Avon Canal. The line, which was originally built as a branch, is quite curvy and allowed plenty of opportunities for 1960s schoolboys to glimpse the locomotive at the head of the train. I used to spend a lot of the journey looking out the window and still enjoy watching the countryside pass by, although don't get quite the same thrill to see the engine. Just after Pewsey I spotted the first of three white horses that we always looked out for on the chalky Wiltshire hills. The largest of these is cut from the chalk just before Westbury.

Non stopping trains miss the busy junction of Westbury by running round the cut off, as do virtually all expresses at Frome, where the avoiding line became the main line. I used Frome several times for work, until sadly my last visit was to buy back stock from the company's receiver. Bruton church was a landmark I recalled from childhood journeys. Sometimes we'd be held up on this section, getting behind a Bristol – Weymouth train, which shared the line as far as Castle Cary. I've never got off here, but have stopped when thousands of muddy and slightly smelly festival-goers were returning from nearby Glastonbury. Freight trains too used to hold us up, a less common occurrence now with fewer on the system and those that remain generally running faster. If we stopped at a signal Dad and I would lean out of the window to see what was going on, something still possible on HSTs but not on most modern trains.

The last time I stopped at Taunton on a day train our entry to the station was delayed by 'swans on the line', bringing mutterings of 'Reggie Perrin' from along the carriage. In the middle of a wild autumn night in 2004 I spent a couple of hours here.

Travelling to meet Deb and the boys in Torquay after watching West Ham at Chelsea, I arrived at Paddington to find that storms had closed the line at Dawlish and coaches were taking passengers from Exeter to Plymouth. We weren't allowed to use the sleeper berths as these were being kept for London-bound passengers, who would join the train to travel back from Exeter. One businessman however made such a fuss that they let him have a bed. He however didn't get to Devon. We were halted at Taunton as a freight train was having trouble climbing Wellington Bank and no one knew if it would make it. After some time the eastbound passengers arrived on an HST from Exeter. They were put in the sleeper and once the freight eventually cleared the summit, the HST took us on to Exeter. The awkward businessman had to be woken from his bed at Taunton but decided to sleep on and return to London. The rest of us gave not a small chuckle when we heard the sleeper had broken down at Bristol and he too had been put on an HST, but that while we made it to the West Country, he was back at Paddington! In contrast I actually got to my destination earlier than expected. To save me being dumped off a bus in the night at Plymouth, the buffet steward from the sleeper kindly gave me a lift to Torquay.

We had a few 'interesting' journeys in our childhood. My red book describes one in August 1974, when our ten coaches pulled by a Class 50 stopped for 38 minutes at Westbury. There had been a derailment at Taunton and we were diverted via Yeovil, arriving at Exeter St David's facing east. With a 33 minute stop for the locomotive to run round, we eventually arrived at Newton Abbot five hours after leaving Paddington. At Easter the same year *Western Empress* had to be replaced at Reading, but such was the availability of locomotives, after stopping for just thirteen minutes, we departed in the charge of a Class 47. Nowadays they are so few and far between that it wouldn't be unusual to wait a couple of hours for a rescue engine to arrive.

In August 1968, as we waited on the 8.30 from Paddington, a huddle of suited men and press photographers walked down the platform. We were being joined by Prime Minister Harold Wilson en route to his son's wedding in Dawlish. Dad took us along the platform and as we looked into his coach Mr Wilson waved to my five year old sister. Part way to Devon the train stopped. There was a problem with one of the coaches which had to be shunted out. The Prime Minister was delayed and Dad recalls a fast run with the driver making every effort to get him to the church on time.

Just west of Taunton we passed the junction for the West Somerset Railway. Since we travelled to Minehead in 1967 the line has been closed and reopened as Britain's longest steam railway. Unfortunately, like too many preserved railways, for regular traffic the link to the main line remains closed.

The climb up Wellington Bank scarcely slowed our HST, although steam and diesel locomotives pulling long trains found it more of a struggle. It was descending here that in 1904 *City of Truro* was reported to be the first engine to reach 100mph. Exiting Whiteball Tunnel under the Blackdown Hills signalled arrival in Devon, another milestone which we'd always look out for on our journey west.

Tiverton Parkway is the only new station on the line, replacing Tiverton Junction which closed in 1986. With the branch to Tiverton having closed, very few trains stopped, but although even further from the town, the new station is well used. Parkway stations, located close to motorways, are a fairly recent but successful addition to our railway system. We used to enjoy overtaking cars on what was initially the A38 Cullompton Bypass and became the M5, Dad tutting at the occasional driver who broke the speed limit to race us.

From Exeter to Newton Abbot we always looked out of the window on the famous stretch of railway along the Exe and Teign estuaries, with open sea between them. At Powderham Castle we'd look for deer in the grounds, often spotting the herd under the trees. Then our eyes were to the left and the sea. Approaching Dawlish Warren we'd spy the wreck – just a mast poking out the sea at high tide, but a black shell when the waters fall. My parents remember it when they passed by as children.

For the stretch along the sea wall one can hardly fail to watch the passing view. People walking on the beach stopped to wave, as they will to a train and perhaps a boat, but no other form of transport. Dawlish station overhangs the beach and every so often waves crashing over the wall force the line to be closed. One stormy day Mum was stuck in a tunnel for four hours as they waited for the tide to fall. A neighbour had to meet us from school, but she was home in time for tea and the excitement of seeing her train on the BBC News.

I remember an old style speed limit sign with cut out yellow numbers showing 40mph along the sea wall. The modern red number on a white board indicates that it's now 60mph, and the trains are perceivably much faster as they negotiate the curves and five short tunnels to Teignmouth. Still a working port, Teignmouth marks the end of the open sea and was our sign to start packing up. Newton Abbot was just eight minutes away.

It still seems strange not to alight, but I stayed on the train to Torquay. At Kingskerswell I looked up to the hill and *Mimosa*, the house my grandparents lived in, and where we have many happy memories of helping in the garden, football on the lawn and just being with Grandpa and Grandma. The station here, which we used when I was very young, closed in 1964, although the old overgrown platforms remain, so we frequented Devon General's maroon Number 12 double decker buses.

The delayed departure from Paddington meant we were running six minutes late, but thankfully the guard hadn't bothered with the far too frequent and unnecessary apologies that we so often even get with a short delay. Approaching Torquay the train passes the Abbey View Holiday Apartments where we stayed several times with the boys. When Kieron was young, a wave from the Torbay Express driver provided rather more excitement than it would now!

We've been coming to Torquay for as long as I remember. It is probably familiarity and memories that make it one of my favourite places. The town has changed, but less than many. Parts have improved, but without going through the run down stage that many resorts suffered. In some ways it's gone a bit more up market, with fewer family cafes and a marina bringing in yachting types, but hen weekends and large numbers of young people in pubs and clubs make evenings very different to forty years ago. Big improvements are the cill that keeps water in the inner harbour, and pedestrianisation of the main street and most of the harbourside.

I walked along the coast path to Daddyhole Plain, then back down to the main beach where hundreds of foreign students were enjoying a not very quiet evening. In summer Torquay is highly cosmopolitan, with students from across Europe coming to language schools. Some of the locals complain, but it adds atmosphere and vitality to the town.

I stayed two nights at the excellent Torcroft Hotel, which I'd used when travelling to Burgh Island for *No Boat Required* and visiting Torquay United for *Stand Up Sit Down*. My most important criteria for an overnight stop are walking distance from railway station, friendly staff, quiet room and good breakfast. The Torcroft passes with flying colours.

My travels on revived Devon railways are covered in the next chapter, so we shall move on to the journey home.

Newton Abbot station has changed from the times our grandparents used to meet and see off us. The four platforms which had been in place since

1927 were reduced to three in 1987, with level access to the car park. No longer did passengers have to climb steps to the bridge and pass the ticket barrier before descending to the booking hall. Stairs up from the bridge level led to the offices of publisher David & Charles, co-owned by David St John Thomas who has become a best selling railway author and wrote one of my favourite books, *Remote Britain*.

In World War Two the station was badly bombed, the junction seen as an important target by the Germans. Fourteen people died on a raid in 1940. For many years *Tiny*, an old broad gauge locomotive, stood on the platform providing a link with the past, but this now resides in the museum of the South Devon Railway at Buckfastleigh. A fine set of semaphore signals stood at the western end of the station. When the line was resignalled these were bought by David St John Thomas as a gift to the town, and still stand at the entrance to the industrial estate that was built on the old goods yard and works.

It was from the old Platform Four that we usually caught a train home. I'd watch intently for the first sight of it sweeping under the bridge to see whether we had a 'Western'. Sometimes Paignton and Plymouth portions would be joined in the platform, giving a longer stop and less of a rush to find seats.

Today I waited near the front – in a rare treat I was to travel home in the restaurant car. And what a treat it was. Far grander than the gammon and chips I had the first time I'd eaten dinner on a train, coming back from my grandfather's funeral in 1987. First Great Western operate just four restaurant cars, but their silver service Pullman Dining is the finest on Britain's railways. Tables were beautifully laid, with complimentary glass bottles of mineral water and hard backed menus. My first drink arrived as we skirted the Teign. Lunch orders were taken alongside the Exe. The steward advised that my choice of lamb comes pink, but said they could serve it well done, although '*it would break the chef's heart*'. Hot bread rolls with pats of butter arrived after Exeter and my rump of lamb as we approached Taunton. Served with Cornish potatoes and perfectly cooked vegetables, it was superb. Portions were ample so I was glad to have declined a starter and saved room for an elderflower tart covered with fresh strawberries – excellent.

Nine passengers were dining – a mix of business people and older travellers with the appearance of being comfortably off – and me! With superb food, attentive staff and the English countryside passing by the window, it made for a lovely atmosphere. It wasn't cheap, but no more than one would pay in a good restaurant, and with the bonus of that ever changing view. The two lunchtime restaurant services from Plymouth return in the early evening. The steward told me both would be full. The Pullman restaurant is a travel experience that I'd recommend everyone try at least once in their life.

For a final comparison of journeys old and new I've gone back to my red book, comparing the fastest point to point timings (in either direction) of seven runs between 1973 and 1975, with the best on this 2012 trip (yes I dutifully recorded all the stops as I used to!).

	1973-75 (Minutes)	2012 (Minutes)	Change
Reading – Paddington	29	24 $^{1}/_{2}$	-16%
Reading – Newbury	17	14 $^{1}/_{2}$	-15%
Westbury – Taunton	47	44 $^{3}/_{4}$	-5%
Taunton – Exeter	27	22	-19%
Exeter – Newton Abbott	21	18 $^{1}/_{4}$	-13%

Such limited data can only provide an indication of performance, but suggests acceleration by around 15%.

From old timetables I've then looked at average timings from Newton Abbot to London, the following table being based on the first five departures after 8am (ignoring any unusual services such as via Bristol).

Timetable	Average Time (Minutes)	Average Stops
1962	221	4
1976	204	6
1986	179	6
1996	170	7
2007	167	5
2012	168	5

The number of stops has to be taken into account, but if five minutes are added adjusting for one less calling point in 2012, the average works out at 15% faster than 1976, matching my station to station timings.

Acceleration from 1962 to 1976 reflects the change from the under-powered *Warship* diesel locomotives which replaced steam, to the Class 50s that took over from the *Westerns*. The further step change to 1986 shows the effect of HSTs, with some reduction ten years later down to track improvements. For the last fifteen years timings have remained constant, with any acceleration negated by extra recovery time. Fuel economy has now rightly become a concern and with 'defensive driving' and drivers closely monitored, timings tend to be more uniform. With talk of electrification or tilting trains, the next fifty years can expect to see further reductions. It will though be a sad day if the restaurants and Travelling Chefs that help make travel to the West Country such a pleasure are lost on the way.

CHAPTER EIGHTEEN

THREE REVIVED RAILWAYS

Okehampton, Meldon & Kingswear

In 1960 Devon had some seventeen branch lines all or partly in the county, and two main routes to Plymouth. Now there are just the two routes from London, main lines to Plymouth and Paignton, plus three branches, one of which ends in Cornwall. Several lines however have been revived, with services ranging from miniature trams at Seaton, steam trains from Totnes to Buckfastleigh and 'National Rail' trains to Okehampton. The rest of my trip to Torquay I spent visiting three of these lines, all of which I'd travelled on in my childhood.

The four coach Pacer forming the 9.54 to Exeter, bumped, rocked and squealed its way round the curves that I'd glided over in an HST the day before. The guard was kept busy selling tickets. There'd been a long queue for the machine at Torquay and when I'd finally reached the front it didn't offer tickets to Okehampton. The line that closed in 1972 now has a service on Sundays in summer, funded by the County Council and operated by First Great Western.

My father and I had used the line shortly before closure, when walking on Dartmoor. On the return journey the driver had invited us into the cab of the 'train like our Romford train'. I remember watching the speedometer reach 70mph and the driver telling us how when he took charge of expresses between Paddington and Reading *'the needle is on the ninety all the way'*. He talked about the work that had recently been carried out to remove a speed restriction at Castle Cary, but that most drivers felt happier to keep a bit under the new 90mph limit.

At Exeter St David's twenty passengers joined the Pacer that pulled into Platform One. The destination blind was blank, but if proposals to fully reopen the line go ahead they'll need to make some new ones. We were to follow part of the old 'Southern' route to Plymouth, so set off northbound from Exeter, initially heading towards London, before branching off at Cowley Junction. After crossing the Exe it was a pleasant run beside the River Yeo and through Crediton, where six more passengers joined, before leaving the Barnstaple line just after Yeoford.

I must just mention my last trip to Barnstaple. I'd travelled from London to meet the rest of the family, before driving on to Bude and was intrigued at some of the unusual activity on the train. At Barnstaple all became clear. The BBC were filming probably the best known episode of *James May's Toy Story*, when they tried to run a Hornby railway all the way from Barnstaple to Bideford. The *Top Gear* presenter who likes trains (as opposed to the one who doesn't!) was there on the platform and a crowd of locals had come out to watch. Having travelled up from Exeter I can however tell one little secret – Oz Clarke, who had supposedly just brought James's favourite engine all the way from London, actually got on at Chapelton, the stop before Barnstaple!

Other than glimpses of Dartmoor as we approached Okehampton, the views from the train weren't as good as one might expect. With the single line tightly hemmed in between trees, it was hard to believe that expresses from Waterloo to Plymouth once ran on double track here. No one got on or off at Sampford Courtney, the only intermediate station, but we still got the full automated safety announcement.

Okehampton station, beautifully restored in Southern green, was a hive of activity. Sausages were being cooked on a barbecue on the platform, the café was doing a roaring trade and trains stood in both platforms; the '143' shortly to return to Exeter and a rather noisy two car green '205' unit ready to head off to Meldon. More of that later, but first I had a walk to complete.

In 1971 we'd walked fourteen miles to Cranmere Pool, a remote spot (although lacking a pool) in the centre of northern Dartmoor. Today I completed a more modest eight, climbing to High Willhays, the highest point in southern England, with superb views in all directions. It was good to be able to walk from train to moor, something that wasn't possible after Okehampton closed, until 1994 when Ivybridge on the Plymouth line reopened. A quick mention for my father here – he arrived at the new Ivybridge station on the first train to call there and was the first person to use it to walk to Dartmoor.

I misjudged the distance back so walked the last mile at a great pace, keen to catch the 17.10 Meldon train, but before that the station buffet which closed ten minutes earlier. Arriving hot, hungry and thirsty, I made it just in time, although the dithering of the lady serving almost made me miss the train. To my frustration, she stood watching my pasty warming in the microwave, rather than get the drink or take my money, so it needed a dash over the bridge to catch the train. They might have waited though – I was the only passenger.

The heritage Dartmoor Railway runs along a couple of miles of the original Plymouth route, as far as Meldon Quarry, for which the line was kept open for freight. Running on the edge of the moors and passing Okehampton Castle, it's a more scenic ride than the journey up from Exeter. Trains terminate at a new station, a short distance from Meldon Viaduct which spectacularly spans the River Okement. A cycle path now crosses the bridge, part of the eight mile Granite Way along the old trackbed to Lydford. A path from the station leads up onto Dartmoor and a family were waiting for the train having been on the moors. With just fifteen minutes here though, I had time for just a quick walk part way over the bridge.

It was forty four years since I'd last crossed it, shortly before the line was closed beyond Okehampton. We'd set out to walk on the moors from Bridestowe, but had to curtail as I was scared of the strong wind, so returned along the road to Lydford. We'd brought a little spirit stove to cook bacon, but hadn't used it because of the wind and I recall asking my father if they allowed frying on Lydford station. He didn't think they did but I remember wondering why anyone would mind if we set up our stove at the end of the platform.

Back at Meldon Quarry I chatted to the driver who agreed that it was good to see that trains other than steam were preserved and running on heritage lines. He said it was a couple of years since the railway had had a steam engine, but some visitors are disappointed to find diesels running. The '205' unit had spent its working life in the South East and would never have run in Devon. It is one of our more unusual trains, with the appearance of being third rail electric, but actually having a large and noisy diesel engine in the end of one of the coaches. Whilst the outside was painted in 1960s green, the interior retained signs of its more recent use, with 'London Connections' maps on the walls. With slam doors and luggage racks over the seats, if I didn't look at Dartmoor out of the window I could have been back in 1970s suburban London.

The 17.59 to Exeter was dispatched by a man in a perfect Southern Railway uniform, with green jacket, tie – and a white sun hat: not quite how First Great Western trains are sent off at Paddington!

Torquay booking office was closed again the next morning but a member of staff was helping passengers who struggled with the machine. Wouldn't he have been better to have opened the office I wondered? I got my ticket just in time for the 10.01 to Paignton. We were scheduled to take ten minutes for the two miles by the sea to Paignton. Those going the other way take five minutes – another example of padding to artificially improve punctuality? Hence we were early and stopped outside Paignton. The guard made the standard apology 'for any inconvenience caused' even though we still arrived on time.

The Paignton to Kingswear line is a rare preserved railway that exists as much to provide a service as to give people a ride on a steam train. Unlike most steam railways, there's little in the way of museums and locomotive sheds to look round, the company concentrating on running an intensive summer service to Kingswear, from where the majority of passengers take the short ferry trip to the historic town of Dartmouth. Three coach parties were unloading outside. Passengers were met in the large entrance hall by a lady explaining the various trips available by train and boat. Unusually for a preserved railway it doesn't rely on volunteer labour and is a profit making organisation. It certainly gave the impression of a serious commercial operation, not just 'men playing trains'. The company owns just four steam and one diesel locomotive, but in the height of the summer runs nine trains a day, a ride on this most scenic coastal line being a must for Torbay holidaymakers.

It's a trip I've made many times, most frequently with my youngest son when a ride on a steam train was still his favourite day out, something that stopped when he reached about ten and trains were no longer 'cool'. I recall just one journey prior to British Rail closing the line in 1973, when in the absence of the steam factor, far fewer passengers used the line, although at least they had the possibility of travelling all year round. Trains started running again very shortly after the line 'closed', but the winter diesel service lasted just one year. To keep it going would have required a far smaller subsidy than the line received prior to closure, and what a shame that the council and railway operators cannot work together to provide a service throughout the year.

Our seven well filled coaches were hauled by the immaculately turned out steam locomotive *Lydham Manor*, which was built at Swindon in 1950 and withdrawn after just fifteen years service. After residing in Barry scrap yard for several years, she was bought and restored by the Dart Valley Railway and now spends busy summers pulling trains by the seaside.

The line is one of the most scenic in the country. After passing the sidings that were once filled with coaches for the many locomotive hauled trains that ran to the English Riviera, we stopped at Goodrington, where screams from children on outdoor water slides competed with puffing from the engine. People stopped to wave as we passed above the beach, the engine working hard as we climbed towards Broadsands Viaduct and on to the line's summit at Churston. A branch from here to Brixham closed in 1963 – my father recalls that the guard's van used to smell of fish. Colour light signals control the train, but the guard still used a traditional green flag to wave us off, not the rigid 'lollipop' now used by dispatchers on National Rail.

Next stop was the newly opened Greenway Halt, where passengers alight for Agatha Christie's house, a short walk through the woods. Emerging from Greenway Tunnel we were by the River Dart, which the line follows to Kingswear. It's arguable as to whether the first part of the ride by open sea or the latter alongside the wooded river, is the most picturesque.

Most passengers took the ferry to Dartmouth, arriving at a unique 'railway' station. It looks like a railway station, was run by the railway company, but never received a train. Initial plans to bridge the Dart failed to materialise, so Dartmouth passengers completed their journey by boat.

With limited time before my train back to London, I reboarded to return to Paignton. This time I travelled not in a fifty year old British Rail compartment coach, but an observation car that was almost a hundred years old and had started life as an ambulance coach in the First World War. It was one of two to have been used on the Devon Belle from Waterloo to Ilfracombe, and later in the Scottish Highlands. The other has recently been restored and sees use on the Swanage Railway. With twenty seven comfortable seats and large windows on three sides, this was the ideal way to enjoy the superb ride back along the South Devon coast.

In pouring rain a Cardiff bound '158' took me from Paignton to Newton Abbot, for the HST back to London and as described in the previous chapter – lunch!

CHAPTER NINETEEN

HAMPSHIRE & DORSET

London – New Milton – Lymington & Swanage

Although I travelled in steam days, my first memory of visiting Southampton is just after third rail electrification in 1967. My father and I went round the *Queen Mary* on her last visit to her home port before the ship was withdrawn. I recall having afternoon tea in the restaurant car as we returned to London and am told that when the steward brought round a tray of cakes I took two, but eyes being bigger than tummy, was only able to eat one.

Today there was no chance of afternoon tea, or even a buffet, refreshments comprising merely a trolley. I was on the 11.35 from Waterloo to Weymouth, a five car 'Desiro 444' electrical multiple unit, built in Austria. No longer are most of our trains made in England. On a summer Saturday, virtually every seat was taken in Standard Class and my five pound upgrade to First, excellent value. The air conditioning was noisy, but very welcome on a hot day. The trains are functional, but with the feel of commuter stock despite the 143 mile run. Closure of the buffets in favour of trolleys didn't help, although generally railways say sales are higher from the latter. People are reluctant to leave laptops and luggage, and more likely to buy a cup of tea if someone walks by asking them, but of course the choice is less. East Coast are now the only operator to regularly run trains with both buffets and trolleys.

The Southampton trains on which I travelled as a child had the appeal (for small boys) that passengers could look into the empty cabs at the centre of the train where sets were linked, and see the speedometer. I would make regular trips to check the speed, watching for the needle reaching the magic 90mph and sometimes a little more.

They were replaced in 1988 by the smart new 100mph 'Wessex Electrics'. These popular trains enabled timetables to be accelerated, taking just 58 minutes non stop for the 70 miles from London to Southampton Airport Parkway. With extra stops journeys are now slightly slower. In April 1988, with dispensation to exceed 100mph, a special run to Weymouth was accomplished in a fraction under 2 hours, beating the old record by more than 45 minutes. The top speed of 108mph represents a world record for a third rail train.

Our childhood journeys usually involved 'The Drain', the Waterloo and City Line from Bank to Waterloo. This and the Devils Bridge narrow gauge steam line in North Wales, were British Rail's most unusual railways. The Jubilee Line now gives us a quicker route to Waterloo, although it's so busy in the evening rush hour that I tend to avoid it. How did all these passengers travel before it was built? The answer of course is that far more people use both the underground and surface trains than in the 1960s.

In terms of passenger numbers Waterloo is by some way our busiest station, with over 91 million entries and exits in the year ending March 2011. Various refurbishments have resulted in a much brighter concourse than that we used in the 1960s, and the recent opening of a balcony with a range of good quality catering outlets is a welcome addition to the station. The famous four faced clock, under which people have met for almost a hundred years, still hangs from the roof in the middle of the concourse. Two platforms were lost for domestic services when the Eurostar terminal opened in 1994, but despite international trains moving to St Pancras in 2007, they are now unused. One is due to be brought back into service in 2014, but for such a busy station to have platforms lying idle reflects poorly on how our railways are run.

The view of London as the train leaves Waterloo has changed over the years, with the London Eye perhaps the most notable addition. The iconic Battersea Power Station remains, although no longer generating electricity. New buildings have obscured the view of the Oval cricket ground as the train passes Vauxhall. A sign at Clapham Junction announces 'Britain's Busiest Railway Station'. Around 2,000 trains pass through here very day with more than a hundred an hour stopping at peak times.

Once clear of London's outskirts, the route passes through fairly unremarkable scenery, with not a great deal of interest to view until

Southampton. Most trains stop at Winchester and either Basingstoke or Woking. Today we called at the latter, where on my last trip we'd sat for over an hour due to a suicide further down the line. I'd arrived at New Milton two hours late and when I returned in the evening trains were still delayed. South West Trains however kept us informed and even sent a member of staff to talk to everyone on the train to make sure they were OK. I have found them to be one of our better operators and can't recall having written even one letter of complaint.

At Basingstoke the 'Southern' line to Exeter branches off. My only through journey on this was behind a steam engine on our 1963 holiday to Woolacombe, a destination I didn't return to thanks to Dr Beeching's foolish closure of the Ilfracombe branch. I've made many business trips as far as Andover, the first in 1990 behind a Class 50 locomotive. Today's '159' DMUs have reduced the journey time and are comfortable, if a little noisy.

Virtually all trains now stop at Southampton Airport Parkway, linking with the terminal a few yards away. What a shame though that the airport's busiest destination is Edinburgh, with around 200,000 journeys a year, and that cross country rail still struggles to compete with planes. Fares are similar but through trains take around seven hours. It's quicker and often cheaper to go via London – and you get more than a choice of three sandwiches for sustenance.

The original station here was built in 1929, not to serve the airport but a transit camp opened in the hangars for mostly Russian refugees waiting to sail to America. Atlantic Park Hostel Halt later closed, but in 1966 Southampton Airport Halt opened to serve the airport, although it was some years before it saw large numbers of passengers.

A recent addition to the view as trains approach Southampton Central is St Mary's Stadium, which in common with many changes to our railways, has higher capacity but less atmosphere than The Dell which it replaced.

As a young child I travelled to Southampton on a number of occasions but the *Queen Mary* trip is the first I remember. I recall the plush bedrooms, long corridors and being told the ship was almost a quarter of a mile long (it was actually about a fifth). Whilst memories are dim, I'm glad to have been on a ship which along with the *Queen Elizabeth*, dominated transatlantic passenger travel until the dawn of the jet age in the late 1950s.

A few months earlier we'd had our only South Coast holiday, staying at Milford on Sea, which we'd reached by bus from New Milton station. Today I was repeating the journey to New Milton, one which I've done often in recent years to see my Aunty Dora, who after ninety-three years living within the same square mile of Southampton, now resides in a retirement home. On each visit I learn snippets of her long and interesting life. Today she was to tell me of bank holiday trips on paddle steamers to the Isle of Wight. Her father George worked in the payroll office of the docks and as these were owned by the Southern Railway they always holidayed at places on the South Coast or the West Country that could be reached by the company's trains using privilege passes.

Leaving Southampton the line runs parallel with the docks, where containers piled high on ships were being loaded onto trains. This is one of the relatively rare places where locomotives can be seen waiting in sidings, once a common sight across the country. From here it's a lovely ride through the New Forest, where ponies, and more often than not deer, are seen through the window.

New Milton is an ordinary town, but Milford on Sea a pleasant seaside village with views to the Isle of Wight. As usual for our holidays we spent time on the beach and made trips out by train. The two which I recall best I've repeated in part, forty-five years on.

After a couple of hours with Aunty Dora I caught the next London train, but got off at Brockenhurst. From this village in the heart of the New Forest we'd travelled on the branch to Lymington, then caught the ferry to Yarmouth on the Isle of Wight.

For four years until 2009 the trains used on the branch were similar to those we'd travelled on in 1967 – slam door Mark One electric units. Hundreds of such trains, which were the mainstay of London commuter services, were scrapped after safety legislation banned their use. Although they had a good overall record, they were considered less safe than modern rolling stock and had a tendency for coaches to override onto each other in the event of a serious collision (as occurred in the 1988 Clapham disaster). After modifications, including fitting of central door locking, an exception was made to allow two units to run on the self contained Lymington branch. These were painted in the green that was used on the Southern Region until BR made everything blue and white. The branch was marketed a 'Heritage Route' and I often saw trains being photographed by enthusiasts as I passed by on my way to New Milton.

South West Trains replaced them with modern electric units at weekends, but with none spare in the week, '158' Sprinters run from Monday to Friday. While passengers on much longer runs elsewhere in the country have to make do with overcrowded Pacers, these diesel units which were designed for longer runs, shuttle up and down the 5½ mile electrified branch. Such is the way of our privatised railway.

It's a nice ride across heathland, stopping at Lymington Town, then crossing the harbour to Pier Station. Quite a crowd got on at Town for the half mile hop to the ferry, but with no time for checks on the two minute journey I wondered how many had bothered to pay the £2.30 return fare (two thirds of what I'd paid from Brockenhurst for a tenth of the distance).

After getting off at Lymington Town on the return, I must have missed the sign that said 'posh people only'. With three marinas it is a yachting town and the shops and restaurants reflect the up-market visitors it attracts. We'd been promised a month's rain in a day but so far it had stayed dry. Ignoring brooding clouds I set out for a walk down the river. Within minutes the heavens opened. Most of the month's rain seemed to have fallen in half an hour. Thirty minutes later I was back at Lymington station – soaked! Inevitably as I walked onto the platform the rain stopped.

Our second trip in 1967 was to Wareham, where we changed to the branch to Corfe Castle and Swanage. Later that year British Rail announced that the line would close, however vociferous local opposition forced a Public Inquiry. After hearing evidence that buses couldn't handle the weight of summer traffic, the Inspector ruled that it should stay open. It was not electrified and served by Class 205 diesel electric units, a preserved example of which I'd recently seen on the Dartmoor Railway. A shortage of such trains and the governments refusal to allow BR to buy more, led to further pressure for closure, and the Secretary of State eventually overturned the Inquiry's decision. The line closed in January 1972.

Within four months the Swanage Railway Society was formed, with the aim to run all year round 'community' services, subsidised by the operation of steam-hauled heritage trains in the tourist season. British Rail responded by ripping up the track. Without backing from the County Council (who wanted to use the trackbed for a bypass at Corfe) and Swanage Town Council (who wanted to demolish the station), progress was slow, but by 1979 trains were running on a short length of track in Swanage. In 1995 the line was opened through Corfe to Norton, where a park and ride facility helps reduce traffic on the busy road to the coast.

On 3rd January 2002, thirty years to the day after the line closed, a temporary connection was made restoring the link with the main line at Wareham. Later that year a Virgin Voyager became the first through train to visit Swanage, but although the link was later made permanent, only occasional charter trains run over it.

The line is a popular tourist attraction and in summer provides a genuine transport service, but although the founders' aims of an all year round service linking Swanage with the main railway system are yet to be achieved, progress is being made. Government money has been promised to upgrade the track and heritage DMUs are expected to start operating to Wareham in the summer of 2015. It took British Rail seven weeks to lift seven miles of track, but forty three years later it seems that it won't be too long before passengers will be able to change at Wareham for Swanage as we did in 1967.

Taking advantage of our youngest son being on school exchange in Berlin, a few months before my New Milton trip Deb and I had spent three days in Swanage. Of course I repeated my childhood journey, not in a steam train, but another train from my past – a 'train like our Romford train'. The Class 108 'first generation' DMU was similar to trains we'd travelled on all over the country until withdrawal in 1990. This was as nostalgic to me as the steam locomotives were to older generations – two or three green coaches, seats behind the driver and a characteristic engine noise – they were fine for short runs but always seemed to be wrongly geared for high speed or hills.

Like all the line's stations, Swanage is beautifully restored and painted in the traditional Southern green. Herston Halt, a request stop on the town's outskirts was rebuilt in 2009 by volunteers from the 11th Signal Regiment, 300 of whom then exercised their right to march through the town with swords drawn and bayonets fixed. Corporal Jones would have loved it – 'they don't like it up em!'.

Travelling on the last train of the day, I had no time to explore Corfe but waited on the picturesque station close to one of England's most famous ruined castles, for the DMU to return from Norton. I was the only passenger coming back. The guard said I needn't feel guilty at the train running just for me – the driver was enjoying himself too!

Postscript

Shortly before this book went to press my Aunty Dora was taken into hospital in Lymington. I made four trips down to see her.

On the first, I was caught out by the perils of modern ticketing – complexity, illogical restrictions and misinformation, so bought a ticket for £20 more than was necessary. Being midweek, a diesel '158' was running on the electrified Lymington branch.

On the second, the train from London was slightly late, arriving at Brockenhurst ninety seconds after the Lymington train was due to depart. It wasn't held. My conversation with the gentleman in the booking office elicited several possible reasons why, then admitted the real one: South West Trains get fined if the train arrives late, so they choose to let it leave for Lymington rather than wait for passengers.

On the third, I noticed the superfluous automated announcements at Lymington Town. '*The next train at Platform One*' (there is only one platform), '*is for Brockenhurst, calling at Brockenhurst only. Customers for London should change at Brockenhurst.*'

On the fourth, I encountered a guard who called me sweetheart and a surly passenger who believed his dog was entitled to occupy a seat.

Such are the vagaries of modern train travel.

And I gained one more snippet from Aunty Dora's long life. Aged ten, in July 1925 her father took her on the first day of operation of the Totton to Fawley branch line.

CHAPTER TWENTY

TO THE FAR NORTH

London – Aberdeen – Inverness – Forsinard – Altnabreac

My final journey started as had my first – on a sleeper from London. This time I was on the way to Aberdeen, enjoying chocolate pudding and custard in a busy lounge car. The steward recommended lemon pudding but I stayed with the chocolate that I'd last sampled returning from Fort William in February. Sharing my table was Janet, a charming lady who runs the tourist information centre at Gairloch on the west coast and who ordered five copies of *No Boat Required*.

The lounge car is shared with Fort William passengers, one of whom was a quite elderly lady. As she sipped a gin and tonic she told us she wasn't travelling alone – her 101 year old mother was back in the cabin! They travel regularly to stay with family in London, the only way the mother, who apparently sleeps well, can manage the journey.

My first journey on a sleeper had been returning from holiday in Aberdeen in 1962. Aged eighteen months, I'd apparently said 'cot on train' and fallen asleep as we crossed the Forth Bridge. Tonight I got even less sleep. The man in the next cabin was a snorer and kept me awake for hours. After a while I detected a pattern and thought that perhaps counting snores rather than sheep would send me to sleep. After a burst of action there'd be a lull for about fifty seconds, then the rasping sound would return. Banging on the wall sometimes resulted in a lull but within a couple of minutes he'd be at it again. I'd vowed to confront him at Aberdeen but soon after Edinburgh the noise stopped. He'd got off. I slept until Stonehaven, waking to a view of the sun rising over the North Sea.

Aberdeen certainly meets up to its name as the Granite City. Its solid grey buildings seem to invite dismal weather, although the locally quarried granite is said to sparkle in sunshine. North Sea oil has brought prosperity to the city, which has one of the busiest commercial heliports in the world and a large harbour with boats servicing the rigs. I came here one December afternoon after a meeting in Glasgow, walking several miles along the beach where patches of frozen snow lay on the sand. It was for the beach and surrounding scenery that my parents chose to come here and although it seems an unusual choice, fifty years ago the city was marketed as a family holiday destination.

Today I had time for just a short look at the city before travelling back south for a meeting in Dundee. I'd chosen to stay on the sleeper rather than alight in Dundee at 6am, a decision also influenced by there being a left luggage facility in Aberdeen. It makes a big difference not having to lug a bag round all day, but the man who checked my rucksack told me it may be closing. Clearly receipts don't cover the cost of the person who looks inside bags before putting them in a locker, but are the checks really necessary?

After enjoying a ridiculously cheap breakfast roll, I joined the 9.07 ScotRail '170' to Edinburgh. These are comfortable trains with large windows and it was an enjoyable ride along another spectacular but uncelebrated section of coastal railway. With rugged cliffs, steep gorges and rocks jutting into the sea, it reminded me of the line north from Berwick. The ruined churches surrounded by walled graveyards and distant views of the Breas Hills were however more characteristics of northern Scotland.

At Montrose we crossed the tidal Montrose Basin, a nature reserve which plays host to a range of birdlife, including up to 60,000 migrating geese each year. The station at Arbroath, the next stop, recently celebrated its centenary with a re-enactment of the scene on Christmas Eve 1911 when 'quite a crowd of excited citizens' had gathered to watch purchase of the first ticket by Mr Sutherland Banks, proprietor of the Imperial Hotel. A large mural on the platform commemorates the historic signing in 1320 of the Declaration of Arbroath, a letter to the Pope declaring Scotland's independence. The mural was moved to the station in 2009 after being destined for a skip. Also on the station is a plaque in remembrance of Matthew Kerr, the founder of Kerr's Miniature Railway, which runs parallel to the main line by the beach and is Scotland's oldest small railway.

At Carnoustie we passed the famous championship golf course. Two small stations serve the courses, Golf Street and Barry Links, both of which are amongst the least used in Britain and are served by just one train a day in each direction, although were considerably busier when the British Open was last held here in 1999.

With time to spare after my meeting in Dundee, I walked the mile or so to the Tay Bridge, which carries the railway across the Firth of Tay. The 2¾ mile bridge opened in 1887, replacing the original cast iron construction which collapsed as a train crossed on a stormy night in December 1879. All seventy five people on board perished in the icy water. The Inquiry found that the bridge did not allow for high winds and lessons were learned that still ensure the safety of railway travellers more than a hundred years later. In 2003 the bridge was strengthened and refurbished, with workers in the exposed conditions using hand tools to scrape more than a thousand tonnes of bird droppings from the ironwork lattice.

After returning to Aberdeen and another brief look at the city, I joined the 15.30 to Inverness. ScotRail provided a trolley for the 2¼ hour run, with bottles of water almost half the price of those in WH Smiths on the station. Those on the train were a reasonable size, whereas in a sign of our wasteful consumer society, Smiths now choose to sell drinks and crisps in packs larger than most people want.

This area of Scotland was once well served with railways, but only the line to Inverness escaped Beeching's axe. As a toddler I travelled from Aberdeen to Ballater, on the route used until 1965 by royal trains taking kings and queens to Balmoral. We continued to the royal castle by bus, walking round the grounds, something that security no longer permits. My parents had bought Holiday Runabout tickets and we travelled extensively, one day riding behind a diesel locomotive to Fraserburgh, where we changed to a DMU for the coastal branch to St Combs. Another day we changed at Maud Junction to visit Peterhead, which like Fraserburgh, is still a thriving fishing port and perhaps deserving of getting its railway back. One line we didn't go on (maybe my mother put her foot down?) was the branch from

Pitcaple to Macduff, which was then open only for freight, but passengers could travel in the brake van on payment of a First Class fare.

The Inverness line runs mostly through farmland with patches of semi-moorland as it follows the meandering River Bogie either side of Huntley. Thanks to the previous night's snoring monster I struggled to keep awake.

Most passengers were using intermediate stations, quite a few boarding at Elgin and travelling to Forres and Nairn. Also well used was Keith, in the heart of Scotland's whisky distilling country. It is the terminus of a heritage railway to Dufftown, although trains now start from Keith Town station. In 1961 we'd changed at what was then Keith Junction and travelled to Dufftown, from where we boarded a four wheel railbus on to Boat of Garten, which is now served by the Strathspey steam railway to Aviemore. In the opposite direction from Keith we travelled on the line to Banff, changing to a steam train at the wonderfully named Tillynaught Junction. What a shame that I was too young to remember riding these railways in an often forgotten corner of Scotland, which with their network of rural branches typified a railway age now past.

I like Inverness, principally for its river and castle that looks down on it, as the town itself is nothing special. Indeed the centre by the main bridge has been ruined by 1960s buildings, which raised the same question I ask myself in so many British towns – how could the Council have possibly thought that such concrete monstrosities could improve their town?

My B&B accommodation was probably the best value in all my travels. Moira at Fairfield Villa made me very welcome and provided a room that met all my needs. Quiet, comfortable and with the absence of the pile of unwanted cushions that one has to routinely remove from hotel beds before sleeping.

After a good dinner in the Castle Tavern, I enjoyed one of my favourite city walks – along the river to the Ness Islands, over the suspension bridges and back on the north bank. With mountains in the distance and fly fishermen by the river, Inverness is a fitting place to be Capital of the Highlands.

Over breakfast I chatted to two German ladies who were heading for Loch Ness, then popped into the tourist information centre, accessed up a flight of steps on one of the 1960s carbuncles. There must have been fifty people inside, the vast majority foreign tourists enquiring about Loch Ness.

Rather than returning to London, on this, my final trip, I was allowing a little self indulgence – a night in the wilds and a ride on a line I hadn't travelled on before. I joined the 10.38 to Wick.

As I sat at a table in the two coach '158', the guard announced the stops. There were two lists; first the stations where the train always stops and second the request halts. In another of the eccentricities of British railway lines, Georgemas Junction featured twice. Until the early 1990s the line was operated with locomotive hauled trains and the rear portion would be detached here, with another locomotive taking it to Thurso, while the rest of the train continued on to Wick. When four car '156' Sprinters took over the line they too divided at Georgemas Junction. Now the line is normally operated with two coach units which can't be split, so Wick passengers are taken to Thurso and back, before proceeding on to the terminus. It adds twenty three minutes to their journey, but a special dispensation means they're not charged for the additional miles!

As we slipped out of the curved platform the line turned sharply left, taking us over the River Ness on a steel bridge that was erected with great haste in 1990. This was to replace the previous 127 year old stone bridge that had been swept away by a flood tide the previous year, leaving 50 yards of twisted rails spanning the raging torrent. By the next day four of the five arches had gone and two hundred yards of track skimmed the surface of the water. Fortunately trains to Wick and Kyle of Lochalsh had already crossed safety so there were no casualties, although severance of the only rail connection to the North required passengers to be bussed to Dingwall, from where a special timetable operated using those trains stranded above the gap.

A swing bridge takes the line over the Caledonian Canal and the sea loch that links it to the Beauly Firth, the train making an audible clunk as it negotiates the short gap in the rails. From here it runs along the coast to the village of Beauly, where we stopped at the reopened station, which has one of the shortest platforms in Britain. Just one door on the train is opened but the station is remarkably well used. After reopening in 2002, 75% of commuters switched from road to rail, and in 2008 its annual usage of 36 journeys per head for the population of 1,164 ranked as one of the highest in Britain. Today two ladies boarded, booking to the summer only request stop of Dunrobin Castle.

At Dingwall the lines to Kyle of Lochalsh and the Far North diverge. The Kyle Line is a superb run, which Deb and I did on a locomotive hauled train in 1984, when we caught the ferry across to Skye. I used it again when visiting Gavin Maxwell's Sandaig Islands, writing in *No Boat Required*:

'From Inverness I headed west on a little train to Kyle of Lochalsh, another famously scenic ride, which featured in Michael Palin's series of 'Great Railway Journeys'. The 80 mile route runs from coast to coast, starting by the Beauly Firth and ending opposite the Isle of Skye. Heading inland from Dingwall we started to climb over the Highlands, reaching the still waters of Loch Garve which mirrored surrounding hills and trees. At Garve a coach party boarded, a sea of grey hair clustering around a single door as if the train were a coach. Their driver waved them off then set out to follow the train to Kyle.

The line follows the River Bran, which runs through lochs and meanders across a glacier-cut U shaped valley – a geographer's paradise. A buzzard flew alongside, only yards from the train window and a lone deer stood by the river's edge. More mountains reflected in the glasslike waters of Loch Achanalt. Ruined crofts reminded of the Highland Clearances when landowners cruelly evicted their tenants because more money could be made from grazing sheep. I made a note of Achnasheen as a place that I shall one day return to and walk along this beautiful valley.

The two coach train was surprisingly busy, with hardly a spare seat. Tourists heavily outnumbered locals, American and German accents mingling with those from England and Scotland. To the lady sitting opposite me however this was a vital transport link. She was returning from art college in Inverness to her home on the island of Benbacula, a journey that would take 8 hours, involving train to Kyle, bus to Uig on Skye, ferry to North Uist and finally a bus over the causeway to Benbacula.

Approaching the west coast the line runs along Loch Carron, twisting and turning around inlets of this sea loch that extends 13 miles inland. Although we had reached the sea at Strathcarron it was another 45 minutes before

*the train pulled into Kyle of Lochalsh, from where ferries once ran to Skye.
It is now bypassed by most visitors who drive straight over the bridge.'*

I'd considered going to Achnasheen today, but decided instead to experience
our most northerly railway, stopping a night at the remote settlement of
Forsinard.

Just beyond Dingwall station we passed Victoria Park, home to Ross County
Football Club, who improbably play in the Scottish Premier League. From
here the line runs by the sea again, following Cromarty Firth through
Alness and Invergordon, then across farmland to Tain. I'd come here to visit
a tidal island on the RAF bombing range, but the lack of any car hire
facility in the town meant I'd had to drive from Inverness, before crossing to
some remote spots on the west coast. Some kind of simple to use nationwide
car hire facility at railway stations, similar to the excellent bike scheme in
London, would allow more people to use the train for the bulk of journeys
when they need the flexibility of a car for the last bit. In my youth major
stations had Godfrey Davies car hire, but now even some large cities don't
have hire facilities at their railway stations.

From Tain the train dives inland following the Dornoch Firth towards
Lairg, while the road takes the direct route over a bridge which opened in
1991. A campaign to divert the railway over the bridge failed, but the
government did agree to a design modification with more gentle approaches,
so that trains could potentially use it at a future date. If the line is ever built
the tracks would share the bridge, with cars stopped as trains cross. It
would save forty minutes on the journey although users of the 'Lairg Loop'
would lose their railway unless this was retained as a branch.

Perhaps conscious that we were heading in the wrong direction, the driver set
off at a fair lick, beats of the jointed track registering 77mph along the sea
wall. It was a lovely ride alongside sandbanks teaming with bird life. After
stopping at Culrain we crossed the Kyle of Sutherland, with a superb view up
the river, but no one requested a halt at Invershin the other side of the Oykel
Viaduct. The two stations are just 750 yards apart (thirty-four chains in the
ancient units still used by the railways), making these two of the closest on the
network. Following pressure from the Friends of the Far North Line (FoFNL)
a footbridge was constructed alongside the lattice girder bridge so pedestrians
can walk across, but for cars it's an eight mile journey via Bonar Bridge.

From Invershin we started climbing up the Shin Valley to Lairg. This isolated village is the northern terminus for the 'Invernet' commuter train from Inverness, a successful service bringing workers into Inverness from three directions. Running east through the hills we passed the request stop of Rogart without halting. Camping coaches by the track, once a common site in holiday areas, offer hostel accommodation. With a ten per cent discount to those arriving by train, this is another place to add to my list of 'will visit one day'.

Now we were heading south east, away from Wick, but back to the sea. Golspie, our next stop, is just seventeen miles by road from Tain. Our forty mile loop inland had taken an hour. The next fifteen miles was one of the wildest stretches of coastal railway I'd seen. I had expected valleys, mountains and moors, but this run alongside the rugged North Sea coast was a bonus. I saw not one person, but many birds, several groups of seals, and most excitingly, otters at the water's edge. Although often called 'sea otters' they are actually the same species that inhabit freshwater further inland. Around half of Scotland's otter population are thought to live by the sea, but the true sea otter lives only in the north Pacific.

The convoluted route continues with a ninety degree turn inland, following the fast flowing River Helmsdale into hills which were starting to turn purple with heather. Now the scenery was getting wilder. This was the real Scotland, which those whose visit includes just Edinburgh never get to see, but there were few tourists amongst the twenty or so passengers on the train.

No one got on or off at Kildonan, which was the unlikely centre for a gold rush in 1868. Within six months of the announcement that gold had been found, 600 hopeful prospectors had arrived, with two shanty towns growing up in the glen. At the time the railway had been built only as far as Golspie, so adventurers had to hike the last thirty miles. As the price dropped and finds were less than hoped, the rush soon subsided, but flecks and the occasional nugget are still found and panning equipment can be hired in Helmsdale.

Soon we were heading north again and entering the Flow Country – 1500 square miles of wilderness, the largest area of blanket bog in Europe. The railway cuts a lonely tract across this inhospitable landscape, leaving the road at Forsinard, where wooden snow fences protect the track. From here it veers east towards Altnabreac, which rivals Corrour as the most isolated station in Britain.

It was at the tiny settlement of Forsinard where I was to spend the night. The train waited to pass a southbound service but I was the only passenger alighting from either. With just a handful of houses plus a hotel, Forsinard isn't the busiest of stations. Ten miles from the nearest shop, its isolation exceeded the small communities of Drumbeg and Salon on the west coast where I'd stayed on my tidal island journeys.

I set off to explore. I'd planned a walk along what my map showed as a track running several miles into the heart of the bog land. Just a semblance of the track though headed east and when my foot sank in to the ankle, I gave up. I'd only bought the map the previous day but a more modern one in the hotel showed it as just a path. John, the hotel proprietor and a most interesting man, told me it was once used for bringing in the deer. After sitting for a while on a rare rock to eat my lunch, I found a track the other way that took me close to the railway and its bridge over the Halladale River. We'd crossed the watershed and this was flowing north towards its mouth at the very top of Scotland.

Next I returned to the railway station. Not for trains but to the RSPB visitor centre in the waiting rooms. Here I picked up a leaflet for the Dubh Lochan trail, which was one of the most remarkable walks I've ever done. A mile long path of stone slabs winds its way across the bogs, passing tiny pools where a myriad of bog bean shoots pointed skywards. For miles all I could see was acre upon acre of this moss covered boggy peatland, with mountains rising in the distance. Even the weather had been suitably dramatic – cycles of an hour of sunshine, five minutes of heavy rain, beautiful rainbows arching across the sky, then back to sun. Back at the RSPB centre I wrote in the visitors' book – '*An incredible place. Thank you to the RSPB for making it accessible. Worth the year's membership fee alone*'.

Forsinard Flows is the RSPB's biggest reserve and it is largely thanks to them that this amazing place was saved from destruction. Otters, water voles and Atlantic salmon flourish in the water, arctic hares and red deer graze on the moorland, and a wide range of bird life including golden eagles, merlin and short eared owls thrive in the varied habitats. However, after remaining largely untouched for millennia, the Flow Country has undergone a massive change in land-use over the last sixty years. Much of the blanket bog was drained in an attempt to make the land more productive, and huge areas planted with non-native conifer trees, driven by inappropriate forestry grants and tax breaks. Following a major campaign the tax incentives were removed in 1988, stopping the conifer planting, and a programme of restoration is bringing back the lost bogs, leading to the return of wildlife.

Hungry after an afternoon walking around this amazing environment, I returned to the hotel. Forsinard Hotel was one of eight built by the Duke of Sutherland as places for his men to stay when collecting rents. It's the only one still open and staying there was quite an experience. In thirteen years owners John and Kim have taken it from semi-derelict to a successful establishment where the welcome and food compliment the magnificent location. Most guests come for the deer stalking or fishing, both of which are expertly organised by John who owns the rights for surrounding land and lochs. That 87% of guests are repeat customers says much for the hotel.

After enjoying a superb steak looking out across the moors, I moved to the bar, spending a most enjoyable evening in the company of John and one of the night's other two guests who was staying for the fishing. The third guest, an elderly man, had come by train (as do several each week). He used to work for the railways and travels up on a free pass, spending time playing the piano for which I was told he has great talent. The fishing guest also comes every year from Edinburgh, spending a week alone pitting his wits against the trout, as relaxation from busy business life.

A cockerel woke me in the morning. From my bedroom window I watched the early southbound train approach Forsinard station through murky drizzle. Passengers on this line experience the full range of weather.

In the severe blizzards of 1978 a train was lost in deep snow north of Altnabreac. Almost 24 hours after they'd left Inverness an RAF helicopter eventually located them, rescuing seventy passengers. The log from Inverness Control records (which I reproduce with thanks to FoFNL) makes interesting reading:

"Meanwhile, a report was received from Georgemas at 23.09 to say that the 17.15 Inverness to Wick, which had left Forsinard at 22.20, had not yet arrived. Wick loco to proceed to Georgemas ready to assist"

"00.50 After telephone conversation with Georgemas signalman, Outdoor Superintendent (OS) instructs LD 26031 into section accompanied by signalman. Guard left to man Georgemas telephone. Loco to proceed at extreme caution, sounding whistle continuously, headlight switched on and keeping very good lookout."

"07.50 LD 26031 arrived back at Georgemas. Had reached MP 135 (approx 1 mile north of Altnabreac) and stuck in a drift. Men had dug her out and returned not having seen anything of the 17.15."

"08.00 LD ordered back to Wick for crew change. Pick up P'way Inspector (PWI) and re-enter Forsinard section to find the 17.15."

"09.35 Georgemas signalman reports message received on lineside phone from driver of the 17.15 that five coaches are derailed just beyond a rocky cutting approx MP 133½. Two locos and one coach have gone forward approx 1½ miles and are stuck in snow drift. 70 passengers on coach. No injuries. About 2 miles of track damaged in rear of derailed coaches."

"09.45 Georgemas PO phone now out of order. Messages being relayed via Thurso police station."

"11.05 Georgemas. LD re-entered section at 10.00. Lineside phone message from PWI to say LD derailed one pair of wheels and stuck in snow drift approx 1½ miles north of stranded locos and coach. OS contacted General Manager requesting helicopter rescue of passengers."

"17.03 Wick. Station Assistant Wick reports from Thurso – no PO phone communication from Wick – three helicopters airborne with food and blankets and will lift as many passengers as possible from Saturday's 17.15."

"17.33 Wick. All passengers from train landed, some at Halkirk and some at Wick Airfield. All well and, after refreshments, proceeding home. PWI and some rail staff eventually uplifted at 21.00."

I enjoyed a large and tasty breakfast, watched through the window of the dining room by half a dozen deer at edge of a small wood about fifty yards away. After thanking John for a most memorable stay I returned to the station, not yet travelling south, but one stop further north to the even more isolated Altnabreac.

I was the only passenger waiting at Forsinard but shared the platform with a chicken who was enjoying morsels dropped from the RSPB bird feeder. Soon we were both joined by a man in a ScotRail uniform who arrived by car. He normally works in the booking office at Keith, but was driving north to cover staff shortage at Thurso. He'd stopped at Forsinard to photograph the station. As we chatted he asked me to come to his car to look at something. In the boot were two 1950s Hornby models of steam locomotives in Caledonian colours – the sort of engine that once worked the Wick line. The models were third rail powered and valuable. That's why they were in the car boot. There'd been a spate of burglaries in Keith, so he didn't want to leave the model trains and a selection of other railway memorabilia, which were getting a ride to Thurso.

The train arrived thirty minutes late. One of the two engines had failed on the northbound service, so rather than send the single engined train to the remote northern part of the line, it had waited to pass the southbound service that I'd seen earlier from my bedroom window. Passengers had been transferred to this train which then returned north.

The guard was nowhere to be seen (he eventually emerged from the rear cab) so I knocked on the driver's cab door asking him to stop at Altnabreac. They don't get many requests for this remote little station. In fact no one seems to know why it was built here. It pre-dates the hunting lodge a mile away, which seems the only obvious source of trade, but as it once had a passing loop and water tower (the latter remains), may have been established for purely operational reasons. A tiny school in what is now a cottage close to the station once provided some business and John from the Forsinard Hotel occasionally sends shooting parties to the estate here. Men boarding the train with rifles caused a little concern amongst those not used to stalking and he's now managed to educate his guests to at least cover them as they travel.

A notice on the platform advised that the nearest taxis are at Halkirk. Should you wish to use one you'd presumably have to walk five miles along tracks to the road, before the eleven mile drive to the village which is close to Georgemas Junction. The station house has recently been vacated and trains now serve just two very isolated cottages. Not surprisingly Altnabreac is one of the least used stations in Britain, its occasional users tending to be walkers or those who enjoy visiting obscure locations. I qualified on both counts.

I walked three miles, first between trees, then along Loch Du, passing the impressive former hunting lodge and out onto the open moors to Loch a Mhuilinn. As I reached the loch the sky darkened, the wind picked up driving waves across the water onto little sandy beaches and within seconds heavy rain was falling. Such a dramatic change in the weather seemed entirely appropriate for this wild and isolated but immensely beautiful spot. Five minutes later the sun was shining and shadows lifting from the mountains to the east. My overriding thought as I returned to the station was, when can I come back?

Altnabreac isn't somewhere you'd want to miss a train, so I'd returned with plenty of time to spare, retrieving my rucksack from the little wooden shelter where I'd had no qualms about leaving it. I had seen no one in my three hours here and so far from civilisation I was at last free from announcements threatening to blow up luggage should I turn my back on it for an instant. The bomb squad couldn't get me in Altnabreac.

I'd read notes from a walker warning that as they are so rarely required to stop drivers tend to rattle through at 60mph. His advice was to jump up and down and gesticulate wildly, but a simple extension of the arm brought the train to a halt for me.

It was another long but enjoyable journey back to Inverness, although with '158s' considerably quicker than the old locomotive hauled trains. These took an hour longer to reach Inverness from Thurso. The current service is probably the best the line has ever seen, with four trains a day, all with refreshment trolleys, plus the commuter services at the southern end. Beeching would have closed this and the Kyle line, but what a loss that would have been to the communities and tourists who use what are now rightly considered to be amongst the world's greatest railway journeys.

My disappointment at reaching Inverness and having to head home was of a different kind to one of the train's other passengers, a young Canadian man. He'd spent the whole journey in friendly conversation with an attractive American girl and must have thought his luck was in. As they walked onto the concourse at Inverness however she bade him just a brief goodbye and headed off into the town. The poor young man was left standing, a picture of disappointment.

As I sat in the sleeper lounge car awaiting departure for London, one of our more famous trains pulled in. *The Highland Chieftain* had left London at 12.00 and after travelling 581 miles, was arriving at Inverness bang on time, eight hours and eleven minutes later. One summer evening, just before East Coast stopped proper at seat dining, I'd picked it up at Stirling after a day of meetings around Glasgow. It was a last chance to fulfil an ambition – dinner on an express train travelling through the Highlands of Scotland.

Tonight I sat in the lounge car until Pitlochry, one of my favourite Scottish towns, where I've been several times after meetings, on each occasion climbing part way up Ben Vrachie, then boarding the sleeper just before 11pm. Tonight it was the same steward as had been working the Aberdeen train on Sunday. He remembered me and his recommendation of lemon pudding. I needed little persuasion. It was excellent.

CHAPTER TWENTY ONE

THREE TREATS TO FINISH

Having completed my British travels I realised that I'd missed two of the experiences that no self-respecting railway book should omit – breakfast on the train and the Settle to Carlisle line.

Breakfast

Even in the supposed dark days of British Rail, when the railways and their catering were the butt of every comedian's jokes, the 'Great British Breakfast' was recognised as an exception. Few would argue that to enjoy sausage, bacon and eggs while speeding across the country on the way to meetings or holidays, is not one of the more civilised ways to start a day.

Dining cars initially survived privatisation and over the last twenty years I've enjoyed breakfast on trains travelling from all six main line London termini north of the Thames. One by one though operators have phased out restaurant cars, replacing them at best with complimentary at seat dining for First Class passengers, and at worse with nothing. There are now no service trains where any passenger can wander down to the dining car and have breakfast served at their seat as they travel. As I complete this book, East Coast and Virgin offer 'free' breakfast to First Class passengers only. Those travelling First Class on some First Great Western and a few southbound East Midlands Trains services can pay for a breakfast, but only on the Welsh Premier Service from Holyhead can Standard Class passengers enjoy breakfast served on a plate.

So having travelled 9,818 miles around Britain, none of my journeys had given the opportunity for that great institution – breakfast on the train. To put this right I bought a First Advance ticket for the 9.03 from Kings Cross to Leeds.

Tea and coffee were offered as we entered Gasworks Tunnel outside Kings Cross. A few minutes later a trolley came by with toast, croissants and juice, and orders were taken for breakfast. I chose the full works – sausage, scrambled egg, mushrooms, tomato and two slices of bacon.

Waiting for breakfast to arrive I realised that there were no other passengers in Coach K. This raised a conundrum. If you're the only person in the Quiet Coach, do you have to be quiet?

Breakfast arrived after Stevenage. It was good but not brilliant. I've enjoyed many better on trains. When GNER and, for a while, National Express ran the East Coast line, breakfast was an altogether grander affair. There was a sense of occasion with announcements requesting those who wished to dine to make their way to the restaurant car. Diners would be shown to a seat and given a menu to peruse. Options included fresh fruit salad, cereals or porridge to start, the full English, smoked salmon with scrambled eggs, or the famous British Rail kipper, plus as much toast and marmalade as one wanted.

Today there was no fruit or cereals and the kippers, which I last enjoyed on a train to Norwich, are no more. The main course was brought to me already plated. The silver service where two stewards served passengers from stainless steel platters has gone. Toast is supposed to be limited to just the one slice, although I was allowed a second when the trolley passed by on the way back to the kitchen. Most importantly, the food just isn't as good. On most trains it's no longer cooked by a chef but simply reheated by a 'Customer Service Assistant', with the menu designed that (in theory) either can produce meals to the same standard. Hence the best breakfasts are now on First Great Western, where each one is individually cooked by the Travelling Chef.

So breakfast on the train; yes it was a treat, but not what it used to be.

England's Highest Station

At Leeds I boarded the 12.49 to Carlisle, joining a mix of locals with shopping, families with luggage and walkers with backpacks, for a ride on

England's most scenic main line. It was a trip I'd made four times before, but always in locomotive hauled trains, which made for a more pleasant environment than today's two car '158'. The ambience wasn't helped by the noisy under-floor engines, or a lady making a call through her laptop so we could all hear both sides of the conversation.

My last journey had been in 2004, when I came back this way from Scotland. It was the penultimate day of a locomotive hauled service which Arriva Trains ran for a year to provide extra capacity. The train was full, passenger numbers boosted by enthusiasts taking what was one of the last opportunities to ride behind one of these early 1960's (Class 37) locomotives on a main line service train. My first two journeys were both on rather sparsely filled trains– with my father in the late 1970s and my wife on our honeymoon in 1982.

From Leeds' busy and recently modernised station, we passed through historic Yorkshire towns – Shipley, Saltaire, Bingley, Keighley and Skipton. Through the window, rivers, canals and mills added interest to the mix of towns and countryside. At Keighley a little girl asked if we were there. Her mum told her rather firmly that it would be another two hours. Last time I'd been here had been with my youngest son at the height of his train interest, when we'd travelled on the Worth Valley Railway, spotting landmarks from *The Railway Children*.

After Skipton we were in the Yorkshire Dales. For some distance the railway forms the National Park boundary but doesn't actually enter it until just after Settle. The train stopped, seemingly in the middle of nowhere. After a while the guard announced that the driver had gone to speak to the signalman. Old fashioned lineside phones are still used to communicate here. Soon he returned and we were on our way. There had been a problem with a level crossing.

There was a further delay at Hellifield as staff helped a man in a wheelchair alight from the train. He'd been shopping in Skipton. Hellifield is just a small village but has a railway station more befitting a large town. There's even a privately run buffet. It was once a major interchange, with passengers and goods travelling from the industrial North West on the line through Blackburn. This remains open for freight, diversions when the West Coast route is closed, occasional charter trains and on summer Sundays, DalesRail trains from Preston and Manchester. These are mainly used by walkers and were instrumental in proving a market to reopen eight small stations between Settle and Carlisle which had closed in 1970.

Just before Settle, the line to Lancaster and Morecambe leaves to the left. This too is highly scenic but often eclipsed by its more famous neighbour. I'd travelled on it from Morecambe to Clapham the previous year, walking part way up Ingleborough. The views from the train were excellent, but the ride on a very bouncy Pacer was not!

The market town of Settle nestles under limestone hills and marks the start of the most spectacular part of the railway. Its station is just perfect. With restored buildings, well tended gardens, beautiful flower displays, a preserved signal box that is occasionally open to the public and a shop run by FoSCL (Friends of the Settle Carlisle Line), it is a tourist attraction in its own right.

Quite a few passengers join here, often driving from further afield as Deb and I had when we stayed in the Lake District in 1989. Then the platform had been packed, with coach parties dropped here and picked up at Carlisle, and it had been a relief when a locomotive hauled train arrived. British Rail had the flexibility to run longer trains to match demand, but there's little stock spare on today's railways.

The 72 mile Settle to Carlisle route had its origins in railway politics. In the 1860s the Midland Railway company was locked in dispute with the rival London and North Western Railway over access rights to the latter's tracks to Scotland, and decided that the only solution was to build their own route. The line was constructed by over six thousand navvies, many of them Irish, who toiled in inhospitable terrain, working through some of the worst weather England can provide. Many died through accidents and disease, and were buried, often in unmarked graves, in local churchyards. Huge camps were established to house the navvies and the Midland Railway helped pay for scripture readers in an attempt to temper their often drunken and sometimes violent behaviour.

To keep the gradients down to no steeper than 1 in 100, a requirement for fast running using steam locomotives, massive engineering works were required, with fourteen tunnels and twenty two viaducts. Even then the terrain imposed a 16 mile climb from Settle to Blea Moor, almost all of it at 1 in 100, and known to enginemen as 'the long drag'. The route was never as fast as the East or West Coast lines, so the Midland competed by offering extra comfort and of course the best scenery. With today's cramped Pendolinos, I wonder if there would still be a market for a comfortable train to take tourists to Scotland this way?

Leaving Settle with the train almost full, we started to climb past a patchwork of dry stone walls. Horton-in-Ribblesdale is another perfectly restored station. I wondered how it compared to the 1950s and 60s when it won the Best Kept Station award for seventeen consecutive years. The 'Three Peaks' can all the climbed from here and there's an excellent view of the flat topped Pen-y-Ghent from the station.

Green fields were giving way to the rough grass of higher moorland, but as we reached the line's best scenery the man sitting opposite failed to raise his head from a newspaper. The next stop was Ribblehead, another beautifully restored station. The waiting room here was once used as a chapel, with monthly services held by the Vicar of Ingleton. Music was provided by a harmonium, concealed behind a billboard, which had been brought to the railway by a missionary who came to minister to navvies during the line's construction. British Rail used to charge two shillings for use of the room, which saw as many as fifty worshippers for harvest festivals.

When the station reopened in 1986 only southbound trains could stop, as the other platform had been demolished to make way for sidings to a nearby quarry. A new wooden platform opened in 1993, partly funded by the Settle and Carlisle Railway Trust, which cares admirably for buildings along the line.

Just beyond the station is one of the most famous railway structures in Britain – Ribblehead Viaduct. Twenty four massive stone arches take trains a hundred feet above the moors. One and a half million bricks were used in its construction and the swampy ground meant that foundations had to be sunk twenty five feet into the peat. The curve adds to its beauty, but it is mainly for its location in this remote and beautiful part of England that the viaduct is so outstanding. Cars were parked by the narrow road that runs beneath it and a tea van had set up in a lay-by to serve those who'd come to see this iconic railway structure. Children waved as we crossed and walkers stopped to watch the train.

Soon we were passing through another Victorian engineering wonder – the 2629 yard long Blea Moor Tunnel. Hundreds of navvies dug the tunnel with only muscle and dynamite, using steam engines at the top of shafts to haul out the spoil. Terrible weather took its toll, with several men drowned in the cuttings on Blea Moor during a rainstorm in July 1870. Brick to line the tunnel was produced at a brickworks sited near to Ribblehead Viaduct. The tramway that transported spoil up to six huge heaps is still visible, as are three shafts which were left to ventilate the tunnel.

I left the train a few minutes later, alighting at Dent, the highest railway station in England. In the heart of the Dales, 1150 feet above sea level and with just one house close by, this is one of our most isolated stations. The village of Dent is five miles away and 600 feet lower. The line was engineered to express standards throughout, with local traffic of secondary importance, so many stations were miles from the villages they purported to serve. Wooden snow fences protect the station, which is another that is superbly preserved, with stone waiting rooms on both platforms. The northbound shelter is new as the main buildings are rented out as holiday accommodation. A sign next to a preserved gas lamp proudly displays the station's altitude.

It would have been unthinkable to come here without staying for a walk. And what a wonderful walk it was – along the lane for a mile or so, then following a track round the hillside and on to Dent Fell. From here I looked down the valley to Artengill Viaduct and watched a little blue two coach train cross, then disappear into Blea Moor Tunnel. Deb and I had walked from Dent on our 1989 trip on the line, but after coming back today I decided that this was yet another place to return to again one day.

We are fortunate that trains still run here, the line having being saved from closure after a high profile campaign run by the Friends of the Settle Carlisle Line. I'd joined the Friends in 1982 after being given a leaflet at Appleby station, when we'd passed through at the time of the line's lowest ebb. Through trains from London had been withdrawn five years earlier and the replacements from Nottingham further curtailed to start from Leeds. Just two trains a day ran each way and it seemed that the line was being deliberately run down for 'closure by stealth' – reduce the service until few travel, then say there's no demand.

Campaigners pointed to the line's potential for tourism, freight and as a diversionary route, but in 1984 British Rail gave notice of its intention to close due to heavy financial loss. Crucial to its case was the cost of maintaining the line's tunnels and viaducts, notably Ribblehead Viaduct which the government said would require £6 million to repair. Amid accusations of dirty tricks, experimental repairs on one arch however showed that the total cost would be much less than claimed.

Publicity of the threatened closure led to a huge rise in traffic, with passenger numbers increasing five fold from 1983 to 1988. More than 32,000 objections were received and 2,000 people spoke at the Inquiry, but in 1988 the government announced that it was minded to close the line unless a proposal could be found to operate it privately. No such proposal was received.

A year later however, in a decision which he has since referred to as his greatest achievement in politics, Minister for Transport Michael Portillo announced that consent to closure was being declined. It was a victory for rail travellers and local people, and an example that if enough people are prepared to make the effort, common sense can prevail.

It was very much a community effort to save the railway, but one of the objectors has been remembered above all others. On the 20th anniversary of the line's reprieve a brass statue was unveiled on Garsdale station commemorating Ruswarp, a border collie – a fare paying passenger and bona fide objector, who had signed with a paw print. Ruswarp (pronounced 'Russup') was owned by Graham Nuttall, co-founder of the Friends. The two were inseparable companions and on 20th January 1990 they went walking in the Welsh hills. They failed to return. Graham's body was found on 7th April. His faithful dog had stayed at his side for eleven winter weeks. The case attracted nationwide attention and Ruswarp was honoured by the RSPCA. Weakened by his long ordeal on the mountainside, Ruswarp lived just long enough to attend his master's funeral.

Back at Dent station, I was interested to read a notice put up 'in the interest of public safety' advising passengers what they should do if they miss the last train. It's not a place you'd want to be stranded in mid winter. There's a pub a mile away that offers basic bed & breakfast, otherwise it's a 4½ mile walk.

At the due time of 17.32 I heard a train approaching. As I gathered up my rucksack ready to board, round the bend came a large diesel locomotive pulling a long line of wagons. It was going rather slowly. Ten minutes later there was still no sign of a passenger train. There's no departure board but a notice says that passengers may call the signalman for information.

I lifted the receiver and was answered by the signalman at Blea Moor, one of our most famous and remote signal boxes. It isn't attached to a station or accessible by road, so signallers have to walk three quarters of a mile along a narrow track from near Ribblehead viaduct. As passengers enjoy the scenery from the warmth of a train, perhaps they should give a moment's thought to the signalman who will have got up at 4am and walked to his post in the dark, whatever the weather, to ensure that trains can run. The answer to my question was that the signalman was just putting the now failed freight train into his siding, but my train should arrive in eight minutes. It came in six.

As I had been when alighting earlier, I was the only person using Dent station, but the train was busy. I sat opposite a family who'd been to Carlisle, as do the majority of tourists, although walkers use all the smaller stations too. A few minutes later we were passing Blea Moor where the freight train waited in a siding. At Skipton the guard announced that to make up time we'd be running non stop to Leeds, so passengers for intermediate stations had to change here. Several got off, without a word of complaint. If this were London commuters there'd have been much sighing and muttering.

We set off at a fair lick, the driver seemingly on a mission. Time was made up and we arrived at Leeds just two minutes late. The train was due to return on a commuter service as far as Ribblehead just ten minutes later. A slight delay to the few passengers who had had to change at Skipton meant everyone else would be on time.

A few months later I used the line again, travelling from Leeds to Glasgow for work. The online booking site told me to go via Edinburgh or Preston, and it was only when entering 'via Appleby' on advance options that the cheaper, more scenic and just as fast Settle – Carlisle option came up. While those who didn't have the experience to challenge the computer's recommendation took a more roundabout route, I enjoyed a truly spectacular ride through the Yorkshire Dales. On a freezing day the fields were white with frost, long icicles dangled from stone cuttings and snow covered the hill tops.

On a December morning I'd expected the train to be quiet, but it was far from it. As we travelled north local people joined at every stop, most heading for a day's shopping in Carlisle. At Appleby an elderly man sat opposite me. He'd sold his car – there was no need to keep it with such a good train service and connections to London and Scotland. One hundred and three passengers alighted at Carlisle. What a contrast to my journeys thirty years earlier. Thanks to the sterling work of local people and in Northern Rail, a train operator who wants to run trains rather than close them down, a line that was dying now thrives. It raised just one question though – how many more lines across the country could have continued to serve travellers had successive 1960s governments had a more open minded policy to the railways?

And finally a quick word on my journey the day after visiting Dent – on to Accrington for a meeting, using the other end of the line I'd travelled on from Preston to Burnley earlier in the year. The views were good, passing through Halifax and Hebden Bridge and along pretty Pennine valleys. The train back though was awful – a three car '158' with smelly toilets and out of order air conditioning. It was badly in need of refurbishment, and on a very hot day, after 82 minutes in this sauna, so was I. What a relief to get into a lovely cool East Coast train back to London.

A Day Out With Ben

Ben is my eight year old nephew. He loves trains and an occasional treat is a day out with Uncle Peter. Today we were celebrating his birthday, with a ride behind an Inter City electric engine, then a steam locomotive.

Ben has autism, so life isn't always easy for him and he finds it hard to cope with change or the unexpected. His day didn't start well. My sister was bringing him from Didcot to London, but First Great Western hadn't put out the seat reservations and the train was packed. Ben lay on the floor. It looked like a tantrum but he just couldn't cope with all the people. He'd expected a seat and there wasn't one. A kind man understood what was happening and gave up his. Ben calmed down and all was well.

We met at Kings Cross. Ben liked the new concourse where we waited for the platform number to come up on the board. With a wave to his mum we went through the barrier and like generations of small boys before him, walked to the front to look at the engine. It was Ben's first trip from Kings Cross and his first ride behind an electric locomotive. He loved it. Fifty minutes later and with hardly a break in his conversation, we pulled into Peterborough. From here it was a short walk to the Nene Valley Railway. This heritage steam line was a new experience for Uncle Peter too.

The railway's website had said that *Number 22*, an industrial tank engine, would be hauling trains today. Fortunately it added a rider that locomotives were subject to change, so Ben understood when *City of Peterborough* pulled into the station hauling six coaches. But who could be disappointed at a ride behind this fine locomotive, which once used to haul the *Pines Express*.

Ben chose a compartment and we ate our sandwiches as the train took us at a gentle pace through surprisingly good scenery alongside the River Nene. A fifty-five minute stop at Wansford gave us time to look at the locomotives in the yard, where *Number 22* seemed to be undergoing repairs, and walk over the bridge to view the coaches in Platform Two. These were continental stock, as are some of the line's locomotives. By the mid 1970s other heritage railways had claimed most of our remaining steam engines and all that was available were rusting hulks. European stock was selected for easy availability without the need for restoration, so the company could concentrate on track laying.

The coaches in the platform however gave us a mystery. How was the engine going to get to the other end of the train to take us back to Peterborough? We asked the guard. Ben wasn't quite sure what to say to his answer that they lift up the engine and put it down at the other end! Then he told us the real answer. Wansford isn't the end of the line. Trains run on to Yarwell Junction, where there are two tracks and the locomotive can run round. The lines from Peterborough to Northampton and to Rugby once diverged here, although there was no station. The current station was built by the Nene Valley Railway and is picturesquely situated between the river and a lake.

As the engine ran round I provided a little entertainment for a family sitting in one of the compartments. While Ben was concentrating on taking photos I stepped back to get one of my own, not noticing a large plant pot behind me and ending up sprawled backwards over a wooden seat. Ben was oblivious but the family on the train must have wished they'd been filming, with £250 to be made at my expense from *You've Been Framed*!

With six coaches to choose from, Ben went for familiarity and selected our same seats for the return journey. At Peterborough we took some photos, Ben posing by the engine as his uncle used to forty years earlier. He'd loved his ride on the Nene Valley and had felt comfortable with the friendly staff and a compartment to ourselves.

Back at the main line Ben decided that he wanted to return to London in the Quiet Coach. He understood that he'd have to be quiet and promised he would. True to his word, at last his conversation stopped and a tired young boy almost fell asleep. A not so young Uncle Peter was glad of the respite!

At Kings Cross we had a little worry. We'd arranged to meet at Trafalgar Square but Ben wasn't familiar with the Piccadilly Line. He'd have been fine if we had told him in advance, but with little warning he was worried. He pressed himself against the back wall of the platform. Once on the train though Ben was at ease again, fear of the unknown being replaced by the excitement of riding a new underground line.

Reflecting on our trip, I thought how life for Ben mirrors our railway system. When all goes well everyone is happy, but it only takes a tiny problem to spark a chain of events that causes stress for all involved.

A trip with my nephew behind a locomotive that had been withdrawn from British Rail service when I was about Ben's age seemed a fitting end to my travels around Britain. Now I was to turn to the continent, taking the train to Milan to compare European rail travel with that in the UK and to Belgium where we had our only oversees childhood holiday.

CHAPTER TWENTY TWO

THROUGH SWITZERLAND TO ITALY

London – Paris – Montreux – Milan

This was my fourth visit to Milan, each time for a work meeting, travelling by train and varying the route. As with most of my trips to Europe, I was to experience a few new places as well as revisiting more familiar ground. One of the advantages of running my own business is the flexibility to take a little longer over such trips, to have an enjoyable journey and to see interesting places. So many business people travel, but see just airports and hotels. By taking the train though one can experience a country, meet some of its people and enjoy its scenery.

As in the UK, the cheapest European train tickets have to be bought in advance and are only valid for booked trains. To allow flexibility, and at not much more cost, I bought an Inter Rail ticket, choosing to pay the extra 50% for the First Class option. There are various versions of this ticket, which is no longer restricted to young people, and mine was valid for five days. It can be used on most trains, but supplements are charged for some, notably the French run TGV and Thalys, and through trains to Italy. Everything can be booked online, but I prefer to avoid trawling through websites and buy from Ffestiniog Travel who offer expert advice, with profits supporting the Ffestiniog Railway.

Travelling by Eurostar isn't always the most relaxing of train journeys, but neither is it as bad as the long waits, queues and crowds of air travel. At worst it usually takes fifteen minutes or so to get through security and passport control, which for those used to flying must seem a doddle. The thirty minute check in, baggage x-rays and metal detectors are nothing compared to airport security with shoes removed and liquids forbidden. Rail passengers though are used to just turning up and stepping onto a train.

Passengers wait in the station undercroft, which once stored beer barrels brought to London from Burton-on-Trent. Its pillars were positioned to allow just enough space for three of the largest barrels to be stored between them. The waiting area was busy, but gained an air of tranquillity once the train to Euro Disney boarded. I was surprised how many families were travelling in term time.

Once on board the advantages over plane travel continue. There's far more leg room, the ability to walk about and a café bar with a moderate range of food and drink. There was the usual mix of nationalities and passengers in the coach; four businessmen to one side and to the other a family with two young girls. Their table was covered with little pink plastic cups and saucers, and the eldest girl provided a running commentary for most of the trip.

The best part of the journey starts soon after exiting the twelve mile tunnel to Dagenham, running alongside the Rainham Marshes nature reserve, swooping over the M25 and diving into the Thames tunnel. After a quick stop at Ebbsfleet it's pleasant Kent scenery all the way to the Channel Tunnel. Once into northern France though it's pretty dull – huge flat fields with long straight roads and avenues of trees, but little in the way of hills, hedgerows or woodland.

I arrived at Paris splattered with water courtesy of an over-enthusiastic hand drier that blew water everywhere. What other passengers thought as I came out of the toilet with damp patches down the front of my trousers I don't know!

There was a bit of a commotion on the concourse at Gare de Nord, with people running out of the station. A lad approached me with a clipboard asking if I'd sign what looked like a petition for the 'deaf and mute'. Gullible I may be (I've handed over small change in response to many a plausible tale of woe at railway stations), I refused his request for money. He wasn't happy, pointing to the list above who'd all 'given' ten Euros. Then suddenly he legged it. A policeman was approaching. I watched the ongoing spectacle for a while. Outside the station was a group of around fifteen lads with clipboards. They'd approach tourists and no one seemed bothered to stop it, but when they tried to harvest the presumably richer pickings inside the station, the police chased them off. A lad of about twelve was caught by one policeman, but all they did was chuck him out, no doubt to sneak back in a few minutes later. At least the lads were making a bit of effort and taking a few Euros from gullible foreigners, rather than snatching bags or picking pockets.

Paris isn't my favourite city – too busy and too many cars. Usually I've just walked the short distance to Gare de l'Est and caught a train towards Strasbourg, but today was heading further south on the TGV to Geneva. I always get lost on the Paris Metro (of course blaming the lack of signs not my sense of direction), so thanks to *seat61.com* was glad to find it's only two stops on an RER suburban train.

The atmosphere at Gare de Lyon was less frenetic than the always busy Gare de Nord, and with fewer foreigners it seems the youth of Paris don't consider it worthy of their scams. The station was built for the World Exhibition in 1900 and is considered a classic example of architecture of its time. The clock tower resembles London's Big Ben. Inside the station is the famous Le Train Bleu restaurant, crammed with sculptures, gilt and vast paintings. It was here that Rowan Atkinson struggled with seafood on his journey to Cannes in *Mr Bean's Holiday*.

The 15.10 to Geneva was virtually full, even in First Class, which is less exclusive in Europe than the UK. The price differential is smaller and rather than being mainly patronised by business travellers and the fairly well off, is also used by families and young people. TGVs always seem to be busy, France having shown that if you provide fast trains at reasonable prices, people will use them in preference to road or air.

Twenty minutes from Paris there was a marked acceleration as we joined the 186mph high speed line. The 'meal' we'd been promised arrived soon after – a tiny drink and chicken or salmon roll. French train catering is worse than the UK and as I was to find, far inferior to Swiss and German. There was a bar coach, where about twenty people stood drinking and chatting, but the food selection wasn't up to much. Nor was it cheap – 4.90 Euro for a Kit Kat and bottle of water. The TGV Lyria trains are a joint

French – Swiss enterprise, but as with Eurostar, it seems that the French influence the catering. On French trains I use the same policy as planes – don't rely on getting anything and if there's something reasonable count it as a bonus.

It was a pleasantly quiet ambiance on the train, any mobile calls being made in the vestibule and the majority of passengers tapping away at laptops. Hardly anyone spoke and I had just a brief conversation with the Swiss lady opposite who was returning home to Geneva.

Whilst slightly more hilly than east of Paris, for two hours the scenery was nothing special. Again the fields were vast and it seems the days of Frenchmen farming half an acre and claiming European subsidies for their two cows, pig and half a dozen hens, may be over. The population density is very low, but every few minutes we'd pass a little village, each with a church in the centre and walled cemetery at the edge.

The train slowed as we left the high speed line, then further as we negotiated a curve onto the single track Haut-Bugey line. For 126 years this was an increasingly neglected local line, but in 2006 was closed for reconstruction and electrification, and now forms part of the TGV network, shortening the journey to Geneva by twenty minutes. Passing through eleven tunnels, over countless bridges and alongside beautiful lakes, the train threads itself through the mountains in a spectacular journey – a contrast with the rest of my travels through France in both speed and scenery.

Arriving on time in Geneva, there was time for a brief walk before boarding the 18.42 to Milan. Today however I was to travel for just an hour, stopping overnight in Montreux on Lake Geneva, before continuing on to Italy. Switzerland is my favourite country and I was keen to take the opportunity to explore another place.

The hour's journey gave just enough time for dinner in the restaurant car, an excellent meal of roast pork in red wine sauce. Although announcements were being made in English, the menu was in French, German and Italian, but my very limited language skills were just enough to decipher it by translating odd words from each of the three versions. The price was similar to a UK restaurant car, but the food whilst good, not quite to the same standard. Unlike in the UK, in Europe passengers can use the restaurant for just drinks or snacks, and whilst all eighteen seats were occupied, only one other person was dining. Instead of the refined atmosphere of our restaurants, there was a happy chatter of office workers enjoying a drink as they travelled home, most getting off at Lausanne, the first stop.

Deb and I had briefly visited Montreux en route to Zermatt, a beautiful town at the foot of the Matterhorn. After flying to Geneva, we took the train to the car-free resort, and spent a week exploring mountains by cable car and rack railway.

Arriving in the dark, it wasn't until morning that I saw the city's beauty – and what beauty. Morning mist hung over the blue lake, with the sun's rays breaking through over the waterfront and snowy mountains opposite: a truly splendid vista, far beyond my literary skills to adequately describe.

Montreux is a very rare station having railways of three different gauges – the standard gauge line from Geneva, the Golden Pass line to Interlaken and Luzern, and the rack railway up the 6,699 foot Rochers-de-Naye. With just a morning to spare, I took the little 2 foot 7½ inch gauge train to the top of the mountain – a spectacular ride with views down to the lake and across the snowy peaks. A group of Americans got off at Glion, a typically Swiss mountain station, with a panoramic walk along the mountainside. Now the train was quiet. As we ascended, locals joined at little halts, putting their skis in a truck at the front. Seeing them well wrapped it dawned on me that whilst warm by the lake, it was likely to be cold higher up in the snow. How wrong I was – in bright sunshine it was almost hot enough for sunbathing. In a world of whiteness groups of Swiss school children were having skiing lessons, travelling by train as ours would get the coach for swimming.

I'd expected to walk to the summit, but with the path covered in snow and skiers there was no access to the mountain top. The best Alpine walking is often found just below the snow line. The terminus station forms part of the usual ugly building that tend to be put on mountain tops, perhaps in such a hostile environment strength having to come before aesthetics. Unless one had come to ski or pay a fortune to eat a dubious looking selection of food, there wasn't actually much to do other than admire the views. A tunnel under the mountain comes out at a viewpoint on the

Montreux side, with a shear drop of maybe 2,000 feet. From this lonely but spectacular spot looking down on the lake, I watched the little train crawl up the mountain, before walking back through the tunnel for it to take me down from this winter wonderland. There was just one other tourist, the other passengers being returning skiers and locals picked up on the way to shop in Montreux. Although busier in the summer (when the fares are double), this little railway provides a service all the year round for both recreation and day to day business.

Keen to sample a range of trains, rather than wait for the through Milan service I caught an Inter City to Brig. Locomotive hauled, this reminded me of a typical British early 1970s train. All the seats were around tables with excellent visibility as we skipped along the Rhone Valley, but not too fast to enjoy the views of vineyards and mountains. Most of the stations retained their original buildings, with not a bus shelter in sight, and such is the extent of the Swiss rail system that at many I could have changed for another train into the mountains.

Most stations had goods sidings or loading platforms, and here as in much of Europe, there are far more freight trains than the UK. Wagonload freight, with trains carrying mixed cargos, which is now hardly seen in the UK, is still common in Europe.

Approaching Brig, a line from Bern can be seen descending into the valley. I'd used this on my second trip to Milan, travelling via Basle. It's a scenic route, passing through Spiez above Lake Thun, although the recently opened Lotschberg base tunnel means that express trains no longer make the spectacular climb to the old tunnel at Kandersteg.

On that Milan trip I'd stayed overnight at the historic town of Brig, a stop that travellers have made for more than two hundred years. Its position at the head of the Simplon Pass led to the town growing when a carriage road was built through the pass in 1807, and again when the Simplon rail tunnel opened in 1906.

The 15.44 to Milan was a modern Pendolino tilting train, although without the cramped interior and small windows of Virgin's Pendolinos. This was a comfortable train with good sized windows and just a few airline seats, the rest nicely positioned around tables. As we entered the

Simplon Tunnel I walked down to the restaurant car, joining five other diners. A Frenchman in the corner seemed to have escaped from a cartoon, wearing the regulation stripy jumper and beret. All he lacked was a string of onions. The eighteen Euros for a cold meat platter I justified purely on the basis of research. My findings – excellent. As well as the restaurant, a refreshment trolley passed up and down the train, although this too was somewhat pricey – Euro 3.80 for a bottle of water, more than three times what I paid on Milan station.

I'd expected to enjoy this late lunch with alpine scenery passing the window, but engineering work meant single line working, and we spent twenty minutes stopped just outside the tunnel waiting for a freight train loaded with brand new Fiat cars to pass. Announcements in three languages explained the problem. The stop at the border station of Domodossola was extended to allow customs police to walk through the train. With open borders it's less common to see such checks, but it seems that both the Swiss and Italians want to keep an eye on who's coming and going.

Leaving the high Alps, the line runs along the western shore of Lake Maggiore with views to the beautiful Borromean Islands. The trouble with travelling by train through such scenery is you keep wanting to get off! I did stop for a couple of hours at the main lake resort of Stresa on one trip to Milan, enjoying a walk along the lake.

After three hours travelling a little lad further down the carriage was getting restless and kept toddling up the aisle with his mum. Each time he'd stop and stare at me for a while, then turn round and go back. Not speaking a word of Italian all I could do was smile – and wonder why it was me who he chose to stare at!

The approach to Milan was slow, lateness meaning we'd lost our path. Already I could see changes from Switzerland, with more graffiti and the strange sight of a family of 'gypsy' types cooking with a pot over an open fire yards from the track and inside the railway fence. In Britain such trespass would lead to all trains being stopped. Whereas every Swiss train had been smart, Italy had a wide range, from sleek Eurostars to some very scruffy old stock.

Arrival at Milan's immense Central Station was forty-one minutes late.

With cavernous stone halls, wide staircases and huge steel canopies, this is one of Europe's great railway stations. The imposing 207 metre wide façade topped with winged horses, 72 metre high vaulted booking hall and plethora of stone sculptures, were designed to be awesome, Benito Mussolini wanting the station to represent the power of his fascist regime.

On my first visit to Milan I spent an entire evening at the station, having realised on the train from Zurich that I'd forgotten to bring my return sleeper ticket. Such a large station has several enquiry offices, all with long queues and always with the answer that I needed to go to another office. The largest had that system where you collect a number on arrival and wait for it to be called. After a while I calculated the rate at which people were being seen, went off for half an hour, but on returning found things had speeded up and I'd lost my place. When eventually I got to speak to someone there was an impasse. The train was fully booked, so I couldn't buy another ticket, even though I knew there would be a spare berth – my one. The next day Deb faxed a copy of the ticket to my hotel. Now knowing the berth number, but suspecting the fax wouldn't be accepted, I sneaked aboard the Paris sleeper and quickly locked my cabin door. Only once the train pulled out of Milan could I relax. After pretending to be asleep and not answering knocks on the door, eventually I had to let the steward in. He wasn't entirely happy, but sold me a new ticket and Ffestiniog Travel managed to get me a full refund on the original.

The Italian sleeper was a similar standard to those in the UK, but inferior to the German ones I've used to Munich and Hamburg. The best experience was a German City Nightline from Milan to Cologne, a route which no longer runs, where Ffestiniog Travel booked me a First Class berth with en suite shower and toilet. The facilities were somewhat better than the French sleeper I used a few times to Zurich and Chur, where toilet arrangements consisted of a pot that tipped its contents through a hole onto the track.

This time my evening was spent wandering round Milan, with a ride on one of its famous old orange trams. These are gradually being replaced by modern high capacity vehicles which glide rather than rattle their way through the city's streets. The city's efficient Metro also has a mix of old and new trains, although all with the hard plastic seats favoured by European subway systems. Unusually some lines are overhead electric and some third rail. Unlike London, mobile phones work on the trains, taking away that excuse of 'I must have been in the tunnel', for not getting a message.

My meeting had been put back until Friday afternoon, so I had a morning to myself. I wanted to see inside the cathedral (last time they'd refused me entry for wearing shorts), but other than that wasn't too bothered by Milan's tourist sights. Leonardo da Vinci's *Last Supper* I'd seen on my first visit, being fortunate to get a ticket, but not being a connoisseur of art, wondering what to do after the first two of the allotted fifteen minute viewing time. Today I wanted to see a more ordinary Italian town, away from tourists, and to sample one of the country's Inter City trains.

Hauled by an electric locomotive, the 9.10 Inter City from Milan Centrale to La Spezia was a mix of old and new coaches. Most had compartments and all seats in the open coaches were arranged round tables. My First Class coach was modern, with an unusual little quirk – blinds inside the double glazing and a button to move them up and down. I could have played with it for hours! Refreshments consisted of just a trolley and although not a tourist route, announcements were all in both Italian and English. Italy has some fast new trains serving major cities, but I liked this Inter City, which was similar to the British trains of my youth, right down to the basic toilet that you could see the trackbed through.

After leaving the suburbs of Milan, we passed through Italian countryside, where pale brick buildings added interest amongst the large fields. Most impressive was the 15th century monastery Certosoa di Pavia, an outstanding building worthy of more than glimpsing from a passing train. I alighted at Pavia, 25 miles south of Milan. With cobbled pedestrianised streets and a smattering of interesting buildings, it is well worth a short visit. For the return journey, which was 22 minutes late, I sat in Second Class, a rare opportunity to experience a compartment as we so often did as children.

Milan's gothic cathedral took six centuries to complete and is the world's fourth largest. Emerging from the Metro station, one cannot fail to be impressed by either the scale of a building that can comfortably hold 40,000 people, or the beauty of its towers, spires and ornate statues. With knees suitably hidden, this time I could explore the vast naves of the interior. To be honest though, I think it's best appreciated from outside. Inside it's dark and remarkable for size rather than beauty.

My meeting at Parabiago, sixteen miles from the city centre, was easily reached using Milan's suburban railway. This extensive system comprises ten lines, most of which converge to run in a tunnel under the city. Trains are all double decker, either smart new units, or quite old locomotive hauled coaches. Most of the system's 213 miles, plus the metro and trams, are covered by a day ticket that cost just 4.50 Euro; excellent value and less than half the cost of London's Travelcard. I found the whole system to be efficient, and whilst busy, without the huge passenger numbers that can make travelling around London such a trial.

Italy's railways are very much a mix of old and new. The older trains are reminiscent of British Rail, right down to the tendency to be late! The new ones are cleaner and faster, but although busy, don't have the British failing of putting in so many seats that travelling ceases to be comfortable. I had just one complaint about travelling in Milan – perhaps everyone is less hurried than here, but there's no system for standing on the right on escalators and for someone used to nipping around on the underground it's most frustrating having to wait behind two gossiping Italians.

CHAPTER TWENTY THREE

BACK THROUGH GERMANY

Milan – Luzern – Frankfurt – Brussels – London

I saw something at Milan Central that used to be common in Britain, but I probably hadn't seen for thirty years. Later in the day I saw the same happening at Luzern. Both were nothing spectacular, just a shunting engine pushing two coaches into a platform. What it signified however highlighted a change in the flexibility of our railways that so far has had less impact in Europe.

When we travelled on long distance trains in the 1960s and early 70s, if a lot of passengers were expected extra coaches would often be added. My red book shows that we went to Devon on trains ranging from eight to thirteen coaches, with the length of the train reflecting demand. There was no point in pulling sparsely filled coaches across the country, but nor was it necessary to cram passengers in when extra carriages could be provided. Virtually all British trains are now fixed formations or units and it's less easy to adjust the number of seats to demand. Units can be coupled together, but frequently there aren't spares available. Whilst coaches could sit in sidings for use as required, new trains are expensive and operators can't afford to buy more than will be regularly needed (and often not even enough for that). Most new trains in Europe are also fixed units, but unlike the UK they still run many services formed of locomotive with coaches, and the inherent flexibility that provides.

There's an interesting story behind the ETR 470 train that formed the 9.10 to Zurich. In 1993, Cisalpino, a joint Italian and Swiss company, was formed to run fast tilting trains through the Alps. I first used it from Stuttgart to Zurich, but this route was discontinued in 2006 due to problems of punctuality, cleanliness (overflowing toilets) and nausea from the tilting. Problems continued and in 2008 eighty three Cisalpino trains failed to reach their destination. In 2009 the project was abandoned and the trains divided between the two owners. They continue to run from Zurich to Milan, but have been replaced on other lines by the ETR 610 Pendolinos that I travelled on from Brig. These too had their problems, entering service two years late and being found to be too heavy for the Milan to Zurich route. To prevent damaging the track they'd have had to run so slowly that conventional non tilting trains would have been just as fast. Just imagine what the media would have made of all this had it happened in the UK.

The route through the Gotthard Tunnel to Zurich is probably my favourite Alpine main line. After half an hour of ordinary scenery the train reaches Lake Como, stopping at the popular resort of Como at the southern end of the lake. On one of my Milan trips I spent a very pleasant evening here, taking the funicular railway to Brunate and enjoying dinner sitting outside a restaurant looking over the lake.

The Italian customs officials who boarded at Como asked if I had more than ten thousand Euros on me, but seemed happy to accept that I had just a hundred or so. I was spared the thorough searching of luggage that Swiss officials at Chiasso decided was necessary for the only other passenger in the First Class coach. We'd both got booked seats, but rather than spread passengers around the train they'd put us opposite each other, although with the train quiet on a Saturday morning I chose to sit further down the coach. That way I could keep moving to the side with the best views. Soon after leaving Lake Como these were on the left as we passed Lake Lugano, where the water was dead flat on a still morning, although mist meant we could barely see the mountains the other side.

Signals at Como had caused a slight delay and my planned five minute connection at Arth Goldau was going to be a test as to whether Swiss trains really do always run to time. As we climbed into the mountains the guard assured me that we'd be OK for the Luzern connection. The views weren't their best in the mist but it was still a splendid ride between snowy mountains. We emerged from the nine mile Gotthard Tunnel to sunshine and snow. The line spirals downwards with spectacular scenery, although much of this route will be bypassed when the Gotthard Base Tunnel opens in 2017. At thirty five miles this will be the world's longest rail tunnel and will considerably reduce journey times.

After passing along the banks of the lovely Urner See lake, we arrived at Arth Goldau five minutes late. The Luzern train was waiting in the adjacent platform and the guard walked down to make sure I knew where to go. I've very rarely been on a Swiss train that's late and their reputation for punctuality and keeping connections seems fully deserved.

I could however recall plenty of occasions when British connections haven't bothered to wait, one of the worst experiences being at Hereford. The train from Shrewsbury was late, arriving about a minute before the Birmingham train was due to depart. We were amongst several passengers who hurried over the bridge, but just as we were walking along the platform the train moved off. Passengers were not exactly happy but the staff didn't care. My letter of complaint to Central Trains got a standard reply, which made what appeared to be reasonable points about being unable to hold connections due to knock on delays from lost paths, but ignored my point that the train waited several minutes in Ledbury, its first stop, so a one minute late departure would be made up there. Perhaps the key is that in Switzerland the railway wants to ensure passengers get the best service, but here the priority is to make money and avoid fines for lateness.

More recently my parents had an even worse example at Hereford. Their train from Ledbury was a few minutes late and they were in danger of missing the nine minute connection to Shrewsbury. They asked the guard if he'd phone through to get it held, but his response was that they wouldn't hold it as, *'this isn't British Rail'*. After rushing over the bridge at Hereford, they got to five yards from the Shrewsbury train, then it moved off. A member of station staff said they should have asked the guard from Ledbury to phone and he'd have held it. Sometimes it can be frustrating travelling by train!

I was taking the conventional route to Luzern. On my last trip to Milan I'd stayed overnight in Luzern, travelled by boat along the lake, on a rack railway to the top of Rigi mountain, then down to Arth Goldau on another rack train. This was in January with everywhere covered in thick snow. The people I was visiting thought I was strange to be travelling from London by train, but when told how I'd come over the mountain didn't seem to know what to say! Today's train was hauled by one of Switzerland's ubiquitous red electric locomotives. I sat in Second Class, but the guard suggested I moved as First Class was a panoramic coach with large curved windows allowing extended views of the mountains.

Luzern is a popular tourist destination and like Montreux there were many American voices as I walked by the lake. Although mid March, it was very warm and I was soon carrying my jacket and wishing I'd brought shorts. I was however glad to have been able to leave my bag in left luggage, a facility available at most European stations, but now rarely in the UK. It's such an advantage to be able to break a journey and explore somewhere without the burden of luggage, but with Britain's obsessions about security and making money, only a handful of our stations now offer the service.

The third leg of my journey home took me on another locomotive hauled train through northern Switzerland to Basle. This was another comfortable train where every seat was round a table. The scenery was less mountainous, but still very pleasant, passing green fields, gentle hills and the blue waters of Lake Sempach. The train had come from Locarno and on a four hour Saturday afternoon run had both a refreshment trolley and restaurant car. In the latter I enjoyed a rather nice Swiss cake (a panettoncino).

After just a few minutes in Basle I boarded the 15.04 to Hamburg, one of Germany's superb ICE (Inter City Express) trains. With hourly services linking most German cities and many running to bordering countries, this is probably the best network of high speed trains in Europe and has led to the closing down of many short-haul flights. Most run partly on new high speed lines at up to 186mph, and partly on conventional lines. Unlike the TGV, there are no supplements for rail pass holders and although seats can be booked, this it not essential. They are 'turn up and go' services, although as in the UK, the cheapest fares are non flexible tickets bought in advance.

All are electric of course, as like much of Western Europe, Germany's main routes are mostly electrified. I was however surprised to find that around half the country's mileage remains diesel. The only journey I could recall making behind a diesel locomotive was from Hamburg to Lubeck in the very north of Germany. Although there are plans for further electrification, the UK still lags behind Europe with only 40% of track electrified, and probably the only extensive use of inter city diesels in Western Europe.

The twelve coach train was a pleasure to travel in. Seats are comfortable, mostly round tables, with some airline style, plus a few compartments. Unlike on British trains, even in Second Class (there's no dressing it up as 'Standard' in Europe), seats are individual with none of the spread of a neighbour's large buttocks we sometimes have to endure. At each seat a 'Travel Guide' shows the timings for the train, with lists of connections and their platform for each stop. Windows are large and I enjoyed a beautiful ride as the train ran along a flat plain with the snow smattered Black Forest Mountains to our right. On conventional track, we were running at around 125mph, a speed I find gives the optimum balance for a comfortable ride, good journey time and viewing scenery.

A lady came through First Class taking orders for at-seat food, but I preferred to sample another restaurant car. Even at weekends ICE trains have either a full restaurant or bistro, both with the same menu but the bistro less seats. At 10 Euros my early dinner of fricasseed chicken with rice and mushrooms was excellent value and most enjoyable. With reasonable prices the restaurant car attracts a wide cross section of travellers, and a family were sitting at the next table, their two girls ordering from the children's menu.

As we continued north the speed increased but scenery became less attractive. Notable river crossings were the Rhine at Mannheim and the Main as we approached Frankfurt, my stop for the night. Deb and I had stayed here in 1988, our holiday arranged to coincide with the European Football Championships. We made the mistake of asking the travel agent to book their cheapest hotel, and suffice to say that the Hotel Tourist near the station hasn't been my choice since. On that holiday we'd hired a car and spent most of the trip based at Garmisch-Partenkirchen in the Alps, our only train journeys being up the Zugspitz mountain and through the valley to the border town of Mittenwald. Both are highly recommended.

I'd stayed at the Holiday Inn Express the previous year when travelling on to Stuttgart to stand on a terrace for *Stand Up Sit Down*, and booked that again as a comfortable hotel in a quiet street just a few minutes from the station. To keep costs down on the football trip I'd used Inter City rather than ICE or TGV trains, but the slower speeds and more scenic routes made very pleasant journeys. My return from Stuttgart to Frankfurt had been on an Austrian train, where I'd enjoyed one of my best ever European train meals, with of course apple strudel for dessert.

I like Frankfurt. It's a vibrant city, with some beautiful old buildings around the cathedral. Many of its modern skyscrapers were built with character, not simply oblong blocks, and best of all it has a river. I always feel that cities such as Brussels, Manchester, Birmingham and Milan lack something in the absence of a major river where one can stroll away from the bustle of people and cars. My last visit to Frankfurt had been the previous September, when on a warm Saturday evening many of the city's young people had migrated to the banks of the Main, cooking barbecues, drinking wine and simply enjoying sitting by the water.

On a cool March evening there were fewer people sitting out, but still enough business for a boat that moors on the south bank, selling chips, kebabs and of course sausages. After walking along both sides of the river I ended up in a square by the cathedral, where I sat for a while enjoying a crepe. I took the subway back to the main station, eventually working out how to pay the machine 1.60 Euro for a short hop ticket. It was an underground tram rather than train, but Frankfurt also has an extensive network of S-Bahn suburban trains, which are covered by a 6.20 Euro day ticket, two thirds the cost of an equivalent in London.

In terms of number of trains, Frankfurt Hauptbahnhof (Central Station) is the busiest in Germany and its 350,000 passengers a day is one of the highest in Europe. The façade reminds me a little of Kings Cross, although more ornate, and the German's haven't hidden theirs behind a 'temporary' 1970's canopy (which thankfully is soon to be removed). Even late on a Saturday evening stalls were selling a wide range of attractively presented and appetising food. Station food varies considerably around Europe. In Germany it's usually excellent, with many shops and stalls selling both hot and cold fare. Switzerland, notably Basle, offers a good choice, if somewhat expensive, but Milan was poor. In Britain it's very variable, although few stations now offer sit down hot meals, and probably only St Pancras (the best station in Europe?) betters what I've found at Frankfurt, Munich or Stuttgart.

My night in a quiet hotel was rudely interrupted by the fire alarm and a message telling guests to leave immediately. The fire brigade arrived just as

I'd descended four flights of stairs with hundreds of other guests in various states of dress (one lady was wrapped in just her duvet, but several Chinese were fully dressed and carrying their suitcases). As firemen entered carrying axes it was soon apparent that the alarm was false. Guests drifted back to bed, but needless to say it was ages before I got back to sleep.

The 10.16 from Frankfurt to Brussels was one of Germany's ICE 3 trains, which unlike older versions are powered by under-floor motors rather than a locomotive at each end. Like our old diesel multiple units, passengers in the front coach can watch the driver through a window into the cab, and enjoy forward views of the track. And just like on a plane, it's a little annoying when a passenger with the best view chooses to read a paper which they could do at any seat.

Displays in the coaches show the train's speed and on the new line to Cologne I watched it creep up from 291 to 300kph, then touch 302kph, 189mph. How exciting it would have been to have had this in our trains when I was young. The line runs parallel with a motorway for much of its length, and isn't nearly as scenic as the old route through the Rhine Gorge that the Inter City train had followed when I'd last travelled to Frankfurt. The high speed line includes some gradients that in railway terms are very steep (1 in 25, or 4% in the new terminology that few understand), and only the ICE 3 trains have the necessary power-to-weight ratio to negotiate. It is however very fast. We took just 22 minutes for the 79km from Montabaur to Cologne / Bonn airport, an average of around 135mph.

Last time I travelled back from Frankfurt I'd caught this same train but not realised it ran on to Brussels, so bought a ticket only as far as Cologne and another on the Thalys train to Brussels. These silver and red trains look impressive, but inside are nothing special, and with the French SNCF as the majority shareholder, offer disappointing catering. In contrast, even on a Sunday morning, my ICE had a bistro with hot meals. I couldn't leave Germany without having some sausages, so enjoyed an excellent and reasonably priced lunch of six Nuremburg sausages, with potatoes and salad.

I had an interesting conversation about the difference between British and German railways with two gentlemen in the restaurant. Their experience was that our trains weren't as good, which they put down to them being privately operated. We came to the conclusion that the underlying aim of the British railway operators is to make money, whereas in Germany it's to provide a service.

From Cologne the train runs on a mixture of new high speed line and upgraded standard track. We sped through the town of Duren, where a few years ago I'd used the Rurtalbahn narrow gauge railway to visit a customer, then on to the picturesque town of Heimbach in the Eifel Hills. This little known railway along the River Rur is well worth a visit. Soon after Aachen, where I'd once arrived on a little diesel train from Heerlen in the Netherlands, we crossed into Belgium, stopping at Liege with its futuristic new station.

Approaching Brussels there was a short announcement, but nothing unnecessary. In Europe there are few of the health & safety and 'thank you for travelling with' announcements that infest our trains. ICE don't consider it necessary to tell passengers to take their luggage with them at every stop, but the display shows a picture of a case and umbrella under the simple words 'Forgotten anything?' as the train approaches stations.

On a busy Eurostar back to London I reflected on the differences between British and European trains. The latter obviously vary between countries, with the fastest journeys I've experienced in France and Germany, but the best scenery in Switzerland. Other than the high speed lines and cheaper European fares, I'd say the biggest difference in travelling is the trains themselves. Europe has the wider loading gauge, stock and line capacity not to have to cram passenger in. In Second Class there's more space, a nicer ambiance and greater comfort than our Standard Class, and whilst the difference is less in First Class, so is the European price differential. As in the UK, catering varies considerably, but the widespread provision of restaurant cars in Germany and Switzerland, puts Britain to shame. In many ways European railways retain the best bits of travelling by train, which have been lost in Britain over the last couple of decades.

CHAPTER TWENTY FOUR

BELGIUM

London – Brussels – Ostend – De Haan – Vichte – Namur

Just one of our childhood holidays was abroad. Not to Spain, France or other countries our friends went to, but to Belgium. Being our family we didn't do it conventionally, travelling by train and boat, and staying at a holiday village owned by the ferry company Townsend Thoresen. Hence everyone else had cars, but we walked up the lane from town of De Haan. Not that we stayed in the village other than to sleep in our four night stay – we were busy travelling around Belgium by train. It was 1976, the hottest summer since records began, but our holiday was the very week the months of unbroken sunshine ended.

We'd caught a train to Dover, then the ferry to Zeebrugge, the same port and ferry company that were so tragically involved in disaster when the *Herald of Free Enterprise* capsized eleven years later. From here we'd travelled on the unique but surprisingly little known, Belgian coastal tramway. At forty two miles and running the entire length of the country's coast, this is the longest tramway in the world.

On each of our three full days holiday we'd caught the tram to Ostend, then explored Belgium; Bruges one day, Brussels and Antwerp the next, then a longer trip to Dinant in the Ardennes. Two business trips to Belgium gave me the opportunity to repeat some of our travels.

With the company footing the bill, I paid thirty pounds extra for Standard Premier tickets, Eurostar's intermediate class, which on a busy train was good value for extra space and a quieter environment. Eurostar allow seats to be selected when booking on line and my single window seat was a comfortable way to travel. The complimentary breakfast of croissants, rolls, yogurt, drinks and a little pot of marmalade, was a welcome bonus. Approaching Brussels, I chatted to a lady who was travelling to Leiden. Although a six hour journey, she lived near Kings Cross and said it was as quick as flying.

Hotels in Brussels tend to be either not very good or expensive, so I was delighted to find the Euro Capital a couple of years ago. This is of reasonable standard and price, but just two minutes walk from Midi station. The only problem today was that they'd lost my booking. Fortunately there were spare rooms and within an hour I was checked in, changed and back at the station for the 15.05 to Ostend. My excellent value 'Any Belgian Station' Eurostar ticket allowed First Class travel and the locomotive hauled coaches were pleasantly comfortable. Like most Belgian trains, it wasn't a particularly fast ride through not very inspiring scenery.

At Ostend I made the mistake of assuming that a coastal tramway would run by the sea. The main line station is set back a way from the shore, so I walked along the dockside, coming out at a wide promenade above a sandy beach. It was very pleasant, but there was no sign of the trams. After much wandering, I eventually found where the line runs through the town and bought a five Euro ticket for 'De Kusstram'. Then I waited. They are supposed to run every fifteen minutes, but it was half an hour before one showed up. It was packed. After trundling through the streets of Ostend, we stopped a few yards from the station, a stop I hadn't noticed when I'd arrived nearly two hours earlier.

Here a party of schoolchildren boarded and I still had no seat or view. Stop by stop the tram emptied as we left the city's outskirts and travelled through villages along the less populated coastline. Now I could look out, but not at the sea. Although the line runs close to the beach, it's behind huge dunes and only on a few sections do you get a view of the English Channel.

Thirty six years after we'd stayed there, I instantly recognised De Haan's three storey tram station, with its tiled roof, overhanging eaves and ornate brickwork. Of the town I recalled nothing, other than arriving back one evening and having a portion of chips, as meals out were too expensive for a family budget (or was it that train tickets took precedence over food?). It's actually a lovely little town; a planned resort designed in the late 19th century and which remains unspoilt.

For the return journey I sat at the back, with a view down the track. Unusually, many of the trams can be driven from one end only, so loops are required so they can turn back. My nostalgic return to the De Haan had been but a taster and I shall add to the list of 'one day', a few days exploring the coast of Belgium by tram.

Back in Ostend I did what we hadn't been able to on holiday – enjoyed an excellent meal in a restaurant opposite the station. I have a vague memory of walking along what was probably the same row of restaurants in 1976 and of disappointment at being told they were beyond our means.

More than comfortably full, I caught the 20.02 to Gent, which was one of the strange rubber fronted trains that have recently appeared in Belgium. The only similar one I've travelled on was a service from Sweden to Hamburg, that I boarded at Lubeck in Germany. Unfortunately, on that occasion my ticket wasn't valid and at the very moment the guard came to check it I spilled a bottle of Coke over the table. As we discussed payment of the supplement, liquid slopped from side to side, spilling over the edges and barely stemmed by my feeble attempts to mop up with a single tissue.

The centre of Gent is thirty minutes walk, or a tram ride from the main station. I'd come here one evening when staying in Brussels the previous year and found it to be a most attractive city, with historic buildings around squares and canals. The centre rivals Bruges, but without the hordes of tourists was a more enjoyable place to wander. On a late summer Friday evening the young people of Gent had gathered by the canal, drinking wine and chatting in the same way that young Frankfurters had by the Main.

The train on to Brussels was an unusual arrangement of two sets of double deck coaches, with an electric locomotive in the middle. Like Italy, Belgium has a mix of old and new trains, with from what I've found, a reasonably reliable if not particularly fast service. In general the older local trains are less comfortable than ours, but longer distance services quite nice to travel in, not having our high seat density, although lacking refreshments. Trains which Belgian Railways call 'Inter City', fall short of ours in both speed and service.

My meeting next day was near Vichte, a village in West Flanders between Lille and Gent. Another locomotive hauled 'Inter City' took me to Oudenarde, where I changed to a local train. As I got off the guard told me which platform to wait for the three coach electric unit that pottered through deepest Belgium. As we meandered past farm houses and little villages, I thought again how travelling by branch line takes you into the heart of a country. It was even a little hilly in this very rural area and quite comfortable on my upholstered First Class seat. Second Class passengers had hard plastic seats, with the difference in classes more noticeable than is usual in Europe. In Britain though it would be strange to find First Class at all on such a rural train.

Confusion over who was meeting me meant I waited almost half an hour at the quiet little station in Vichte. With effusive apologies I was eventually picked up, my hosts exhibiting surprise that I'd come by train. I've become used to arriving at out of the way places that rarely see a business passenger and being told by those I'm visiting that they've never had anyone come by train before. After a couple of hours talking glue and an enjoyable lunch where I'd declined the local speciality of rabbit (they couldn't understand that one might not like the idea of eating rabbits but apparently don't tend to keep them as pets in Belgium), I retraced my journey back to Brussels.

The return to England on Eurostar was the first time I'd used Standard Premier on an evening service and I was interested to see what the advertised light meal would be. Suffice to say that the steward handing out the trays gave passengers little menus 'to tell you what you're eating'. It was poncy food at its worst:

Brie & carrot wrap with mushroom caviar
Poached salmon medallion and cauliflower with walnuts
Brussels 'cuberdon' mousse (with dodgy green bits on top)

I ate just a buttered roll. The French should never be allowed to take charge of catering.

At Lille it was announced that passengers should have tickets ready as the French authorities were carrying out checks – to catch those escaping from France in search of decent British food?

Deb was picking me up at Ashford, where I encountered more officialdom. A swift exit saw me at the front of the immigration queue, but we all had to wait several minutes for their computer to boot up. My passport accepted, I was then called over by a member of Kent Constabulary. 'Where had I been?' – 'Brussels'. What for? – 'Business meeting'. What was my business? – 'Adhesives'. There then followed a discussion about what type of adhesives we made. Once he discovered that it was water based adhesives for use on labels and tapes I was allowed to enter the country. Presumably manufacturers of other glue are barred.

As few trains stop at Ashford, I suspect that Mr Kent Policeman was justifying his existence and stopped me as I was in jeans with a rucksack. I have little doubt that if I'd have travelled onto St Pancras with the best part of a thousand other passengers I wouldn't have been stopped, and had I looked the businessman part with suit and briefcase there would have been no questions at Ashford.

On the subject of immigration, the following week we had a delivery at work from the Czech Republic. When the lorry's doors were opened a dozen men with rucksacks jumped out and legged it. It took the police an hour and a half to arrive. I just hope that none of them make the wrong kind of glue.

For the second trip a couple of months later I boarded the Eurostar at Ebbsfleet, and what a contrast to the crowds of St Pancras. With no queues, I was through security in a couple of minutes and sitting comfortably in the quiet waiting area that looks out across the tracks. Arriving at Brussels in mid afternoon, I had a few hours to explore another Belgium city. Brussels itself I know well, from many visits attending Labelexpo, the 'largest label converting event in the world'. I can't say it's more exciting than it sounds, but it is a big affair in the world of glue, with 28,636 visitors attending from 123 counties. I considered getting a train to Antwerp, with its highly impressive station, but as I'd been there quite recently decided on Namur, a city I'd never visited.

We'd passed through Namur on our holiday trip from Ostend to Dinant, a journey that takes three hours (plus we had the tram ride from De Haan to Ostend). Although we'd stayed by the beach, most of the holiday was spent travelling round Belgium. I don't recall disliking it but we must have been tolerant children – there's no way our sons would have put up with it!

From Brussels it took me just over an hour to Namur, in another double deck locomotive hauled train. Namur was a disappointment. Having seen photos of the huge citadel overlooking the river I assumed it was a tourist destination. It's not. I couldn't even find a shop selling post cards. It's a fairly ordinary city with few buildings of note and not somewhere I plan to return to.

The train back was interesting though. The *Vauban*, an historic train that runs from Zurich to Brussels. With no refreshments, twenty-two stops and taking 8 ¼ hours for a journey that can be done two hours quicker with one or two changes on high speed services, this isn't a train that many use from end to end. I'd caught it once before, returning from Metz in France after West Ham's 1999 InterToto Cup final. After breaking my return journey in Luxemburg, I'd travelled back to Brussels in the comfort of a compartment in Swiss railway coach.

Today it was late. In Europe, rather than amending the departure time, indicator boards tend to show the number of minutes a train is running late. As I waited on the platform the board changed from nine, to sixteen, to twenty-six and finally thirty-eight minutes late. When it eventually glided into Namur the train did look a bit special, with mostly Swiss coaches. Boards on the doors showed the *Vauban* name and how it links some of Europe's key cities : Zurich – Basel – Strasbourg – Luxembourg – Brussels. In First Class most of the passengers were businessmen and in Second almost all had luggage. This was a train for travellers not commuters. Right at the back I found an empty compartment with the same dark beige seats that I'd sat on in 1999. It's not a train for people in a hurry and I enjoyed my hour watching Belgium as we trundled towards the capital. For once it didn't matter a bit that we arrived thirty-five minutes late.

On my previous trip a strike had meant there were no Metro, trams or buses running in Brussels. This trip's inconvenience occurred the next morning. The 9.41 to Kortrijk was cancelled. There was no announcement and it simply disappeared off the indicator board. The next one was an hour later. I was late for my meeting. European railways aren't always better than ours.

CHAPTER TWENTY FIVE

REFLECTIONS

Sometimes authors start with a title and use that to guide them as they write. I've worked the other way, writing as inspired by the journeys and looking for a theme reflecting changes through my fifty years of train travel that suggested a title.

My first thoughts were something related to faster trains. Before embarking on the book I would have said that one of the main changes in our railways is that trains are now faster. It has been interesting to look at past timetables and discover that other than the upgraded West Coast Main Line and the new high speed line to Kent, many journeys are however little faster than they were thirty years ago, and some actually slower.

A more significant change though is frequency, with many more trains running. Few European cities can match the three trains an hour that Manchester and Birmingham now receive from London, illustrating the dividend from investment in the route. More people are travelling by train than at any time since the 1920s and in many places the network is at capacity.

British Rail had a reputation for lateness which might have provided me with a theme. Punctuality is said to have improved over the last ten years, but headline figures only tell part of the story. In 2011/12 30% of trains arrived more than fifty-nine seconds late. The *Daily Mail* headlined the story '*Network Fail : One in Three Trains Runs Late*'. Can *Mail* readers predict the exact time of arrival every time they go somewhere in their cars? Network Rail define on time as within five minutes for short distance and ten minutes for long distance. By these criteria they recorded 92% of arrivals 'on time'. The *Mail* described the figures as 'depressing'.

I disagree – nine out of ten trains arriving close to their scheduled time seems to me quite reasonable and a punctuality that road would find hard to match.

As ever though, statistics show only part of the story. They are based on arrival at the train's destination and ignore stations on route. Timetables now often contain far more 'padding' than the recovery time included in BR days. It is obviously easier to arrive on time if an extra ten minutes is added to the schedule, but at the expense of the overall journey time. It's arguable as to whether passengers want the fastest journeys or a greater chance of the train arriving on schedule, but with fines for late arrival, train operators take the latter option.

I've used my 10,000 miles of travel on British trains to make my own analysis of performance, which I've compared to the journeys in Europe. Using neither the *Daily Mail* nor Network Rail criteria, I've used what seems to me a reasonable measure – arrived within 5 minutes of schedule, and journey delayed by more than 30 minutes.

	UK	EUROPE
Total Number Of Trains	145	40
Within 5 Minutes	124 85.5%	36 90.0%
Delayed By More Than 30 Minutes	8 5.5%	3 7.5%

These figures, albeit based on limited data, show fairly similar performance in the UK and Europe. If however I was to include another journey to Italy made just before the book was completed, returning from Venice on the sleeper, the figures would favour the UK. It is not without reason that Italians say they can't rely on their trains.

Within five minutes seems on time to me but it is the long delays that cause most inconvenience. Out of interest, the causes of my eight delays to the overall journey exceeding half an hour were:

Missed Connection: First Great Western: Liskeard – Looe
'Operational Difficulties': C2C: Upminster – Tilbury
Breakdown: Greater Anglia: Norwich – London
Suicide: East Coast: Alnmouth – London
Engineering Work: First Great Western: Swansea – Tenby
Strike: East Midlands Trains: London – Manchester
Missed Connection: Northern Rail: Barrow – Seascale
Train Fault: ScotRail: Forsinard – Altnabreac

It is inevitable that occasional delays will occur, but two of these were avoidable and a recurring theme of my travels. For the want of holding a train for a couple of minutes and at no significant inconvenience to other passengers, I could have arrived at both Looe and Seascale on time. For a while *'Missed Connections'* was a possible title but later journeys gave fewer problems.

In the 'old days' local staff usually held branch line connections for a late running main line train. Now central control centres make the decisions, which as I experienced, usually means the train doesn't wait. It is a difficult balance between a short delay for those already on the train, to save the few changing having to wait for perhaps an hour. Knock on effects of delaying the branch train from returning in time to meet the next main line departure have to be considered, as do the consequences further down the line. It was right not to hold a train at Hereford when this would mean losing its path through Birmingham, but less understandable when it would have simply meant a shorter stop at Ledbury.

Reconsidering what I wrote about Thorpe-le-Soken in *Essex Coast Walk*, I can understand the need to ensure London trains aren't delayed, but perhaps there could be more flexibility on Walton trains, even if it meant the driver having to walk a bit faster when changing cabs at the terminus. The major factor that now enters the equation is punctuality targets (with punctuality bonuses for control staff) and fines for late running, and it is this that can sway the balance away from the best decision for passengers.

On this subject I shall leave the last word to a sarcastic post on the *www.railforums.co.uk.*

'But surely fining operators for considering customer needs is one of the benefits of privatisation? I've had it a couple of times where my train has run late and the connection has been allowed to leave as I and other passengers run down the platform towards its closing doors. As I watch it depart and think of the extra hour I'll have to enjoy the delights of Darlington station of a late evening I am comforted by the pretty paint scheme of the departing pacer and the knowledge that I'm paying them far more in taxpayer subsidy than in the bad old days of BR.'

The early 1980s British Rail television adverts in which Jimmy Savile proclaimed *'This is the Age of the Train'* suggested possible titles, but recent revelations mean no one would want their product to be associated with Savile. Reflecting on my fifty years of rail travel, I realised it covered three distinct 'ages of the train'.

The first was the tail end of the longest era in our railway history – of steam trains, thousands of miles of rural branch lines, station masters, porters, green flags, parcel vans, local freights and prestige crack expresses. I count myself fortunate to just recall the traditional British railway.

The second was one of transformation under British Rail. Other than the change from steam to diesel, on the lines that escaped Beeching, the railway experience in the mid 1960s was not that different from several decades before. The 'Modernisation Plan' that hastily scrapped steam, rightly cut out some of our wasteful practices, but mostly it wasn't until electrification, HSTs and new multiple units, that passengers saw a big change in travel. Not all will agree, but I'd suggest that in many ways the latter days of British Rail were the finest years of modern long distance train travel. BR was in its best ever state when it was scrapped and many of the improvements put down to privatisation may well have taken place anyway had it been allowed to continue.

The third, privatisation, which was supposed to revolutionise the railway, but in some ways has taken us back to the pre 1923 grouping of trains run by different companies who don't work together. Connections aren't held and many tickets only valid on set trains. The guard at Taunton who recently refused to accept my First Great Western ticket to Tiverton, because a signal failure at Maidenhead *'wasn't Cross Country's problem'*, epitomised the failings of privatisation. Although some are new, many of our current trains ran under British Rail, but have seen various liveries to suit their new corporate operators. More people travel, but often in less comfort and, unless booked in advance, at higher fares. Profit rather than service is the ultimate goal and anything not specified by the franchise agreement is liable to be cut if it doesn't make money.

Privatisation has given us colourful trains, staff with new uniforms, but with government subsidies far higher than British Rail received. Each company has its Passenger Charter, but prefers to call us 'customers'. Customer Service Departments operate, presumably with the aim to improve the service passengers receive, but as I have found, in practice appear to exist solely to hand out or refuse compensation vouchers. Whether constructive comments are passed on seems somewhat questionable considering the number of times they don't even read the letter, preferring to use a standard reply to answer the question they wished you'd asked!

The changes in train travel start before we even leave home, with tickets often bought well in advance on the internet. I thought of finding a ticket related title, but couldn't get out of my head *'Ticket to Ryde'*, which would have made a great title if the book was about the Isle of Wight railway with its 1938 ex London Underground stock – the oldest trains in regular service on our national railway system.

In the 'old days' passengers turned up at their local station and simply purchased a ticket to their destination. The booking clerk would take a pre-printed thick cardboard ticket, stamp the date and hand it to the passenger, who would show the ticket collector and set off on their journey. The last of these traditional 'Edmondson' tickets, which had been in use since 1842, was sold by British Rail in 1990. Their replacement, the larger APTIS machine printed tickets, lasted less than twenty years, with the final ticket issued at my local station of Upminster in 2007. Modern computer based ticketing is more flexible, but still relies on the knowledge of the person operating it to sell the best option. Far too often the booking clerk (who no doubt now has another job title) has little understanding of the railway system, and fails to provide passengers with best advice. With automated gates rather than ticket collectors we now rely on computers to let us on and off the platform, taking away the discretion and flexibility of a real person.

You will have gathered that I enjoy good food while travelling and for a while I toyed with *'Pork Pie to Panini'* as a title. There is no doubt that in many ways catering has improved from the days of the curled up sandwich of comedians' jokes, which continued many years after the food was actually good.

Catering has changed, on both stations and trains. The cafeteria style refreshment rooms where we occasionally ate very British 1960s meals have gone, to be replaced by a plethora of units selling take away food. Pasties, paninis, wraps and baguettes are commonplace, although it's hard to find a basic cheese sandwich. That few stations now offer a facility for a traditional sit down meal, reflects the change in our eating habits to fast food and 'grazing'. Time is invariably short and people don't want to stop for a meal at the station, so one would think that eating on the move would have become more popular. Sadly this advantage of train over car has been undermined with the decline of the restaurant car.

When British Rail ceased operating in 1997 there were 240 trains a day with restaurant cars available to all passengers. Now, excluding the sleeper lounge cars, there are just four, all run by First Great Western, and as I found returning from Newton Abbot, offering superb service and food.

Some say that hot food should be available to all passengers, but others maintain that complimentary meals help differentiate between First and Standard classes. To the majority of passengers who didn't use restaurant cars, they were an irrelevance, but to those who did dine their loss has reduced both the pleasure and convenience of travelling. To the train operators cost is the overriding concern and few restaurants ran at a direct profit.

I shall leave the last word on the subject to Barry Doe – *'The trouble is that the accountants who run the railways see trains merely as aeroplanes without wings. What they fail to spot is the marketing opportunity of a dining experience that we British regard as very special. On long train journeys, operators have a captive audience and much as they seem not to believe it, passengers do eat. Shame on them for not understanding this!'*

Over the years I must have spent thousands of hours watching the scenery pass by through train windows. Unless one is unfortunate enough to get one of the 22% of Pendolino seats with either a part or no window at all, it is still a pleasure to be enjoyed while travelling. *'Through the Train Window'* would have reflected some of the book's content, but whilst some views have of course altered over the years, most of our countryside remains remarkably unchanged. From a railway perspective, the lines of telegraph wires that ran alongside tracks have largely gone, with cables buried underground, and in some areas greater tree growth hampers views. As I found on so many journeys, the views from our railways of coast, moors and mountains are often spectacular, and the train provides a great way to enjoy seeing our beautiful country.

'Railways Revisited' was a possibility, but it's already been used. I set out to revisit the places we stayed at on childhood holidays and repeat the journeys of my youth. The journeys have changed, some more than others, but on the whole the places we stayed on holiday aren't that different to forty years ago. What has often changed though is the people who go there and how they travel. Resorts like Tenby, Torquay and Llandudno are still popular family holiday destinations, but at others holidaymakers are few and far between. With many now flying to warmer destinations, visitor numbers are invariably lower, but Seascale stands out as a place where no one takes their holiday any more. Some still travel on holiday by train, but most now drive. Summer Saturdays are busy on the railways, but far less so than the days of relief trains queuing up for miles to get into Torquay, with coaching stock used on just a few weekends each year.

One cannot compare changes to train travel without mentioning health and safety. A series of train crashes which highlighted systematic failings, particularly in maintenance, meant that the railways have been subject to even greater safety constraints than the rest of society. With just one passenger killed in the last ten years in train accidents for which the railways could be held responsible (as opposed to those caused by road users), there is no doubt that our railways are now extremely safe. Whether this has been the best use of resources I considered in *Stand Up Sit Down*:

'This illogical approach to safety is not confined to football. For example, a series of railway accidents between 1991 and 2000 killed a total of 58 people, an average of six per year. Of course it was right that action was taken to improve safety, but was all of the huge sums spent the best use of funds? In the same period around 40,000 people were killed on British roads, where expenditure in areas such as crash barriers, lighting or by-passes, would give a far greater value in terms of lives saved. The report of the Ladbroke Grove Rail Inquiry observed that the expenditure to prevent a road fatality is around £0.1 million, whereas the cost per fatality prevented by fitting the hugely expensive TPWS rail safety system was 100 times less value at about £10 million per death prevented. Many more lives could have been saved if this had been spent on road safety or in healthcare. To compound this illogical approach, much of the cost of safety works on the railways has been passed on to rail passengers, with the result that some will now choose to travel by road, and therefore actually face increased dangers.

Simple measures such as insisting all cars are painted in bright colours would save lives, yet there is no pressure to do this. It would be resisted by the consumer, yet with football it seems that customer's opinions are barely considered.'

It is of course right that there is now a far greater safety culture on our railways, but it is the inconsistencies that I question. Trains are not permitted to call at unlit stations, so instead passengers at some rural halts have to walk down dark roads to bus stops. Every year there are collisions at level crossings and whilst Network Rail spends many millions to improve or remove crossings and educate users, those who blatantly ignore red lights receive minor penalties. In July 2012 a bus driver jumped the lights and got his double decker trapped between the barriers at Manningtree. Fortunately the signalman spotted the bus blocking the tracks on CCTV and stopped the trains. The driver received a fine of £300 and nine points on his licence, but was soon back driving buses for another company. The prospect of a long driving ban might focus minds a little more and perhaps save lives of both road users and train passengers.

Just before it closed in 1976 my father and I travelled on the very rural line from Haltwhistle to Alston (it had only survived Beeching because there was no all-weather road). In an arrangement that was clearly routine to those involved, part way to Alston the driver stopped the train in a cutting and the guard let two ladies out. With their shopping bags they climbed up a path to the road above. Health and safety ensures that such unofficial stops could not happen on today's railway, but was there really any risk?

At Upminster large notices have recently appeared asking passengers to hold the handrail as they use the steps. That it will never happen when large numbers arrive on rush hour trains and those who need the rail know this without being told, doesn't seem matter. Maybe announcements requesting people to take care are a good idea in snow or ice, but not every time there's a drop of rain (or even in bright sunshine if no one remembers to tell the computer). No one can argue that we should expect reasonable safety, but how much is about reducing risks and how much simply arse covering?

In the 1960s there were no public address systems on trains. Now only the sleepers don't have them. For safety and to keep passengers informed they are a great benefit, but unnecessary and sometimes plain daft announcements were a regular theme of my journeys.

Do we really need to be told several minutes after leaving every station that *'First Class is at the front of the train'*, or to *'please take a moment to familiarise yourself with the safety information'*? Repeated apologies for every tiny delay eventually become annoying, as does the new railway language – we are *'on the approach to'*, Euston will be our *'final destination'* and of course the *'complete stop'*. And why do trains now arrive *into* rather than *at* a station?

It can be useful to know how many coaches a train will have, but what's the point of announcing the number of carriages when it has already been sitting in the station for five minutes? I'm happy to be informed that there is a buffet but do passengers need to be told of every item on the menu? Where do I actually find the policeman to report *'anything suspicious'* to as my train speeds along a main line or dawdles down a country branch? How many blind passengers actually walk to the buffet to collect the *'safety information leaflet in Braille'*? If I can't leave my *'personal belongings'* unattended do I have to take them to the toilet?

We used to hear a friendly voice telling us which train would be arriving (at the platform – not *alongside* as they now say at Waterloo). Now it's invariably a pre-recorded automated message, which whilst useful to be relayed to unstaffed stations, lack the flexibility to quickly provide the information passengers need when trains are disrupted.

Once on Shrewsbury station I listened to the Heart of Wales train announced – all thirty-three stops followed by the seventeen request stops listed again. Then, presumably as programmed, the whole announcement started again two minutes before departure. As the train with its handful of passengers disappeared down the line, those of us on the station were still being told that we should inform the guard if we wished to alight at the likes of Llangammarch, Sugar Loaf and Pontardulais.

There is one particularly annoying little announcement that sums this up. When British Rail first installed public address the guard would announce the next 'stop' or 'station'. Now the guard (Train Manager, Customer Host or whatever title they have this week) tells us what will be our next *'Station stop'*. Health and Safety, which requires the operator to ensure that passengers don't get out on the track should the next stop happen to be at a signal (even though the doors are centrally locked), combines with the obsession for the random deployment of redundant adjectives to give us the most clumsy announcement of all – *'The next station stop'* it is.

So the big question – has travelling by train got better or worse? Well that depends. If your local station was one of the 4,000 to have closed, it has probably got worse. If your railway still exists, the faster journeys and more frequent trains, probably make travel more convenient than in the 1960s. If you want to travel Standard Class (or Second Class as it was before 1987) in comfort and perhaps enjoy a meal on the way, then your journey would probably have been more enjoyable in the 1980s. If you can book in advance and travel on set trains, then your ticket might be comparatively cheaper, but if paying full fare it is considerably more expensive.

Perhaps I can summarise by going back to the conversation I had with the two German gentlemen in an ICE restaurant car. Their experience that our trains were inferior they put down to them being privately operated. The conclusions we reached, that the underlying aim of the British railway operators is to make money, whereas in Germany it's to provide a service, underpins many of my observations of modern rail travel.

Having looked back at the last fifty years perhaps I should end with a quick view to the future. As we waste our planet's resources and change its climate, no one can predict what changes there will be to life fifty years from now, but our railways will continue to evolve and adapt. Indeed, they should be at the forefront of policy to reduce mankind's effect on our environment, moving freight and passengers from road and air to the far more sustainable electric rail travel.

The announcement of a programme of electrification and a dedicated high speed line which will eventually link the Midlands, North and Scotland to Europe's railway system, are huge steps forward and indicate that the government have at last recognised the importance of our railways. If only they weren't hamstrung by the inefficiency and costs of a botched privatisation which was motivated by political ideology. New trains are being ordered (although whether they'll be as comfortable as the 1970s stock they'll replace is another matter) and lines reopened. It seems that organisations such as *Railfuture* and *Campaign for Better Transport* are being listened to. Fares though must stop rising and politicians must see railways as being for service not profit.

As with the rest of life, our railways have inevitably changed over the last fifty years. Opinions vary as to whether for the better, but what remains true is that the train is the most pleasant, safe and environmentally sound way to travel around our wonderful country. Long may it continue!

USEFUL ORGANISATIONS

Railfuture
Railfuture is the UK's leading independent organisation campaigning for better rail services for passengers and freight, fighting for things such as cheaper fares, reopened lines and stations, and getting more freight off the roads and onto rail. www.railfuture.org.uk

Campaign for Better Transport
Campaign for Better Transport has been campaigning on rail issues since 1973 and is the UK's leading authority on sustainable transport. www.bettertransport.org.uk

Friends of the Settle – Carlisle Line (FoSCL)
Providing support to the Settle – Carlisle railway, with some 3,500 members, FoSCL are the largest rail support/user group in the UK. www.foscl.org.uk

Heart of Wales Travellers Association
The Heart of Wales line has two support organisations. The Heart of Wales Line Forum is its Community Rail Partnership and details can be found on www.heart-of-wales.co.uk. One of the Forum's members is the Heart of Wales Line Travellers Association (HoWLTA). It is approximately 1000 strong and a membership form can be downloaded from www.howlta.org.uk

Cotswold Line Promotion Group
The group is supporting and safeguarding the Hereford – Worcester – Oxford railway line, actively promoting improvements to intercity and local trains serving the community. www.clpg.org.uk

Friends of the Far North Line (FoFNL)

The campaign group for rail north of Inverness, lobbying for improved services for the local user, tourist and freight customers. www.fofnl.org.uk

Barry Doe – Independent Transport Consultant

Bus and rail timetable website. www.barrydoe.co.uk

The Man in Seat 61

Website – How to travel by train from the UK into Europe and worldwide. www.seat61.com

Ffestiniog Travel

Established in 1974, Ffestiniog Travel are one of the UK's leading specialist rail tour operators, providing escorted and tailor made rail holidays to both rail connoisseurs and train travel tourists to destinations throughout the UK, Europe and worldwide. Its dedicated Ticket Only team at Myrailtrip is a one-stop shop for all rail journeys in the UK and across Europe. www.ffestiniogtravel.com

RailUK Forums

RailUK Forums has grown to become one of the most popular forums for railway-related discussion. www.railforums.co.uk

ALSO BY PETER CATON:

NO BOAT REQUIRED
EXPLORING TIDAL ISLANDS

When is an island not an island? Peter Caton takes us to all four corners of England, Scotland and Wales to find out.

Sharing our nation's fascination with islands, Peter sets out to be the first person to visit all forty-three tidal islands which can be walked to from the UK mainland. Along the way he faces many challenges: precipitous cliffs, vicious dogs, disappearing footpaths, lost bus drivers, fast tides, quicksand and enormous quantities of mud, but also experiences wonderfully scenic journeys by road, rail and on foot. He contrasts the friendly welcome from most islanders and owners with the reluctance of others to permit visits, and tells how he was thrown off one secret island.

An entertaining narrative illustrated with colour photographs, *No Boat Required* contains a wealth of information as the author unearths many little known facts and stories. It tells of the solitude of the many remote islands and the difficulties of balancing the needs of people and wildlife. We learn of the islands' varied histories – stories of pirates, smugglers, murder and ghosts, of battles with Vikings, an island claimed by punks and another with its own king. He writes of the beauty of the islands and our coast, and reflects on how these may be affected by climate change.

In *No Boat Required* Peter Caton takes us to explore islands, some familiar but most which few of us know exist and even fewer have visited. He finds that our tidal islands are special places, many with fascinating and amusing stories and each one of them different. It adds up to a unique journey around Britain.

£12.99 343 Pages ISBN 9781848767010 **Published by Matador**

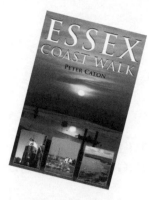

ALSO BY PETER CATON

ESSEX COAST WALK

When Peter Caton set out to walk the Essex coast he had no idea
of the beauty, wildlife and stories that he would find on the way. He
takes the reader up and down the many creeks and estuaries of the
longest coastline of any English county, through nature reserves,
seaside resorts, unspoilt villages, sailing centres and alongside
industry past and present. On the way we read of tales of
witchcraft, ghosts, smuggling, bigamy and incest. We learn of the
county's varied history – stories of battles with Vikings, of invading
Romans bringing elephants, a fort where the only casualty occurred
in a cricket match, burning Zeppelins and of Jack the Ripper.

Whilst an entertaining narrative, not a guidebook, *Essex Coast
Walk* contains a wealth of information, including many little-known
facts and stories. With gentle humour to match the
coastline's gentle beauty, and illustrated with photographs and
maps, the book makes for easy reading.

The book highlights how climate change may alter our coast and
looks at new methods of coping with rising sea levels. It tells us how
tiny settlements grew into large holiday resorts and how other
villages have remained as unspoilt and isolated communities. The
author's thought provoking final reflections consider how the coast
has changed over the centuries and what its future may be.

Written in an accessible style, *Essex Coast Walk* has been enjoyed not
only by those living in the county, but by others who have been surprised
to read of the beauty and history of this little known part of our coast.

£9.99 376 Pages ISBN 9781848761162 **Published by Matador**

ALSO BY PETER CATON

STAND UP SIT DOWN – A CHOICE TO WATCH FOOTBALL

For a hundred years most supporters watched football from terraces, a culture that was an integral part of the game. By the 1980s though, neglected stadia, hooliganism and a lack of concern for safety meant that football had to change, and after ninety-six Liverpool fans tragically died at Hillsborough, Lord Taylor's report recommended that our grounds should be all-seated. Many people however believe that something of the soul has been taken away from watching football and that standing is the natural way to feel part of the game.

In *Stand Up Sit Down* Peter Caton considers the arguments for and against the choice to stand to watch football. He visits the twenty-three English grounds that still have terraces, seeking the views of clubs and supporters, travels to Yorkshire to watch rugby league and to Germany to stand on a convertible terrace.

With extensively researched background, the author analyses the disasters and hooliganism that led to all-seating, and the many changes that have occurred in the game. He considers various solutions proposed to allow standing, and highlights obstacles facing those backing the choice to stand. His own experiences of watching football at all levels add insight and interest. The book ends by asking its own questions and with a whiff of conspiracy.

Illustrated with colour photographs, *Stand Up Sit Down* is a fascinating read, which unearths some surprising facts and raises many controversial issues relevant to all who love football.

£9.99 320 Pages ISBN 9781780881775 **Published by Matador**

CATERING UPDATE

Since completing my journeys I'm pleased to report a few improvements in train catering.

Greater Anglia have brought back chefs on four trains a day, offering a choice of freshly cooked breakast items from the buffet. Sadly not the full restaurant but nevertheless a welcome start to my trips walking the Suffolk coast – my next book. Trolleys also operate so East Coast are no longer the only trains to have both buffet and trolley.

I am led to believe that East Coast's complimentary all day menu now offers improved hot food. Best of all, First Great Western now operate two more restaurants, including one where Standard Class passengers can enjoy a full breakfast.

I am however still to find a Cross Country train with more than three sandwiches.